John Santore, Modern European History

Selected Course Outlines and
Reading Lists from American
Colleges and Universities

Modern
European
History

1789 - Present

Vol. II - Topical and
Thematic Courses

Third updated and expanded edition, 1990

edited by John Santore
Pratt Institute

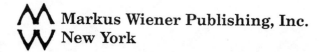 Markus Wiener Publishing, Inc.
New York

For information write to
Markus Wiener Publishing,
225 Lafayette Street
New York, NY 10012

Library of Congress Cataloging-in-Publication Data

Modern European history / edited by John Santore. -- 3rd updated and enl.
   ed.
      p. cm. -- (Selected course outlines and reading lists from American
      colleges and universities)
      Contents: v. 1. Chronological and national courses -- v. 2. Topical and
      thematic courses.
      ISBN 0-910129-94-0 (v.1) : ISBN 0-910129-95-9 (v. 2) :
      1. Europe--History--1789-1900--Outlines, syllabi, etc. 2. Europe--
      History-- 20th century--Outlines, syllabi, etc. 3. Europe--History--
      1789-1900--Bibliography. 4. Europe--History--20th century--
      Bibliography. I. Santore, John. II. Series.
      D359.2.M59 1989

      940--dc20   89-16473
                                                         CIP

Introduction to the Third Edition

Over the last two decades, the teaching of European history in American universities has undergone a remarkable transformation. Beginning almost imperceptibly in the early 1960s, colleges across the country have gradually increased their offerings in social history, and developed whole new areas of historical research. Indeed, since 1970 in particular, courses on such topics as the history of women, labor, and ethnic minorities, regional and local history, the history of medicine and psychoanalysis, and the use of quantitative methods and computers have multiplied rapidly. Even the older political and diplomatic histories are no longer taught from the same perspective, and their future popularity among young historians may very well depend on their ability to adapt to new historical methods and concerns.

The courses presented in these two volumes reflect this changed emphasis among American historians. Designed by some of the country's leading teachers and scholars, they show a marked shift toward social history as a primary or secondary concern. In addition, they also illustrate the growing tendency among history departments to deepen their curriculum by adding courses on special topics, and the astonishing diversity which now characterizes the historical field. Although highly individualistic and difficult to categorize, they provide a prime example of the degree to which contemporary political and social problems affect the teaching of history as a whole.

The courses themselves have been divided into four sections, each representing a traditional area of historical interest or a specific pedagogical approach. Volume I deals with those courses that have been organized chronologically or nationally. Among the chronological courses, special attention has been given to the survey of Western Civilization (of which there are four examples) and a number of critical historical periods or events (such as the French Revolution and the Second World War). In the national section, emphasis has been placed on the Great Powers - Britain, France, Germany, and the USSR. This decision to emphasize the larger nations, it should be mentioned, reflects the current distribution of history courses in the United States. As partial compensation, the volume also includes a selection of offerings on the lesser Powers - Italy, Poland, Spain, Portugal, Austria, Hungary, and the Netherlands.

In contrast to volume I, volume II provides a list of courses in which the materials have been organized topically or thematically. Among them are several which stand at the very cutting edge of current historical research and are thus illustrative of many contemporary historical trends. Included in this list are courses on the history of medicine and mental illness, the development of the European working class and proletarian culture, women in European society and politics, and comparative Fascism, Communism, and political terrorism. In addition, there are also courses on general social and economic history, and selections on diplomatic, intellectual, and military history (including the so-called "new military history") as well.

Finally, some mention should be made about the way in which the courses were selected. In choosing from among the hundreds of syllabi submitted, I have tried to select those which, in my estimation, would be of maximum use to students, teachers, and scholars. As such, I have favored those which display the highest measure of clarity and organization, as well as a mastery of existent literature in the field. Within these parameters, I have also provided the reader with examples of courses taught in the widest variety of formats and at different instructional levels (undergraduate lectures, graduate seminars, independent reading courses, etc.) and have striven to maintain a balance between divergent political and pedagogical points of view. Finally, I have never lost sight of the fact that the basic function of a syllabus is to inform the student about the content, readings, and other requirements needed for the course under discussion, and that its ultimate justification lies in its effectiveness as a pedagogical tool.

John Santore

New York
September 1989

TABLE OF CONTENTS

Volume Two:
Topical and Thematic Courses

Military

1. ISTVAN DEAK, Columbia University*
"The Army in European Society and Politics, 1815–1945" 7
2. CHARLES S. MAIER, Harvard University
"World War II and It's Impact" 10
3. ROBERT MOELLER, Columbia University
"War and Revolution in Europe, 1914–1923" 15
4. CHARLES S. MAIER, Harvard University
"The Second World War" 19
5. STANLEY HOFFMAN and MICHAEL SMITH, Harvard University
"War: A Social Analysis" 24
6. PETER KARSTEN, University of Pittsburgh
"Comparative Military Systems" 31

Diplomatic

7. STEWARD A. STEHLIN, New York University
"Diplomatic History of Europe, 1789–1939" 39
8. JOHN SANTORE, Pratt, Institute
"International Politics, 1900–Present" 43
9. STANLEY HOFFMAN, Harvard University
Michael Mandelbawn, John Odell, and M.J. Peterson,
"International Conflict in the Modern World" 51
10. PETER J. LOEWENBERG, University of California, Los Angeles
"Psychodynamic Considerations on Crisis Management and
Negotiations on the International, Political, and
Interpersonal Systemic Levels" 55

Intellectual

11. JACQUES KORNBERG, University of Toronto
"European Intellectual History, 1789-1914" 59
12. MARTIN JAY, University of California, Berkeley
"European Intellectual History:
From the Enlightenment to the Present" 64
13. PELLEGRINO D'ACIERNO, Hofstra University
"The Problem of the Intellectual in Contemporary Society" 68
14. RICHARD KREMER, Dartmouth College
"History of Science Since 1700" 73

Economic and Social

15. MARTIN WOLFE, University of Pennsylvania
"Society and Economy in Western Europe, 1815-1973" 98
16. CHARLES S. MAIER, Harvard University
"The Wealth of Nations: Economic Problems and Policy Since the 1700's" 106

17. ROBERT MOELLER, Columbia University
"Colloquium on Modern European Social History" 110
18. MARY JO MAYNES, University of Minnesota
"Proseminar in 18th and 19th Century Europe:
Social History" 117
19. JOHN MERRIMAN and PAUL JOHNSON, Yale University
"Comparative American and Western European
Social History" 133

Labor

20. HERRICK CHAPMAN, Carnegie Mellon University
"Labor and the Left in Modern Europe" 135
21. ROBERT MOELLER, Columbia University
"Workers' Lives, Workers' Culture, the Working Class Movement: Topics in
European Labor History, 1780-1914" 145
22. MARY NOLAN, New York University
"Workers and Social Change in Twentieth-Century Europe" 149

Women's History

23. BONNIE ANDERSON, Brooklyn (CUNY)
"Queens, Peasants, Housewives, and Rebels: Women in Modern Europe's His-
tory" 153
24. MARY NOLAN, New York University
"Women in European Society and Politics" 157
25. JUDITH M. BENNET, University of North Carolina, Chapel Hill
"Women in Europe since 1750" 161
26. MARY JO MAYNES and BARBARA LASLETT, University of Minnesota
"Gender and Class" 167

Jewish Studies

27. TODD M. ENDELMANN, University of Michigan
"Modern Jewish History to 1948" 176
28. MARION KAPLAN, Princeton University
Jewish Women in the Modern World 184
29. MICHAEL R. MARRUS, University of Toronto
"The Holocaust" 190
30. TODD M. ENDELMAN, University of Michigan
"History of Zionism and the State of Israel" 206

Medicine

31. GERALD L. GEISON, Princeton University
"Disease and Doctors in the Modern West" 210
32. MARTIN S. PERNICK, University of Michigan
"Sickness and Health in Society: 1492 to the Present" 214
33. MARTIN S. PERNICK, University of Michigan
"Health and Disease in the Age of Victoria, 1830-1900" 223
34. MARTIN MILLER, Duke University
"Madness and Society in Historical Perspective" 237

Ideologies and Movements

35. MICHAEL MARRUS, University of Toronto
"Studies on the European Right" 244
36. ROBERT O. PAXTON, Columbia University
"Fascism: An Undergraduate Seminar" 251
37. STANLEY G. PAYNE, University of Wisconsin, Madison
"Revolution and Fascism in Spain, Italy, and Portugal" 254
38. MICHAEL R. MARRUS, University of Toronto
"Fascism: A Comparative History" 258
39. ROBERT O. PAXTON, Columbia University
"European Lefts Since 1830" 263
40. STEPHEN F. COHEN, Princeton University
"Radical Thought: Marxism" 268
41. JOHN SANTORE, Barnard College
"European Communism in the Era of the Comintern,
1919-1943" 276
42. MARTIN MILLER, Duke University
"A History of Russian Anarchism" 280
43. DONALD H. BELL, Tufts University
"Political Terror in Historical Perspective" 281

Historical Methology and Historiography

44. PETER J. LOEWENBERG, University of California, Los Angeles
"Introduction to Historical Practice" 286
45. JOHN COATSWORTH and EDWARD COOK, University of Chicago
"Quantitative Methods for Historians" 289
46. PETER J. LOEWENBERG, University of California, Los Angeles
"Psychohistory" 294
47. JACOB W. SMIT, Columbia University
"Historiography" 298
48. THOMAS BENDER and MARY NOLAN, New York University
"Historiography" 302

For the table of contents of Volume I, please refer to the end of the book.

*Institutional designations refer to the university or college at which the course was taught, and not necessarily to the school at which the author now teaches. In all but a few instances, the syllabi have been reproduced exactly as submitted, with little modification or change. All college courses, of course, are subject to annual revision and updating.

Istvan Deak
1229 International Affairs
Tel.: 280-4008
Office Hours: Tu. 2-4, Th. 4-6

History W3969y
Spring 1987
Tu: 4:10-6

THE ARMY IN EUROPEAN SOCIETY AND POLITICS, 1815-1945

The purpose of this seminar is to investigate the political and social role military officers played in modern European history. Many nations are governed today by generals or colonels. Some of these officers abide by the constitution of their country; most, however, are dictators. Many are fascists if not openly so, then in their style and methods; others appear peaceable and prefer to wear mufti. Some are outright reactionaries; others are liberals; again others are radicals and revolutionaries. But in each and every case these military rulers, and the soldiers they command, are modelled after the historic example of Europe. Whether Asian, African or Latin American, the military commanders wear European-style uniforms; bear titles and ranks that once had a meaning to Europeans only; and organize their armies according to old Prussian, French or English models. Ironically, Europe itself is free today from military rule, except in Poland.

In this course we shall try to explore, among other things, how the military became subordinated to the civilian government in Europe. We shall look into the origins of the European armies, the birth of the standing army, and the painful process by which mercenaries and noble military amateurs were transformed into loyal servants of the state. But we shall also deal with the social origin of the officers, their ideology, education and way of life, the influence they exercised on politics, and society's handling of the soldiers. Of particular interest are such imperial armies as the British, the Russian, the Habsburg, and the Ottoman which acted as international police forces in an age of violent nationalism. We shall ask whether they can conceivably serve as models for a future international peacekeeping force. We shall learn about the military's role in the initiation of the two World Wars; the rise of the reserve officers; the role officers played in the revolutions and counter-revolutions, and in such modern radical movements as Fascism, Nazism and Communism. Finally, we shall look into the question of the officer's ethical and legal responsibility for the conduct of war.

The seminar is organized chronologically, with emphasis on specific crises in the history of Europe and of the military. The readings are relatively short; please read them carefully. Aside from your active participation in classroom work, you will be expected to write a research paper of at least twenty pages. You will be given a list of English-language sources; familiarity with another language is useful but not necessary. I shall want to discuss your research topic with each

one of you privately, and during the semester you will be asked to
submit a first and second draft for seminar discussion.

All the readings indicated in the course outline are on reserve in
the Columbia College Reading Room. Most of the books should also be
available in the Columbia University Bookstore and in the Bookforum.

TIMETABLE

Jan.20   Introduction

Jan.27-Feb.3   Basic questions of civil-military relationship. The
                    origins of the European armies. Mercenaries, amateurs,
                    the purchase of commissions, and the rise of the standing
                    armies in the eighteenth century.

Readings: Michael Howard, War in European History (Oxford
                    University Press), chapters 1-4.
                    Michael Howard, ed. Soldiers and Governments. Nine Studies
                    in Civil-Military Relations (Greenwood), Introduction.
                    John Keegan, The Face of Battle (Vintage Books), chapters 1-2.

Feb.10   Soldiers of the French Revolution. the Napoleonic Wars and
                    the early Restoration period. The birth of the politicized
                    mass armies.

Readings: Howard, War in European History, chapter 5.
                    Howard, ed., Soldiers and Governments, chapters on France
                    and Germany.
                    Keegan, chapter 3.
                    Gordon Craig, The Politics of the Prussian Army, 1640-1945
                    (Oxford University Press), Introduction and chapter 1.

Feb.17-24   The revolutions of 1848-1849. Regulars versus civilians in
                    uniform. The conflict between national ideologies and
                    supranational dynastic loyalties.

Readings: Craig, chapters 2-3.
                    Istvan Deak, "An Army Divided. The Loyalty Crisis of the Habs-
                    burg Officer Corps in 1848-1849." (Copies will be handed out.)
                    Priscilla Robertson, Revolutions of 1848. A Social History
                    (Harper Torchbooks), Introduction, chapters on France, Germany,
                    the Austrian Empire Conclusion.

March 3-17   From the 1850's to World War I. Universal military service
                    and rapid technological development. Aristocratic privilege
                    and the needs of modern war. The Dreyfus Affair or the last
                    gasp of the politically independent army in France.

Readings: Howard, ed., Soldiers and Governments, chapters on France,

Germany, Great Britain, and Russia.
Craig, Chapters 4-7.
O.A. Ray, "The Imperial Russian Army Officer," _Political Science Quarterly_, 76, Dec. 1961, pp. 576-593.
Brian Bond, _War and Society in Europe, 1870-1970_ (Oxford University Press), chapters 1-3.

March 24-31

The First World War. The decimation of the professional officer corps and its replacement by officers of the reserve. Civilian dictatorship versus military dictatorship.

Readings:

Howard, _War in European History_. Chapters 6-7.
Keegan, chapter 4.
Craig, chapter 8.
Bond, chapter 4.
Denis Winter, _Death's Men. Soldiers of the Great War_ (Penguin Books).
Istvan Deak, "The Habsburg Army in the First and Last Days of World War I: A Comparative Analysis," in Bela K. Kiraly and Nandor F. Dreisziger, eds., _East Central European Society in World War I_ (Social Science Monographs, Boulder), pp. 301-312.

April 7

Revolution and counter-revolution in the post-war years. The Red Army in Soviet Russia and the subjection of the military to the totalitarian state.

Readings:

Craig, chapter 9.
Raymond L. Garthoff, "The Military in Russia, 1861-1965," in Jacques van Doorn, ed., _Armed Forces in Society_ (Mouton), pp. 240-256.

April 14-28

The German army in the Weimar Republic and in the Third Reich. Military collaboration with and resistance to Hitler. The rise of the SS and the annihilation of the Prussian officer corps. The moral and legal responsibilities of the soldiers.

Readings:

Craig, chapters 10-12.
Bond, chapters 5-6.
John W. Wheeler-Bennett, _The Nemesis of Power. The German Army in Politics, 1918-1945_. (St. Martin's Press), Part III.
Eugene Davidson, _The Trial of the Germans_ (Collier Books). Chapters 9-10.

WORLD WAR I AND ITS IMPACT

UNIT ONE: THE PROBLEM OF ORIGINS

Sept. 19: What happened at the Battle of the Marne (September 1914):
          Course Introduction.
Sept. 24: How the armies came to the Marne: Crisis, Mobilization, and
          War.
Sept. 26: Background of the Crisis, I: States, Alliances, Antagonisms.
September 26/27: Section Discussion: Who was Responsible?

Required Reading:
         James Joll, The Origins of the First World War (Longman PB:
         1984. Coop).
         Thucydides, The Peloponnesian Wars (Modern Library or any
         other ed.), Book I, Paragraphs 24-48, 66-92, 118-25, 138-46.

Recommended Reading:
         L. C. F. Turner, Origins of the First World War (Norton PB).

Oct. 1: Background of the Crisis, II: Military Organization, Political
         Systems, Public Opinion and "Social Forces."
Oct. 3: The Continuing Debate: "War Guilt," and Inevitability.
         Lessons from the Italian Intervention (May 1915).
October 3/4: Section Discussion: Was War Inevitable?

Required Reading:
         Steven E. Miller, ed., Military Strategy and the Origins
         of the First World War (Princeton University PB. Coop.
         Originally printed as International Security, summer 1984),
         essays by Kennedy, Howard, Van Evera, and Howard.
                  Plus one of the following:
         Volker Berghahn, Germany and the Approach of War in 1914
         (Macmillan PB), pp. 1-24, 43-64, 85-103, 125-214; or
         D. B. Lieven, Russia and the Origins of the First World War
         (Macmillan PB), pp. 1-101, 139-154; or
         Zara Steiner, Britain and the Origins of the First World War
         (Macmillan PB), pp. 36-99, 154-214, 240-257.

Recommended Reading:
         Fritz Fischer, Germany's Aims in the First World War
         (Norton PB), chapters 1-2. (The most recent, powerful
         indictment of German policy; stresses domestic causes.)
         Jack Snyder, The Ideology of the Offensive: Military
         Decision Making and the Disasters of 1914 (Cornell UP),
         esp. chapters 1-5, 8.

UNIT TWO: STRATEGY AND COMBAT

Oct. 8: What happened at Verdun and the Somme: The Logic of _tatic
         Warfare on the Western Front.
Oct. 10: What happened in Galicia: The Logic of Fluid Warfare
         on the Eastern Fronts.
October 10/11: Section Discussion: Problems of Strategy and Tactics.

Required Reading:
        Martin van Crefeld, Command in War (Harvard UP), chapter 5.
        Alistair Horne, The Price of Glory: Verdun 1916 (Penguin
        PB. Coop), chapters 1-6, 8-11, 15-16, 21, 23, 25-27.
        Marc Ferro, The Great War, 1914-1918 (Routledge PB),
        part II.

Recommended Reading:
        Norman Stone, The Eastern Front 1914-1917 (PB),
        pp. 1-144, 194-232, 282-303.
        Paul Guinn, British Strategy and Politics, 1914-1918
        Clarendon Press).
        John Terraine, The Road to Paschendaele.
Oct. 15: Perspectives on Combat.
Oct. 17: The Human Costs of the War (War losses, demography, desertion
         military justice).
October 17/18: Section Discussion: the Experience of War.

Required Reading:
        John Keegan, The Face of Battle (Vintage PB. Coop),
        chapters 1, 4.
        Carl von Clausewitz, On War, M. Howard and P. Paret, eds.
        (Princeton UP PB): Book I, chap. 1: "What is War?"; chap.
        2: "Danger in War"; chap. 7: "Friction in War."
        Italian Court Martials: Xeroxed material.

Recommended Reading:
        Eric Leed, No Man's Land: Combat and Identity in the First
        World War (Cambridge UP), chapters 1, 3, 5-6.
        Tony Ashworth, Trench Warfare, 1914-1918: The Live and Let
        System (Macmillan).
        A. Babington, For the Sake of Example (Secker and Warburg).
        Douglas Gill and Gloden Dallas, "Mutiny at Etaples Base
        in 1917," Past & Present, 69 (1975): 88-112.
        Guy Pedroncini, Les Mutinieries de 1917.
        Denis Winter, Death's Men: Soldiers of the Great War
        (Penguin PB.)
        Leon Wolff, In Flanders Fields (Longmans).

Oct. 22: The War as Ideal and Myth (Slides).
Oct. 24: The War in Memoir, Fiction, and Poetry.
October 24/25: Section Discussion: War as Ideal and Reality.

Required Reading:
        I. M. Parsons, ed., Men Who March Away: Poetry of the
        First World War (Heinemann PB. Coop), selections to be

5

announced. Or Up the Line to Death (Magnum PB) as
an alternative edition.
Thomas Mann, Letters to Paul Amann (Knopf). Letters
number 1, 2, 4, 5, 6, 9, 11, 18.
        Plus one of the following memoirs:
Guy Chapman, A Passionate Prodigality; or
Robert Graves, Goodbye to All That (Penguin PB), chaps. I,
IV, VI, X-XXV; or
Ernst Jünger, The Storm of Steel.

UNIT THREE: THE WAR BEHIND THE WAR: EFFECTS ON STATE AND SOCIETY

Oct. 29: Party Truces and the Concentration of Executive Power:
        The Transformation of Politics.
Oct. 31: Paying for the War: Finance and Inflation.
October 31/November 1: Section Discussion: What did the war change for
        women?

Required Reading:
        Arthur Marwick, The Deluge: British Society and the First
        World War (Norton PB. Coop), chapters I-VI, VII:ii; VIII:iv;
        IX.
        Sandra M. Gilbert, "Soldier's Heart: Literary Men, Literary
        Women, and the Great War," Signs vol. 8,nr. 3 (Spring 1983):
        422-50.
        Enid Bagnold, A Diary without Dates (Virago PB).

Recommended Reading:
        Jane Jensen, Margaret Higonnet, Sonia Michel, eds., Women
        and War, CES Manuscript, selections to be announced.
        Vera Brittain, Testament of Youth (Widewood Press PB);
        Albert Mendelssohn Bartholdy, The World War and German
        Society (Yale UP).(Not on women; rather the erosion of
        of the settled prewar order.)

Nov. 5: Labor between Cooptation and Revolution.
Nov. 7: What happened in Turin and Petrograd: Social Upheaval, 1917-18.
November 7/8: Section Discussion: The War and the Socialist Movement.

Required Reading:
        V. I. Lenin, Imperialism (PB), prefaces, chapters II, IV,
        VIII, IX.
        Marc Ferro, The Great War, 1914-1918, part III.

Recommended Reading:
        Martin Clark, Antonio Gramsci and the Revolution that Failed
        (Yale UP), esp. pp. 1-73. (The Turin milieu and factory
        councils.)
        Keith Middlemas, Politics in Industrial Society (Andre
        Deutsch PB), chapters 2-6. (The unions' tie to the state.)
        Gerald Feldman, Army, Industry, and Labor in Germany,
        1914-1918 (Princeton UP), pp. 3-38, 63-96, 116-45, 149-68,
        203-217, 253, 349-73, 407-09, 442-533.

Jürgen Kocka, Facing Total War: German Society 1914-1918
(Harvard UP). (A test of theories of social polarization.)

Nov. 12: Woodrow Wilson's War, 1914-18.
Nov. 14: America's War, 1917-18.
November 14/15: Section Discussion: Harvard's War.

Required Reading:
Xeroxed materials on reserve.

Recommended Reading:
Phyllis Keller, States of Belonging, Book I, chapter 4. (On
Harvard's Hugo Munsterberg.)
David Kennedy, Over Here (Oxford UP: PB). (General account.)

Nov. 19: Undefeated but Desperate: Did Germany have to Lose the War?
Nov. 21: What happened in Berlin and Vienna: Defeat and Revolution.
November 21/22: Section Discussion: The "Stab in the Back" and the
German Revolution.

Required Reading:
Arno J. Mayer, Politics and Diplomacy of Peacemaking:
Containment and Counterrevolution at Versailles (Vintage
PB), chapters 1-2, 17, 22, Epilogue.
Francis Carsten, Revolution in Central Europe, 1918-1919
(U.Cal PB), pp. 11-83, 108-143, 210-146, 293-335.

Recommended Reading:
A. J. Ryder, The German Revolution of 1918 (Cambridge UP),
esp. chapter 5, 7-9.

Nov. 26: Global Upheaval and Nationalist Reactions.
Nov. 28: Thanksgiving holiday.

UNIT FOUR: TOWARD THE NEXT WAR

Dec. 3: What happened in Paris: The Constraints of Peacemaking, 1919.
Dec. 5: Reparations, Security and the Fragility of the Versailles
Order.
December 5/6: Section Discussion: Was Versailles a bad Treaty?

Required Reading:
John Maynard Keynes, The Economic Consequences of the Peace
(any edition; most recent is The Collected Writings of JMK,
Cambridge UP, vol. 2: PB).
Marc Trachtenberg, Reparation in World Politics (Columbia
UP), chapter 2.

Dec. 10: Freikorps and Fascists: Postwar Counter-Revolution.
Dec. 12: Monuments aux Morts: Commemoration, Cynicism and Pacifism in
the 1920's and 1930's.
December 12/13: Section Discussion: Veterans and Intellectuals; Pacifism
and Paramilitarism.

Required Reading:
>   Erich Maria Remarque, All Quiet on the Western Front
>   (Fawcett PB).
>   Robert Wohl, The Generation of 1914 (Havard PB),
>   pp. 1-41, 54-72, 160-181, 203-237.

Recommended Reading:
>   John Dos Passos, Nineteen Nineteen (U.S.A. volume 2).
>   Henri Barbusse, Under Fire.

Dec. 17: Lessons Learned too well: Diplomacy and Strategy in Preparation
for World War II.
Dec. 19: Two Wars or One? Comparative Aspects of the Two World War.
December 19/20: Section Discussion: What did it mean?

Required Reading:
>   Paul Fussell, The Great War and Modern Memory (Oxford PB),
>   at least chapters I, III, V, VII, IX.

NOTE: "PB" means that a British or American paperback edition has
recently been in print, but not necessarily that it is still in print.
"Coop" means that the books were ordered for student purchase, but not
necessarily that they shall be available.
      For a clear and imaginative cartographic history of the war,
students should definitely consult Martin Gilbert, Atlas of World War I
(Dorset Press).

WRITTEN REQUIREMENTS

1. A five-page paper, due in class, Tuesday November 12.
      Choose one of the volumes of the Carnegie Endowment series on the
Social and Economic History of the World War, and summarize, for the
country in question, either some demographic effects of the war, the
progress of state regulation of the economy, costs of the war in
financial or human terms, shortages or other difficulties, medical
responses or other developments in human services. More detailed
guidelines will be distributed.

2. A twelve-to-fifteen page course essay, due on January 8.
      This essay should be on a subject of interest to be worked out
with the instructor or teaching assistant. Some suggested topics and
bibliography will be provided later in the term.

3. A final examination on January 15.

Columbia University

War and Revolution in Europe, 1914-1923: Comparative Studies

of Russia, Germany and Italy

    For a brief moment at the end of the First World War,
revolution was on the agenda of many European nations. Not
since 1848 had Europe undergone such a period of turmoil and
political crisis. This seminar will seek to examine the origins and forms of that unusual revolutionary outburst. We
will begin with a treatment of the background to revolutionary
upheaval in the period of the First World War and will then
proceed with three case studies of revolutionary development
---Russia, Germany and Italy---each with a very different
outcome. Course requirements in addition to the weekly required reading assignments will include: a brief oral presentation of one of the week's readings, a mid-term paper
(5-7 pages), and a term paper (15-20 pages) which should offer
a comparative analysis of one of the aspects of revolutionary
situations discussed in the course.

    Those readings which have been ordered in the bookstore
and are available in paperback are marked with *. These and
all others are on reserve in the College Library.

Week I: General Introduction

Week II: Defining the Context: Economic Impact of the First
    World War
    *Gerd Hardach, The First World War, 1914-1918

Week III: Defining the Context: Diplomacy and Peacemaking,
    1917-1919
    Arno Mayer, Politics and Peacemaking, 3-30
    Arno Mayer, Political Origins of the New Diplomacy, 1917-
    1918, 1-58
    Charles Maier, Recasting Bourgeois Europe, 3-52

Week IV: Background to Revolution in Russia
    Alexander Gerschenkorn, "Problems and Patterns of Russian
    Economic Development," in Cherniavsky, ed., Structure of
    Russian History, 282-308
    Leopold Haimson, "The Problems of Social Stability in
    Urban Russia, 1905-1917," in Cherniavsky, ed., Structure
    of Russian History, 341-81

JLH Keep. The Russian Revolution. A Study of Mass Mobilization. 1-64

Victoria E. Bonnell, "Trade Unions, Parties and the State
in Tsarist Russia: A Study of Labor Politics in St. Petersburg and Moscow," Politics and Society, 9, 3, 1980,
299-322

G.R. Swaan. "Bolsheviks and Metal Workers on the Eve of
the First World War," Journal of Contemporary History,
16, 1984. 273-91

Week V: Makers of the Revolution in Russia
William G. Rosenberg, "Russian Liberals and the Bolshevik
Coup," Journal of Modern History, 40, 1968, 328-47

Graeme J. Gill, "The Mainsprings of Peasant Action in 1917,"
Soviet Studies, XXX, no. 1, 1978, 63-78

Marc Ferro. "The Russian Soldier in 1917: Undisciplined,
Patriotic, and Revolutionary," Slavic Review, 30, 3,
1971, -34-512

Paul Avrich, "The Bolshevik Revolution and Workers' Control
in Russian Industry," Slavic Review, XXII, 1963, 47-63

Diane Koenker, "The Evolution of Party Consciousness in 1917:
The Case of the Moscow Workers," Soviet Studies, XXX, no.
1, 1978. 38-62

Week VI: Stabilizing the Russian Revolution
J.P. Nettl. The Soviet Achievement, 39-114

Richard Stites, "Zhenotdel: Bolshevism and Women, 1917-
1930," Russian History, v.4, 1977

Carol Eubank, "The Bolshevik Party and Work Among Women,"
Russian History, v.4, 1977

Alexandra Kollontai, Selected Writings, 151-200

Paul Avrich, Kronstadt 1921, 7-34

William Henry Chamberlain, The Russian Revolution, 1917-
1921, v. II, 430-63 ("The Crisis of War Communism..."
and "The Revolution in Retrospect")

Week VII: Background to Revolution in Germany
Gerald D. Feldman, "The Political and Social Foundations
of Germany's Economic Mobilization, 1914-1916," Armed
Forces and Society, 3, 1, 1976, 121-45

Jürgen Kocka, "The First World War and the Mittelstand,"
Journal of Contemporary History, VIII, 1973, 101-24

Robert G. Moeller, "Dimensions of Social Conflict in the
Great War: The View from the German Countryside," Central
European History, v. XIV, 2, 1981, 142-68

Jürgen Tampke, The Ruhr and Revolution, The Revolutionary
Movement in the Rhenish-Westphalian Industrial Region
1912-1949, 3-70

Dieter Groh, "The Unpatriotic Socialists and the State,"
Journal of Contemporary History, 1, 4, 1966, 151-77

Week VIII: In Search of the German Revolution
  Reinhard Rürup, "Problems of the German Revolution 1918-19,"
    Journal of Contemporary History," 4, 1968, 109-35
  Robert F. Wheeler, "'Ex oriente lux?' The Soviet Example
    and the German Revolution, 1917-1923," in Bertrand, ed.,
    Revolutionary Situations in Europe, 1917-1922, 39-50
  Gerhard P. Bassler, "The Communist Movement in the German
    Revolution, 1918-1919: A Problem of Historical Typology?"
    Central European History, v. VI, 1973, 233-77
  Wolfgang J. Mommsen, "The German Revolution 1918-1920:
    Political Revolution and Social Protest Movement," in
    R. Bessel and E.J. Feuchtwanger, Social Change and Poli-
    tical Development in Weimar Germany, 21-54
  Barrington Moore, Jr., Injustice, 376-97

Week IX: A Failed Revolution in Germany?
  Lothar Albertin, "German Liberalism and the Foundation of
    the Weimar Republic: A Missed Opportunity," in A. Nicholls
    and E. Matthias, German Democracy and the Triumph of Hit-
    ler, 29-46
  Gerald D. Feldman, "Social Policy and Social Conflict:
    Labor as a 'Winner' in the German Inflation," (typescript)
  Renate Bridenthal, "Beyond Kinder Küche, Kirche: Weimar
    Women at Work," Central European History, v. VI, 1973,
    148-66
  Jeremy Noakes and Geoffrey Pridham, Documents on Nazism,
    1919-1945, 31-63

Week X: Background to Revolution in Italy
  Salvatore Saladino, "Parliamentary Politics in the Liberal
    Era 1861 to 1914," in E. Tannenbaum and E. Noether, eds.,
    Modern Italy. A Topical History Since 1861, 27-51
  Alice Keikian, "From Liberalism to Corporatism: The Province
    of Brescia during the First World War," in J.A. Davis,
    Gramsci and Italy's Passive Revolution, 213-38
  Frank Snowden, "From Sharecropper to Proletarian: The Back-
    ground to Fascism in Rural Tuscany, 1880-1920," in Davis,
    ed., Gramsci and Italy's Passive Revolution, 136-71
  Gwyn A. Williams, Proletarian Order. Antonio Gramsci, Factory
    Councils and the Origins of Italian Communism 1911-1921, 1-67

Week XI: Revolution and Counterrevolution in Italy
  Martin Clark, The Failure of Revolution in Italy, 1919-1920
  Adrian Lyttleton, "Revolution and Counter-revolution in Italy,
    1918-1922," and Alan Cassels, "Rise of Fascism in Italy,
    1918-1922: Revolution, Counter-revolution, or Re-arrange-
    ment?" in Bertrand, ed., Revolutionary Situations, 63-82
  A. Lyttleton, The Seizure of Power. Fascism in Italy, 1919-
    1929, 42-93
  Paul Corner, Fascism in Ferrara 1915-1925, Ch. 7, "The Rank
    and File of Fascism," 137-69

11

Week XII: A Contemporary Analysis of Revolution and Count-
Revolution in Italy: The Writings of Antonio Gramsci
*A. Gramsci, The Modern Prince and Other Writings, 28-51
*A. Gramsci, Selections from Political Writings, 1910-
1920, ed. Q. Hoare, selections # 17, 20, 21, 23-26, 28,
48, 51-52, 56-57, 60-64, 66-68, 71-72
*A. Gramsci, Selections from Political Writings, 1921-
1926, ed. Q. Hoare, selections # 2, 3, 5, 8, 11, 13, 14,
16, 19, 25, 27, 29, 36, 52, 53, 55-56, 61-63, 73

Week XIII: Presentation of Oral Reports on Papers

Week XIV: Comparative Persepctives on Causes, Consequences and
Outcomes of Revolution in Europe
James E. Cronin, "Labor Insurgency and Class Formation:
Comparative Perspectives on the Crisis of 1917-1920 in
Europe," Social Science History, 4, 1, 125-52
Carmen Sirianni, "Workers' Control in the Era of World
War I. A Comparative Analysis of the European Experience,"
Theory and Society, 9, 1980, 29-88
Charles Maier, "Political Crisis and Partial Modernization:
The Outcomes in Germany, Austria, Hungary, and Italy after
World War I," in Bertrand, ed., Revolutionary Situations,
119-32
Arno Mayer, "Internal Crisis and War since 1870," in Bertrand,
ed., Revolutionary Situations, 201-38
Barrington Moore, Jr., Injustice, 357-75

Fall Semester 1982-83   Prof. Charles S. Maier
                                         Center for European Studies
                                         Harvard University
                                         456-4303; or Robinson 101
                                         495-2157

History 1338

TOPICS IN TWENTIETH-CENTURY HISTORY:
THE SECOND WORLD WAR

I.   (September 20): Introduction to Course.

II. (September 27): Is there an Issue of Responsibility?

    A. J. P. Taylor, The Origins of the Second World War (PB),
        chaps. I-II, VI-XI.

    Michael Howard, The Continental Commitment: The Dilemma of
        British Defense Policy in the Era of Two World
        Wars, chaps. 5-6.

    Klaus Hildebrand, The Foreign Policy of the Third Reich
        (U. Cal. PB), chaps. 4-7.

    Recommended Reading:

        Esmonde M. Robertson, Hitler's Prewar Policies and Military
            Plans,1933-1939.

        Esmonde M. Robertson, ed., The Origins of the Second World
            War (includes Taylor-Trevor Roper and Taylor-Mason
            debates).

        Gerhard L. Weinberg, The Foreign Policy of Hitler's Germany:
            vol. I, Diplomatic Revolution in Europe, 1933-1936 (1970)
            vol. II, Starting World War II, 1937-1939 (1980).

        Robert Young, In Command of France (a reassessment of French
            policy).

    Recommended for origins of East Asian war and American policy:

        William L. Langer and S. E. Gleason, The Undeclared War, 1940-
            1941, chaps. I-III, XXVI-XXVIII.

        Herbert Feis, The Road to Pearl Harbor (PB).

        Robert Dallek, Franklin Roosevelt and American Foreign Policy,
            1932-1945 (PB).

        Robert J. C. Butow, Tojo and the Coming of War.

III. (October 4): Strategic Options: The Case of the Second Front.

    United States War Department, Office of Military History: The
    U.S. Army in World War II:

        Maurice Matloff and Edwin N. Snell, Strategic Planning for
            Coalition Warfare, 1941-1932, pp. 174-194, 217-244,
            279-293, 328, 347-349, 376-382.

Maurice Matloff, Strategic Planning for Coalition Warfare, 1943-1944, pp. 18-33, 37-42, 68-76, 120-138, 162-184, 280-306, 360-367, 376-382.

AND

History of the Second World War: U.K. Military Series:

J.M. A. Gwyer, Grand Strategy, vol. III, part I, pp. 1-33, 49-78.

J. R. M. Butler, Grand Strategy, vol. III, part II, pp. 419-434, 563-582, 593-600, 617-650, 657-666.

John Ehrman, Grand Strategy, vol. V, pp. 47-57, 105-118, 225.

Recommended:

Forrest Pogue, George C. Marshall: vol. II, Ordeal and Hope, 1939-1942, and vol. III: Organizer of Victory, 1943-1945.

Winston S. Churchill, The Second World War (6 vols. of memoirs).

Robert S. Sherwood, Roosevelt and Hopkins.

Albert Seaton, The Russo-German War, 1941-1945.

Andreas Hillgruber, Hitler's Strategies: Politik und Kriegsführung 1940-1941.

IV. (October 18): Strategic Options: The Case of Strategic Bombing.

Sir Charles Webster and Noble Frankland, The Strategic Air Offensive Against Germany, 1939-1945, vol. II, pp. 3-8, 32-52, 214-268; vol. III, 103-119, 207-244, 283-311.

AND

Alan S. Milward, War, Economy and Society, 1939-1945 (U.Cal. PB), chap. 9.

Recommended:

Max Hastings, Bomber Command.

V. (October 25): Did Intelligence Make a Difference?

F. H. Hinsley, et al., British Intelligence in the Second World War, vol. I, pp. 19-43, 52-85, 89-92, 115-125, 127-145, 159-190, 487-495, 528-548, 315-346.

Roberta A. Wohlstetter, Warning and Decision: Pearl Harbor.

VI. (November 1): Economic Mobilization: The Nazi Effort in Comparative Perspective.

Alan Milward, War, Economy and Society, 1939-1945, chaps. 2-4.

Alan Milward, The German Economy at War, chaps. II-IV, VI.

R. J. Overy, "Hitler's War and the German Economy: A Reinterpretation," Economic History Review, 2nd Series, XXXV, No. 2 (May 1982): 272-291.

Recommended for further comparison of rearmament efforts:

R. A. C. Parker, "Economics, Rearmament and Foreign Policy: The United Kingdom before 1939 - A Preliminary Study," Journal of Contemporary History, vol. 10, no. 4 (Oct. 1975): 637-47.

Robert Frankenstein, "A propos des aspects financiers du réarmament français," Revue d'Histoire de la Deuxième Guerre Mondiale, Nr. 102 (April 1976): 1-20.

Fortunato Minniti, "Il problema degli armamenti nella preparazione militare italiana dal 1935 al 1943," Storia Contemporanea, IX, No. 1 (February 1978): 5-62.

Other recommended reading:

Albert Speer, Inside the Third Reich.

Burton Klein, Germany's Economic Preparations for War.

G. Jansens, Das Ministerium Speer. Deutschlands Rüstung im Krieg.

Gen. Georg Thomas, Geschichte der deutschen Wehr- und Rüstungswirtschaft (1918-1943/45).

W. K. Hancock and M. R. Gowing, British War Economy.

VII. (November 8): The War and Social Change: The Case of Britain.

Paul Addison, The Road to 1945.

Richard M. Titmuss, Problems of Social Policy (History of the Second World War: Civil Series), chaps. I, II, XX section iv, XXV section i.

Recommended:

Angus Calder, The People's War: Britain, 1939-1945.

Keith Middlemas, Politics in Industrial Society, chap. 10.

VIII. (November 15): Patterns of Occupation.

Robert O. Paxton, Vichy France: Old Guard and New Order, 1940-1944 (Norton PB), Prologue, Chaps. I, II, III, V.

Jan Tomasz Gross, Polish Society under German Occupation: The Generalgouvernement, 1939-1944, chaps. I-III, V, VII, IX-X.

Recommended:

Werner Warmbrunn, The Dutch under German Occupation, 1940-1945.

IX. (November 22): Occupation and the 'Final Solution'.

Lucy S. Dawidowicz, The War Against the Jews, 1933-1945 (Bantam PB), chaps. 1, 4, 6-8, 10-16.

Recommended:

Randolph Braham, The Politics of Genocide: The Holocaust in Hungary.

Gerald Reitlinger, The Final Solution.

Karl A. Schlernes, The Twisted Road to Auschwitz.

Hannah Arendt, Eichmann in Jerusalem (PB).

Isaiah Trunk, Judenrat: the Jewish Councils in Eastern Europe under Nazi Control.

Robert O. Paxton and Michael Marrus, Vichy and the Jews.

X. (November 29): How Important Was the Resistance?

M. R. D. Foot, Resistance (Paladin PB), chaps. 1-4, 6-8;
OR
Henri Michel, The Shadow War;
OR
Werner Rings, Life with the Enemy.

H. R. Kedward, Resistance in Vichy France: A Study of Ideas and Motivation in the Southern Zone, chaps. II-III, VII-X.

Recommended:

Walter Roberts, Tito, Mihailovic and the Allies, 1941-45.

André Kédros, La résistance grècque, 1940-1944.

Charles Delzell, Mussolini's Enemies.

Giorgio Bocca, Storia dell-Italia partigiana.

Peter Hoffmann, The German Resistance to Hitler.

XI. (December 6): Culture and Society: The Impact of the War on America.

John Morton Blum, "V" Was for Victory: Politics and American Culture during World War II.

Recommended:

Leila J. Rupp, Mobilizing Women for War: German and American Propaganda.

Thomas N. Havens, Valley of Darkness: The Japanese People and World War II.

XII. (December 13): Aftermaths: Origins of the Cold War (PB).

   Vojtech Mastny, Russia's Road to the Cold War (PB).

   Charles S. Maier, ed., The Origins of the Cold War and
      Contemporary Europe, chaps. 1-2 (Maier & Schurmann pieces).

   Recommended:

      A. W. DePorte, Europe Between the Superpowers, chaps. 1-7 (PB).

      W. Averell Harriman and Elie Abel, Special Envoy to
         Churchill and Stalin, 1941-1946.

XIII. (to be scheduled): Explanation and/or Judgment: The
                         Decision to Use the Atomic Bombs.

   Martin Sherwin, A World Destroyed (PB).

   Michael Walzer, Just and Unjust Wars, chaps. 1-3, 8, 11, 16-19.

   Articles, distributed by Fussell, Sherwin, Walzer, Alsop, Joravsky.

NB: Gordon Wright, The Ordeal of Total War, 1939-1945 (Harper TB)
      should be consulted as a general reference throughout.

Written work: A 6-8 page paper on one of several assigned
questions if due in early November; a term paper (c. 20 pages)
on a topic selected by the student is due in reading period.

WAR

INTRODUCTION	Sept. 20

PART ONE: Why War?	Sept. 22 - Oct. 22

A. War and social thought   Sept. 22-24
B. The lessons of primitive war   Sept. 27
C. The search for causes   Sept. 29 - Oct. 22
     1. Biology: animal warfare and Darwinian mythology
     2. Psychology
         a. Individual psychology: human drives and war
         b. Social Psychology: national character
     3. Geography and demography
     4. Economics and the problem of imperialism
     5. Politics
         a. Domestic politics: regimes and ideologies
         b. International politics: nations in the state of nature

Hour examination   Oct. 25

PART TWO: War in history	Oct. 27 - Nov. 19

A. War and the international order   Oct. 27- Nov. 8
     1. War and international systems
         a. Types of wars
         b. Functions of wars
     2. War and foreign policy
         a. Ends and means
         b. Strategy
B. War and society   Nov. 10-Nov. 19
     1. War and the domestic order
         a. Societies in war
         b. Civil-military relations
     2. War and the individual

PART THREE: War in the nuclear age	Nov. 22 - Dec. 15

A. Violence since 1945   Nov. 22 - Dec. 10
     1. "Neither war nor peaee": the international system
         a. Rules of the nuclear game
         b. Iïuited and revolutionary wars
     2. The control of force
         a. Taming the actors: International Law and Organization
         b. Taming the weapons: Disarmament and Arms Control
B. Society and the military   Dec. 13 - 15

CONCLUSION	Dec. 17

REQUIREMENTS

1. **Sections** - the course will be divided into sections. They will meet every other week for two hours, at times and in rooms to be announced.

2. **Readings** - (starred * items are in paperback)

Part One: Why War?

A. **War and social thought (Sept. 22 - 24)**

   *Kenneth Waltz, MAN, THE STATE AND WAR, (New York: Columbia U. Press, 1959).

   *Hobbes, LEVIATHAN Ch. 1-6, 13-19.

   *S. Hoffmann, THE STATE OF WAR, (New York: Praeger) Ch. 3.

   C.J. Friedrich, ed., THE PHILOSOPHY OF KANT, (Modern Library) "Idea for a Universal History," (pp. 116 ff.) and "Eternal Peace," pp. 430 ff.

   D.J. Friedrich, ed., THE PHILOSOPHY OF HEGEL, (Modern Library) from the "Philosophy of Right," pp. 320-329.

   *M.J. Forsyth (ed.), THE THEORY OF INTERNATIONAL RELATIONS (London Allen and Unwin) Ch. by Grotius. Rousseau and Treitschke.

B. **The lessons of primitive war (Sept. 27)**

   *Leon Bramson and George Goethals (eds.), WAR (New York: Basic Books, 1970) pp. 269-274.

C. **The search for causes (Sept. 29 - Oct. 22)**

   *Konrad Lorenz, ON AGGRESSION (New York: Bantam Books) Ch. 3-7, 13-14.

   *Freud, CHARACTER AND CULTURE (Collier) IX and X.

   *Bramson and Goethals (eds.), WAR, pp. 21-31, 329-345.

   *Heath Series on Problems in Modern European Civilization: THE NEW IMPERIALISM, (Harrison Wright, ed.) Selections from Hobson, Lenin, Schumpeter, Langer, Robinson and Gallagher, Fieldhouse.

   A. Gilbert, "Marx on Internationalism and War", PHILOSOPHY AND PUBLIC AFFAIRS, Summer 1978, pp. 346-69.

Part Two: War in History

A. **War and the international order (Oct. 27-Nov. 8)**

   *Hedley Bull, THE ANARCHICAL SOCIETY (New York: Columbia U. Press, 1977) Chapters 1-5, 8.

   *Michael Howard, WAR IN EUROPEAN HISTORY (New York: Oxford U. Press) entire.

*Arnold Wolfers, DISCORD AND COLLABORATION (Johns Hopkins) Ch. 5-6.

Clausewitz, ON WAR (Howard and Paret, eds., Princeton U. Press)
    Book I, Ch. 1-3, 7 and Book VIII.

*R.J. Art and K. Waltz, (eds.) THE USE OF FORCE (Boston: Little
    Brown) pp. 365-401.

*E.M. Earle (ed.), MAKERS OF MODERN STRATEGY (Atheneum) Ch. 7, 14.

Readings on specific wars: students will choose two of the four following wars

The Peloponnesian War:

*Thucydides, PELOPONNESIAN WAR, Books, I and II, and Book V, Ch. XVIII.

The wars of the French Revolution and Napoleon:

Kyung-Won Kim, REVOLUTION AND INTERNATIONAL SYSTEM (New York:
    NYU Press(entire.

*Charles Breunig, THE AGE OF REVOLUTION AND REACTION (New York:
    Norton, second edition) chapters 1-3.

World War One:

Hajo Holborn, THE POLITICAL COLLAPSE OF EUROPE (New York: Knopf)
    chapters 3-4.

Gerd Hardach, THE FIRST WORLD WAR (Berkeley U. of California Press),
    Ch. 7-11.

*A.J.P. Taylor, THE FIRST WORLD WAR (New York: Capricorn) entire.

World War Two:

*Telford Taylor, MUNICH (New York: Vintage), Parts II-III, chapters.
    24, 26, 29 -33.

Hajo Holborn, THE POLITICAL COLLAPSE OF EUROPE, Ch. 5-6.

*Gordon Wright, THE ORDEAL OF TOTAL WAR (Harper Torchbook) entire.

Alan Milward, WAR, ECONOMY AND SOCIETY (Berkeley U. of Calif. Press)
    chapters 1, 2, 4, 9-10.

B. War and Society (Nov. 10-17)

*S.P. Huntington, THE SOLDIER AND THE STATE (Vintage Book) Part I
and Part III, Ch. 12.

*J. Glenn Gray, THE WARRIORS (Harper Torchbook) entire.
                            or
*John Keegan, THE FACE OF BATTLE (Vintage) entire.

Jean Giraudoux, TIGER AT THE GATES.
                    or
*Brecht, MOTHER COURAGE (New York:.Grove Press).

André Malraux, MAN'S HOPE (New.York:.Grove Press).
                    or
*George Orwell, HOMAGE TO CATALONIA (Beacon Press).

Part Three: War in the nuclear age

A. Violence since 1945 (Nov. 22 - Dec. 10)

*Walter La Feber, AMERICA, RUSSIA AND THE COLD WAR, fourth edition
(New York: John Wiley) entire.

*Michael Mandelbaum, THE NUCLEAR REVOLUTION (Cambridge: Cambridge U.
Press), Ch. 1. 3-4, 6, 8.

*Ground Zero, NUCLEAR WAR (New York: Pocket, 1982), Part I and Ch. 16.

*Independent Commission on Disarmament and Security Issues, COMMON
SECURITY (New York: Simon and Schuster) Ch. 3-4.

*S. Hoffmann, THE STATE OF WAR, Ch. 4-5, 8, 9.

*Michael Mandelbaum in: David Gompert et al, NUCLEAR WEAPONS AND
WORLD POLITICS (New York: McGraw-Hill) pp 15-80.

Walter Laqueur, GUERRILLA (Boston: Little, Brown) Ch. 6-9.

*Walter Laqueur, TERRORISM (Boston: Little, Brown) Ch. 3, 5 and
conclusion.

*Frantz Fanon, THE WRETCHED OF THE EARTH (New York: Grove Press)
Ch. 1-3.

*John Hersey, HIROSHIMA (New York: Bantam) entire.

*S. Hoffmann, PRIMACY OR WORLD ORDER (New York: McGraw-Hill) Part Two.

*Hedley Bull, THE ANARCHICAL SOCIETY (New York: Columbia U. Press)
Part Three.

*Ava Myrdal, THE GAME OF DISARMAMENT (New York: Pantheon) Ch. III,
VIII-IX.

*Lewis Dunn, CONTROLLING THE BOMB (New Haven: Yale U. Press).

B. Society and the military (Dec. 13-15)

Amos Perlmutter, THE MILITARY AND POLITICS IN MODERN TIMES (New Haven:
Yale U. Press) Ch. 4-9.

To be read throughout the term:

Tolstoy, WAR AND PEACE (Penguin or any unabridged edition.)

3. Other Requirements

All undergraduates must

1. Take an hour exam on Oct. 25. It will cover the lectures and readings of Part One.

2. Write a paper of approximately 5,000 words, due Jan. 14, on a topic chosen in concultation with the instructor or with the section leaders. The paper can deal with any aspect of the course. Here are some suggestions which are indications and do not pretend to be exhaustive.

The treatment of war in literature, in art or in the movies (comparisons can be made between countries, or, for a given country, between different wars).

The attitudes of various social groups, leaders or political organizations, toward war, in either World War I or World War II (especially the workers and the intellectuals).

An examination of types of, or of a particular type of, pacifist or bellicist arguments and attitudes (among soldiers or civilians).

An examination of the effects of war on the economy and social order or a nation (for instance, on civil liberties or on the class structure).

The impact of the expectation of, and preparations for war on a nation (the 1930's provide a wealth of examples).

The role of warfare in the creation and evolution of the modern state.

A study of an arms race (e.g. the British-German naval race before 1914).

The psychological and economic mobilization in a nation or in several nations during World Wars I or II (here again comparisons could be made).

The role of ideology in war (e.g. the wars of the French Revolution).

The conflicts between national allegiance and other forms of loyalty (from Antigone to collaborationism).

An examination of the role of the military in policy-making.

A discussion of strategic doctrines.

The effects of technology and technological innovations on war.

A critique of casual explanations and of philosophies of history dealing with war.

A discussion of primitive war.

22

A study of a specific decision, such as the U.S. decision to enter WWI, the decision to use the A-bomb, France's declaration of war in 1792, Churchill's resort to mass air bombings, etc.

Why a particular conflict has been limited or has escalated.

A critique of suggestions and efforts made for controlling war and the arms race, such as just war theory, the international law of war, collective security and disarmament conferences.

A discussion of the relevance of earlier studies of war (say, Thucydides or Machiavelli) to the wars of the 20th century.

A study of peace-making after a war, and of the effects of the peace treaty.

A discussion of the origins of the cold war and of the conflicting interpretations presented in recent years.

A discussion of the relevance of earlier strategic doctrines or studies of war to the nuclear age.

A study of the comparative evolution of nuclear technology and of the strategic policies or doctrines of the superpowers.

A case study of a conflict involving the use of force or of a conflict that stopped short of the resort to force, since 1945.

A study of some of the methods or doctrines of revolutionary or unconventional warfare.

A study of the impact of nuclear weapons on the policy calculations of a state.

A critique of some of the efforts or suggestions for controlling or ending the arms race.

An examination of the role played by international or regional organizations in peace-keeping.

A study of the so-called "industrial-military complex" in the United States or elsewhere.

A comparison of the views of various writers on strategy.

A study of the attitudes toward and images of other nations, in the public of a contemporary nation.

A case study of the spread (or avoidance of the spread) of nuclear weapons.

A case study of decision-making leading to war or in a crisis.

A comparison of nuclear deterrence with previous strategies of deterrence or defense.

A study of the military policies of small states.

A study of the ways in which the superpowers "control" their clients or allies.

A study of some aspect of the dynamics of the arms race.

A study of army behavior during a crisis in post-World War II foreign policy.

A study of the implications of the internationalization of Civil Wars.

A discussion of the possible effects of disarmament.

An examination of the treatment of nuclear war in literature and in movies.

A discussion of the ethical problems raised by contemporary wars or strategies.

An examination of the uses of hostility for nation-building.

A study of different types of military service and military organizations at the present time.

A study of the development and effects of transnational terrorism.

A study of proposed and possible schemes for international or regional security.

3. Take the final examination on Jan. 21

All graduate students have a choice between

1. either writing a 5,000 word paper and taking the final examination, like undergraduates (but not the hour exam)

2. or writing a paper of seminar length (12,000 words), without taking either the hour or the final examination.

The graduate student papers are due Jan. 14.

Professor Stanley Hoffmann   Professor Michael Smith
Center for European Studies   Social Studies
5 Bryant Street   Hilles Library--Lower Level

Office hours will be announced.

HISTORY 201

Graduate Seminar on

COMPARATIVE MILITARY SYSTEMS

Professor Peter Karsten
University of Pittsburgh

This is a reading seminar, designed to stimulate a research project of one's choice, on the nature of military systems throughout the world. Needless to say, while it should appeal to the sociologist and political scientist, it has a strong historical dimension. The literature we will be considering concerns: the social origins of military personnel; their recruitment, their training; the process of value inculcation; inter- and intra-service rivalries; mutinies; coups d'etat, civil-military relations; and the role of the military in "nation-building." We will also spend a week on a related topic, the laws of warfare and war-crimes. You will be asked to read a common reading and one other work each week.

The sorts of questions we will be asking in the next two months may be of interest to you now as you begin the readings. These questions include (but are by no means limited to) the following:

Stanislav Andreski (in Military Organization and Society) argues that the type of military organization or innovation a society adopts may cause sweeping changes in that society's political and social organizations. To what extent is this valid?

The readings reveal relationships between recruitment practices and the roles military systems play in society? What are they?

What consistent evidence exists of a "militarist" who tends to offer his services or to emerge from training?

Why do military coups occur? Of the several different causes which are associated with particular societies or conditions?

How does one evaluate the claim that "the military is a natural nation-builder"?

What values appear malleable in training? Does military training differ from culture to culture? If so, give examples and explain the differences.

What accounts for the emergence of any particular "law" or "rule" of warfare? What accounts for the fact that any particular "law" is not observed as scrupulously by some military personnel as its drafters had hoped?

You will each be asked to select a particular topic, formulate a question or hypothesis (not necessarily any one of those I've just jotted down, of course), and answer it either with an extensive analysis of the existing literature, or with original research.

WEEKLY TOPICS

Week	Subject	Common Reading (in addition to each individual's)
1.	Introduction: the Military & Society	S. Andreski, Military Organization & Society (skim read)
2.	Civil-Military Relations (in general)	S. Huntington, The Soldier & the State, pp. 1-97
3.	Recruitment & Social Background	P. Karsten, Soldiers & Society, pp. 1-20, 51-125
4.	Training & Value Inculcation	P. Karsten, Soldiers & Society, pp. 21-22, 126-144
5.	The "Military Mind" & Inter-Service Rivalries	A. Vagts, A History of Militarism, pp. 1-74
6.	The World of Combat	P. Karsten, Soldiers & Society, pp. 22-31, 145-231
7.	The Laws of Warfare & War Crimes	P. Karsten, Law, Soldiers & Combat, chpts. 1 & 2
8.	Mutinies	C. J. Lammers, "Strikes & Mutinies," Admin. Science Q (Dec. 1969)
9.	Coups d'Etat	Wm. Thompson, The Grievances of Military Coup-Makers
10.	"Nation-Building"	Lucien Pye, "Armies in the Process of Political Modernization," in John Johnson, ed., The Role of the Military in Underdeveloped Countries
11.	Veterans	P. Karsten, Soldiers & Society, pp. 32ff, 232ff.
12.	Office Hours	
13.	Presentation of Papers	

Basic Comparative Military Systems Literature, Organized Topically

1. The Military and Society: General Intro. Readings

Stanislav Andreski, Military Organization and Society
F. Voget, "Warfare & the Integration of Crow Indian Culture," in W.H. Goodenough, eds., Explorations in Cultural Anthropology, pp. 483-509

2. Civil-Military Relations

I. Deak, "An Army Divided: Loyalty Crisis in Haps. Off. Corps, 1848.'
Jahrbuch des I. für Deut. G. VIII ('79)

Claude Welch and Arthur Smith, Military Role and Rule
E. Joffe, Party and Army: Professionalism and Political Control in the
Chinese Officer Corps
Louis Perez, Army Politics in Cuba, 1898-1958
A. Mazrui chapter in Jacques van Doorn, ed., Military Professions and
Military Regimes
Nelson Kasfir, "Civilian Participation under Military Rule in Uganda and
Sudan," Armed Forces and Society, I (1975), 344ff.
C. Moskos chapter [on U.N.] in Van Gils, ed., The Perceived Role of the Military
Charles Moskos, Peace Soldiers and Moskos essay in J.van Doorn and Morris
Janowitz, eds., On Military Ideology
Gabriel Ben-Dor, "The Politics of Threat: Military Intervention...,"
Journal of Political and Military Sociology, I (1973), 57ff
Gabriel Ben-Dor, "Civilianization of Military Regimes in the Arab World,"
Armed Forces and Society, I (1975), 317ff.
Edwin Lieuwen, Mexican Militarism
Anton Bebler, The Military in African Politics
D. Herspring and I. Volgyes, "Political Reliability in Eastern Europe
Warsaw Pack Armies," Armed Forces and Society, VI (1980), 270-296
Jorge Dominques, "The Civic Soldier: The Military as a Governing Institution
in Cuba," 1973 IUS paper
Roman Kolkowicz, "Interest Groups in Soviet Politics: The Case of the
Military," Comparative Politics (April 1970), 445-472.
Cynthia Enloe, Ethnic Soldiers

3. Recruitment

Richard Smethurst, A Social Basis for Prewar Japanese Militarism
Ithiel de Sola Pool, Satellite Generals
Summer Shapiro, "The Blue-Water Soviet Naval Officer" U.S. Naval
Institute Proceedings (February 1971), 19-26
Christopher Duffy, The Army of Fredrick the Great 24-68
Shelby D vis, Reservoirs of Men: Black Troops of French West Africa
John Erickson, "Soviet Military Manpower Policies," Armed Forces and
Society, I (Fall, 1974), 29ff.
H. Moyse-Bartlett, The King's African Rifles
Edward Lowell, The Hessians
Chapters by Dudley, Wiatr, Graczyk, and Cvrcek in Military Professions and
Military Regimes, ed. Jacques van Doorn
D. Ayalon and S. Vryoni on recruitment, in War, Technology and Society in
the Middle East, ed. Vernon Parry and M. E. Yapp, 44-68, 125-152
Coulombe chapter in On Military Ideology, eds., Morris Janowitz and J. van Doorn
Thomas Brendle, "Recruitment and Training in the SDF:," in James Buck ed.,
The Modern Japanese Military System
G. T. Griffith, The Mercenaries of the Hellenistic World
H. W. Parke, Greek Mercenary Soldiers
Peter Karsten, The Naval Aristocracy, chapter 1 and religion (chapter 3)
Peter Karsten, Soldiers and Society, (section on "The Recruitment Process")
Moskos, Davis-Dolbeare, and Wamsley essays in Roger Little, ed., Selective
Service and American Society
Sylvia Frey, "Common British soldier in late 18th century," Societas (1975
(or '76)
Holger Herwig, "Feudalization of the Bourgeoisie: Role of Nobility in
German Naval Officer Corps, 1890-1918," The Historian ('75-'76), 268ff.

Michel Martin, "Changing Social Morphology of French Mil. Est., 1945-75" (Mimeo)
Alan R. Skelley, The Victorian Army at Home
George Chessman, Auxilia of the Roman Imperial Army
Douglas Wheeler, "African Elements in Portugals' Armies in Africa," Armed Forces and Society, II (1976), 233ff.
John Schlight, Monarchs and Mercenaries
Michael Powicke, Military Obligation in Medieval England
Gianfranco Pasquino, "The Italian Army," Armed Forces and Society, II (1976), 205ff
JJ Sanders, Feudal Military Service in England
Fritz Redlich, The German Military Enterpriser and his work force (2 volumes)
F. Kazemzadeh, "The Origin and Early Development of the Persian Cossack Brieade," American Slavic and East European Review, XV, 351-63
D. Mantell, "Doves v. Rawks," Psychology Today, September 1974
G. Kourvetaris, "Greek Service Academies: Patterns of Recruitment and Organization Change," in G. Harries-Jenkins, ed., The Military and the Problems of Legitimacy, 113ff
E. H. Norman, Soldier and Peasant in Japan
E. Waidman, The Goose Step est Verboden
H. Desmond Martin, The Rise of Chingis Khan, 11-47
John Bassett, The Purchase System in the British Army, 1660-1871
Michael Lewis, A Social History of the Royal Navy, 1793-1815
F. Harrod, Manning The New Navy
Richard Gabriel, The New Red Legions, Volumes I and II
G. R. Andrews, "The Afro-Argentine Officers of B. A. Prov., 1800-1860," Journal of Negro History, 64 (1979), 85-100
Steven Cohen, "The Untouchable Soldier: Caste, Politics and the Indian Army," Journal of Asian Studies, XXVIII (May 1969)
Roger N. Buckley, Slaves in Red Coats: The Br. N.I. Regiments, 1795-1815
John Keegan, "Regimental Ideology," in War, Economy and the Military Mind, ed. G. Best, 3-18
Michael Lewis, The Navy in Trasition, 1814-1864
Michael Lewis, England's Sea-Officers
H. Hanham, "Religion and Nationality in Mid-Victorian Army," in Foot, ed., War and Society, 159ff
Norbert Elias, "Studies inthe Genesis of the Naval Profession," British Journal of Sociology, I (1950), 291-309
C. B. Otley essay in Armed Forces and Society, ed., Jacques Van Doorn
P. Razzell, "Social Origins of Officers in the Indian and British Home Army," British Journal of Sociology, XIV (1963), 248ff.
Peter Karsten, et al., "ROTC, Mylai and the Volunteer Army," Foreign Policy, 1 (1971), 135-60

4. Training and Value Inculation

Roghmann and Sodeur, "Impact of Military Service on Auth. Attitudes in W. G." American Journal of Soc. (September 72)
John Farris, "Recruits and Boot Camp," Armed Forces and Society, (Fall, 1975)
James Kelley, "The Education and Training of Porfirian Officers," Military Affairs (October 1975), 124-28
Peter Karsten, The Naval Aristocracy, chapters 2 and 5
W. Cockerham, "Selective Socialization: Airborne Trainees," Journal of Political and Military Sociology, 1 (1973), 215-29
Correlli Barnett, "The Education of Military Elites," in Rupert Wilkinson, ed., Governing Elites, 193-214

Charles Firth, Cromwell's Army
Peter Karsten, "Ritual and Rank: Religious Affiliation, Father's "Calling" and Successful Advancement in the U.S. Officers Corps of the 20th Century", Armed Forces and Society (Fall, 1981)

Law, Radine, _The Taming of the Troops, Social Control in U.S. Army_
Morris Janowitz, "Changing Patterns of Org. Auth." _Admin. Science Quarterly_
  (1957)
William D. Henderson, _Why The Vietcong Fought: Motivation and Control_
Hassanein Rabie, "The Training of the Mamluk Faris," in _War, Technology,
  and Society in the Middle East_, ed. Vernon Parry and M. E. Yapp, 153-163
Harold Wool, "The Armed Services as a Training Institution," in
  Eli Ginsberg, _The Nations Children_, II, 158-185
Herbert Goldhamer, _The Soviet Soldier_
C. Lammers, "Midshipmen...," _Sociologica Neerlandia_, II (1965), 98-122
G. Wamsley, "Contrasting Institutions of AF Socialization," _Amer. Journal of Soc._
  (Sept.72)

5. "Militarism" and Military Ideologies

Hans Herzfeld, "Militarism in Modern History," in _Germany History_, ed.
  Hans Kohn, 108-121
Alfred Vagts, _A History of Militarism_, 1-74
Peter Karsten, _The Naval Aristocracy_, chapters 3, 5 and 6
Hansen and Abrahamsson chapters in _On Military Ideology_, eds. Morris
  Janowitz and J. van Doorn
Martin Kitchen, _The German Officer Corps, 1890-1914_
Francis Carsten, "From Scharnhorst to Schleicher: The Prussian Officer
  corps in Politics, 1806-1933, in Michael Howard, ed., _Soldiers and
  Governments_, 73-98
Stanley Payne, _Politics and the Military in Modern Spain_
Bengt Abrahamsson, "The Ideology of an Elite...the Swedish Military," in
  Armed Forces and Society, ed. Jacques van Doorn, 71-83
Morris Janowitz, _The Professional Soldier_
Roman Kolkowicz, "Modern Technology and the Soviet Officer Corps,' in
  Jacques van Doorn, ed., _Armed Forces and Society_, 148-168
Richard Smethurst, _A Social Basis for Prewar Japanese Militarism_
chapter on Italy in Stephen ward, ed., _The War Generation_
Maurice Keen, "Brotherhood in Arms," _History_, XLVII (1962)
Marcus Cunliffe, _Soldiers and Civilians_ (chapters on volunteers and on North-
  South comparison)
Wallace Davies, _Patriotism on Parade_

6. Inter - and Intra - Service Rivalries

Louis Morton, "Army and Marines on the China Station," _Pacific Historical
  Review_, X (1960), 51ff
Peter Karsten, _The Naval Aristocracy_, chapter 5, part 2
Fred Greene, "The Military View of American National Policy,"
  American Historical Review (1961), 354ff
Ferry Smith, _The Air Force Plans for Peace_
Vincent Davis, _Postwar Defense Policy and the U.S. Navy, 1943-1346_
Robert Gallucci, _Neither Peace nor Honor_
Lewis Dexter, "Congressmen and the Making of Military Policy,' in
  Nelson Polsby, ed., _New Perspectives on the House of Representatives_
Paul Hammond, _Supercarriers and B-36s_

7. The World of Combat

Peter Karsten, _Soldiers and Society_, pp. 22-31, 145-231
John Baynes, _Morale_
John Keegan, _The Face of Battle_
S. L. A. Marshall, _Men Against Fire_
Peter Bourne, _Men, Stress, and Vietnam_
Art Bareau, _The Unknown Soldiers_

J. E. Morris, The Welsh Wars of Edward I
M. Barton, Goodmen: Civil War Soldiers
R. Grinker ard J. Spiegel, Men Under Stress
Cincinatus, Self-Destruction
Pete Maslowski, "A Study of Morale in Civil War Soldiers," Military
    Affairs, (1970), 122-125
Cecil Woodham-Smith, The Charge of the Light Brigade
Albert Biderman, March to Calumny
Eugene Kinkead, In Every War But One
Ron Glasser, 365 Days
John Beeler, Warfare in Feudal Europe, 730-1200
J. Glenn Gray, The Warriors
John Mahon, The Second Seminole War
Peter Paret, The Vendée, 1789-1796
Eric Leed, No Man's Land: Combat and Identity in World War I
Dennis Winter, Death's Men
Shils and Janowitz, "Cohesion and Disintegration in Wehrmacht,' in
    W. Schramm, ed., Process and Effects of Mass. Comm.

8. The Laws of War and War Crimes

Peter Karsten, Law, Soldiers and Combat
Maurice Keen, The Laws of War in the Late Middle Ages
Raymond Schmandt, "The Fourth Crusade and the Just War Theory,'
    Catholic Historical Review (1975), 191-221
Stan H ig, The Sand Creek Massacre
Seymour Hersh, Mylai 4
The Sand Creek Massacre, ed., John Carroll
Leon Friedman, ed., The Laws of War, Volumes I and II
John R. Lemia, comp., Uncertain Judgement: A Bibliography of War Crimes Trials
The Mylai Massacre and Its Coverup, ed., Burke Marshall, et al
W. H. Parks, "Crimes in Hostilities," Marine Corps Gazette (August 1976)

9. Mutinies

C. Lammers, "Strikes and Mutinies: A Comparative Study," Admin. Science
    Quarterly (December 1969)
J. A. B. Palmer, Mutiny Outbreak at Meerut (1857)
Christ. Hibbert, The Great Mutiny, India, 1857
Daniel Horn, The German Naval Mutiny of WWI
John Williams, Mutiny, 1917
50 Mutinies
Carl Van Doren, Mutiny in January
A. P. Ryan, Mutiny at the Curragh
Hayford, The Somers Mutiny Affair
Richard Watt, Dare Call It Treason
Ronald Spector, "The Royal Indian Navy Strike of 1946," Armed Forces and
    Society," VII (1981), 271-284
Peter Karsten, "Suberned or Subordinate? Irish Soldiers in the British
    Army, 1792-1922," AHA paper, 1981
AllanWildman, The End of the Russian Imperial Army....Soldier's Revolt
John Prebble, Mutiny: Highland Regiments in Revolt

30

10. Military Corps d'Etat

William Thompson, The Grievances of Military Coup-Makers

Richard Kohn, "The Inside History of the Newburgh Conspiracy," William and Mary Quarterly (April, 1970), 1987-220

Harold Hyman, "Johnson, Stanton and Grant," American Historical Review, (October 1960), 85ff

Alfred Stepan, The Military in Politics...Brazil

John Ambler, Soldiers Against the State

Ph. Schmitter, "Liberation by Golpe...Portugal," Armed Forces and Society (Fall 1975), 5-33

Luigi Einandi, "U.S. Relations with the Peruvian Military," in Daniel Sharp, ed., U.S. Foreign Policy and Peru, 15-56

J. Rothschild, "The Military Background of Pilsudski's Coup d 'Etat," Slavic Review, XXI (1962), 241-260

Egil Fossum, "Factors influencing....military Coups d 'etat in Latin America," Journal of Peace Res. (oslo), III (1967), 228-251

Douglas Porch, "Making an Army Revolutionary: France, 1815-1848," in Geof. Best, ed., War, Economy and the Military Mind

Morris Janowitz, Military Institutions and Coercion in Developing Nations, ch. 3

Fuad Khuri and G. Obermeyer, "The Social Bases for Military Intervention in the Middle East," in Catherine Kelleher, ed., Political-Military Systems, pp. 55ff

11. Nation - building

Donald Jackson, Custer's Gold

D. Lerner and R. D. Robinson, "Swords and Ploughshares: Turkish Army as Modernizing Force," World Politics, XIII (October 1960)

Henry Bienen, ed., The Military and Modernization [on L.A., Asia, Turkey, Soviet Union, Africa, and Huntington's caveat]

Willard Barber and C. N. Ronning, Internal Security and Military Power: Counterinsurgency and Civic Action in L.A.

Ellen K. Trimberger, Revolution from Above: Military Bureaucrats and Development in Japan, Turkey, Egypt and Peru

Theophilus O. Odetola, Military Politics in Nigeria: Economic Development and Political Stability

Stephen Cohen, The Indian Army: Its Contribution to the Development of a Nation

Charles Corbett, The L. A. Military Force as a Socio-Political Force: Bolivia and Argentina

R. L. Clinton, "The Modernizing Military: Peru," Inter-American Economic Affairs, 24:4 (1971) 43-66

Francis Prucha, Broadax and Bayonet

William Goetzmann, Army Exploration in the American West

Lucien Pye, "Armies in the Process of Political Modernization," in John Johnson, ed., The Role of the Military in Underdeveloped Countries

Jae Souk Sohn , "Political Dominance and Political Failure: The Role of the Military in the Republic of Korea," in Henry Bienen, ed., The Military Intervenes 103-121

S. E. Finer, "The Man on Horseback-1974," Armed Forces and Society, I (Fall, 1974), 5ff

Hugh Hanning, The Peaceful Uses of Military Forces

Moshe Lissak, Military Roles in Modernization: Thailand and Burma

Robert Athearn, W. T. Sherman and the Settlement of the West

12. Veterans

H. Browning, et al., "Income and Veteran Status," American Sociological
Review (1973), 74

Rodney Minott, Peerless Patriots

Steven Ross, "The Free Corps Movement in Post World War I Europe,"
Rocky Mountain Social Science Journal (1968), 81-92

Forrest McDonald, "French Veterans..." Agricultural History (1951)

G. Wooton, The Politics of Influence: British Ex-Servicemen, Cabinet
Decisions and Cultural Change, 1917-1957

Mary Dearing, Veterans in Politics: The Story of the G.A.R.

William Benton, "Pa. Revr. Officers and the Federal Constitution,"
Pa. History (1964), 419-35

Peter Karsten, Soldiers and Society (section on veterans)

Al. Biderman and L. Sharp, "Convergence of Military and Civilian Careers,"
American Journal of Sociology (1968).

N. Phillips, "Militarism and Grass-Roots...," Journal of Conflict
Resolution (December 1973), 625-655

Stephen Ward, ed., The War Generation

Isser Woloch, The French Veteran From the Revolution to the Restoration

History G57.1251   Diplomatic History of Europe 1789-1900   **Professor Stehlin**

Readings:

For each lecture the student is expected to have read in advance the pertinent sections of the following textbook: Rene Albrecht Carrie, <u>A Diplomatic History of Europe Since the Congress of Vienna</u>. (Harper paperback) (revised ed.)

In addition, the student is expected to read the items under each weekly topic. The bibliography contains further readings listed in order to aid the student in delving more deeply into those topics discussed.

The required books are available in the Reserve Reading Room.

1. September 16   Introduction

2. September 23   1. Background of the period
                     2. The French Revolution
   C. Brinton, <u>A Decade of Revolution</u>, pp. 64-87, 90-104, 128-130, 164-189, 206-209, 221-245.

3. September 30   1. The Diplomacy of the Napoleonic Era
                     2. The Congress of Vienna
   G. Brunn, <u>Europe and the French Imperium</u>, pp. 29-32, 36-61, 83-108, 109-139, 157-209
   H. Nicolson, <u>The Congress of Vienna</u>, chapters 8-15

4. October 7   1. Restoration Europe
                     2. The Eastern Question
   H. Kissinger, <u>A World Restored</u>, chps. X-XVII

5. October 14   1. The Revolution of 1848
                     2. The Crimean War
   L. Namier, <u>The Revolt of the Intellectuals</u>, entire book
   B. Jelavich, <u>St. Petersburg and Moscow (Century of Russian Foreign Policy)</u>, pp. 71-113

6. October 21   1. The Second Napoleonic Era
   R. Binkley, <u>Realism and Nationalism</u>, pp. 27-31, 120-122, 124-139, 157-193, 197-214, 227-230
   J. M. Thompson, <u>Louis Napoleon and the Second Empire</u>, chp. VII, chps, VIII-X (foreign affairs)

7. October 28   1. The Unification of Italy
   A. J. Whyte, <u>The Evolution of Modern Italy</u>, chps. I-XI

8. November 4   1.The Struggle for Supremacy in Germany
   E. Eyck, <u>Bismarck and the German Empire</u>, pp. 11-186

9. November 11   1. The New Europe
                      2. The League of Peace
      H. Kohn, Panslavism, Parts I & II

10. November 18   1. The Near Eastern Question
                      2. The Cracks in the Bismarckian System
      E. Eyck, Bismarck and the German Empire, pp. 187-323
      Gordon Craig, From Bismarck to Adenauer, chaps. I & II

11. December 2   1. The end of the Bismarckian System
                      2. The Diplomacy of Imperialism
      L. Lafore, The Long Fuse, pp. 13-127 (2nd ed.)

12. December 9   1. The Crises of Imperialism
      H. M. Wright, ed., The New Imperialism, 2nd ed. 1975 (entire book)

13. December 16   1. The Franco-Russian Alliance
                      2. The Weakening of the Triple Alliance and the
                         Formation of the Entente Cordiale
      H. Feis, Europe The World's Banker, pp. 26-32, 57-59, 78-80, 117,
         156-159, 187-188, 191-242, 258-360
      B.Jelavich, St. Petersburg & Moscow (Century of Russian Foreign
         Policy) pp. 213-256

14. December 23   1. The Rise of New Powers
                      2. Europe at the Turn of the Century
      B. Tuchman, The Proud Tower, chps. 2,4,5,8

History 657.1252

Readings.

For each lecture the student is expected to have read in advance the pertinent sections of the following textbook: René Albrecht Carrie, A Diplomatic History of Europe Since the Congress of Vienna. rev. ed. paperback.

In addition, the student is expected to read the items under each weekly topic. The bibliography contains further readings listed in order to aid the student in delving more deeply into those topics discussed.

The required books are available in the Reserve Reading Room.

Schedule of Lectures and Assignments:

1. February 4
   1. Introduction
   2. Europe at the Turn of the Century

2. February 11
   1. The First Moroccan Crisis
   2. The Formation of the Triple Entente
      and the Annexation of Bosnia
      - _____ Oron Hale, The Great Illusion Chapters I,II, III, VII-XI

3. February 18
   1. The Bosnia Crisis and its Consequences
   2. The Second Moroccan Crisis and the War in Tripoli
      _____ Laurence Lafore, The Long Fuse 2nd edition

4. February 25
   1. The Balkan Wars
   2. The Great Powers on the Eve of the War
      _____ Dwight Lee, The Outbreak of the First World War 4th ed. 197
      _____ Jack Roth: World War I Chps. 1,2,3,6

5. March 3
   1. The Outbreak of World War I
   2. Diplomacy of World War I
      _____ Hans Gatzke, Germany's Drive to the West, pp. 1-84, 126-195, 219-237, 271-294

6. March 10
   1. The Making of the Peace
   2. The Reorganization of Eastern Europe
      _____ F. Czernin, Versailles 1919, Chps. I,II,VI,VII,IX,XI

7. March 17
   1. The War after the War (1920-1922)
   2. The Ruhr Problem
      _____ A. Wolfers, Britain and France between Two Wars. Chapters I-IX, XI-XVI, pp. 265, XVIII-XIX, Conclusion

8. March 31
   1. The Search for Security
   2. Disarmament
      _____ Gordon Craig and F. Gilbert, The Diplomats, Chapters I, 2,5, Wolfers, Chapters X,XXI

9. April 7
   1. Soviet Foreign Policy
   2. The Turn of the Tide
      _____ G. Kennan, Soviet Foreign Policy 1917-1941 just text
      _____ Gordon Craig, Diplomats, Chapters 8,11 no documents

35

10. April 14   1. Appeasement in the Far East
2. The Beginnings of Nazi Foreign Policy
_____Gordon Craig, The Diplomats, Vol. II, Chapters 10,12-15

11. April 21   1. Fascist Foreign Policy and the Italo-Ethiopian War
2. The Two Camps: Democracies vs. Dictatorships Vol. II
_____Gordon Craig, The Diplomats, Vol. I, Chapters 7,9, Vol. 16-2.

12. April 28   1. The Spanish Civil War
2. The Austrian Anschluss
_____Hugh Thomas, The Spanish Civil War, Book III, Chapters 40,42
54,58,60,64,65,69,70 conclusion and diplomatic sections.

13. May 5   1. The Betrayal of Czeckoslovakia
2. Munich and its consequences
_____A. Rowse, Appeasement

14. May 12   1. The Road to War
2. The Outbreak of World War II
_____L. Lafore, End of Glory Chapters 1,4-8

Social Science 461
International Politics
1900-Present

Professor Santore   Spring 1988
Pratt Institute

Syllabus

        The purpose of this course is to introduce students to
some of the main problems in the history of twentieth-century
international relations. It is designed to examine the patterns
of political interaction between and among nations, with an
emphasis on those conflicts and issues which have arisen since
the end of the Second World War. Among the topics which will
be discussed are the origins of the Cold War and the sources of
American and Soviet foreign policies, the international arms race
and the efficacy of nuclear strategy, international terrorism and
the problems of political governance, the conflicts in Nicaragua
and Afghanistan, and the maintenance of the balance of power in
Europe, Asia, and the Middle East. In addition, special attention
will also be given to such perennial problems as the role played
by nationalism, imperialism, and militarism in the formation of
national policy and the degree to which the press and public
opinion influence decisions of war and peace.
        As a strategy for dealing with these problems, the course
has been divided into two parts. Part One will trace the history
of twentieth-century international relations from 1900 to the
present. Part Two will deal topically with the main international
issues of the contemporary world.
        Requirements for the course consist of two exams, a midterm
and final. In order to receive a quality grade in these exams,
students should attend all classes and complete the assigned
readings. The lectures, in particular, are extremely comprehensive
and contain materials necessary for the examinations. Classes
will meet once a week from 9:30 to 12 on Tuesday mornings. The
list of lecture topics and required readings is as follows:

Lecture Schedule

Part I: The Origins of Contemporary International Conflict, 1871-1962.

Session #1: The Historical Setting: The "Old World" at Zenith   -   the
            European vortex of global politics at the dawn of the
            twentieth century.

                    Robert Paxton, Europe in the Twentieth
                    Century, Chap. 1. (on reserve)

            Echoes in the Distance: Emerging threats to Europe's
            prewar hegemony   -   the United States; Japan; Third
            World Nationalism.

                    William R. Keylor, The Twentieth-Century World
                    An International History, pp. 3-40. (Purchase)

37

Session #2: Denouement in Violence: The diplomatic background to
the First World War, 1871-1914.

Laurence Lafore, The Long Fuse, entire (Purchase)

Session #3: World War I: How deep the causes?
- The immediate cause: the crisis of 1914.
- Deeper causes: nationalism; imperialism; militarism;
the alliance systems; the role of the press and
public opinion; the problem of the balance of
power; domestic political pressures; the
question of "international anarchy."

Keylor, pp. 43-55.
Fritz Fischer, World Power or Decline, pp.
3-45. (on reserve)
Joachim Remak, The Origins of the First World
War, pp. 60-96, 132-150. (on reserve)

Session #4: International relations in extremis: wartime diplomacy,
1914-1918.

Keylor, pp. 55-73.
Rene Albrecht-Carrie, The Meaning of the First
World War, pp. 47-89. (on reserve)

The Paris Peace Conference and the search for normalcy
in the 1920s.

Keylor, pp. 74-132.
Albrecht-Carrie, pp. 90-172. (on reserve)

Session #5: Return to Armagedon: The renewal of German and Japanese
expansionism in the 1930s.

Keylor, pp. 133-184, 229-252.
A.J.P. Taylor, The Origins of the Second World
War, entire. (Purchase)
William Roger Louis (ed.), The Origins of the
Second World War: A.J.P. Taylor and His
Critics essays by Trevor-Roper, Hinsley,
and Bullock). (on reserve)

Session #6: The End of European Autonomy:
- World War II: The fighting, 1939-1945.
- Wartime diplomacy and the origins of the Cold
War: Teheran, Moscow, Yalta, Potsdam.

Keylor, pp. 185-205, 152-258.
Gordon Wright, The Ordeal of Total War, pp.
204-267. (on reserve)
John Lewis Gaddis, Russia, the Soviet Union
and the United States, pp. 1-175. (Purchase)

Session #7: The Cold War at Apex, 1945-1962.
- Conflicting visions: the sources of American and Soviet foreign policy.
- The emergence of a "bipolar" world, 1945-1962.

Keylor, pp. 261-331.
Gaddis, pp. 175-241.

Session #8: Midterm.

Part II: Conflict and Issues in the Contemporary World, 1962-present.

Session #9: Decolonization in Africa and Asia:
- The European response: France; Britain; Belgium; Portugal.
- The American Response: China; Iran; Vietnam.

Keylor, pp. 368-397.
Daniel R. Brower, The World in the Twentieth Century, pp. 202-209, 233-259, 283-290. (on reserve)

Session #10: The United States and Latin America: From the Spanish-American War to Allende's Chile.

Keylor, pp. 206-228; 332-335.

Session #11: US-Soviet Relations: From confrontation to detent and back to confrontation, 1962-1986.

Gaddis, pp. 241-279.

From a bipolar to a multipolar world: the Sino-Soviet dispute and the emergence of new power centers.

Keylor, pp. 335-361; 397-402.

Session #12: The Imbroglio in the Middle East:
- Israel, the Arabs, and the Great Powers.
- The problem of international terrorism.

Keylor, pp. 361-368.
Brower, pp. 260-282. (on reserve)

Session #13: The Arms Race and the question of nuclear disarmament: How realistic is the idea of nuclear "deterence?"

Robert Jervis, The Illogic of American Nuclear Strategy, entire (Purchase)

Session #14; Festering Issues: Nicaragua; Afghanistan; South Africa.

Keylor, pp. 405-428.

Session #15: Final Exam.

Suggested Further Reading

General

Rene Albrecht-Carrie, A Diplomatic History of Europe Since the
Congress of Vienna.
Raymond Aron, Peace and War: A Theory of International Relations.
Hans J. Mongenthau, Politics Among Nations: The Struggle for Power
and Peace.
Donald James Puchala, International Politics Today.
Morton Kaplan (ed.), Great Issues of International Politics.
Geoffrey Barraclough, An Introduction to Contemporary History.
Felix Gilbert, The End of the European Era, 1890 to the Present
Hajo Holborn, The Political Collapse of Europe.
David Calleo, The German Problem Reconsidered: Germany and the
World Order, 1870 to the Present.
Gordon Craig, From Bismarck to Adenauer: Aspects of German Statecraft.

1871-1914

L.C.F. Turner, Origins of the First World War.
James Joll, 1914: Unspoken Assumptions.
H.M. Koch (ed.), The Origins of the First World War: Great Power
Rivalry and German War Aims.
Fritz Fischer, Germany's Aims in the First World War.
_____, War of Illusions.
Imanuel Geiss, July 1914.
V.R. Berghahn, Germany and the Approach of War in 1914.
Vladimir Dedijer, The Road to Sarajevo.
J.F.V. Keiger, France and the Origins of the First World War.
A.J.P. Taylor, The Struggle for Mastery in Europe.
D.C.B. Lieven, Russia and the Origins of the First World War.
Fritz Stern, "Bethmann Hollweg and the War: The Limits of Respon-
sibility", in Leonard Krieger and Fritz Stern (eds.), The
Responsibility of Power.
Arno Mayer, "Domestic Causes of the First World War", in Krieger
and Stern, The Responsibility of Power.
Wolfgang J. Mommsen, "Domestic Factors in German Foreign Policy
before 1914", in James J. Sheehan (ed. Imperial
Germany.

1914-1919

Cyril Falls, The Great War.
A.J.P. Taylor, An Illustrated History of the First World War.
B.H. Lidell Hart, History of the First World War.
J.W. Wheeler-Bennett, Brest-Litovsk: The Forgotten Peace, March 1918.
Gerald D. Feldman (ed.), German Imperialism, 1914-1918: The
Development of a Historical Debate.
V.H. Rothwell, British War Aims and Peace Diplomacy, 1914-1918.

Davis Stevenson, French War Aims Against Germany, 1914-1918.
Patrick Devlin, Too Proud to Fight: Woodrow Wilson's Neutrality.
David F. Trask, The United States in the Supreme War Council:
      American War Aims and Inter-Allied Strategy, 1917-1918.
Harold Nicolson, Peacemaking 1919.
Paul Birdsall, Versailles, Twenty Years After.
Leo J. Lederer (ed.), The Versailles Settlement: Was it Foredoomed
      To Failure?
Arno J. Mayer, Wilson vs. Lenin: The Political Origins of the New
      Diplomacy.
_____, Politics and Diplomacy of Peacemaking: Containment
      and Counter-Revolution at Versailles, 1918-1919.

1919-1939

E.H. Carr, The Twenty Years Crisis.
_____, International Relations Between the Two World Wars,
      1919-1939.
Sally Marks, The Illusion of Peace: International Relations in
      Europe, 1918-1933.
Arnold Wolfers, Britain and France Between Two World Wars.
W.M. Jordan, Great Britain, France, and the German Problem.
Pierre Renouvin, War and Aftermath, 1914-1929.
Jon Jacobson, Locarno Diplomacy.
Hans Gatzke (ed.), European Diplomacy Between the Two World Wars.
Hugh Seton-Watson, Eastern Europe Between the Two World Wars.
Derek H. Aldcroft, From Versailles to Wall Street: 1918-1929.
John Hoff Wilson, American Business and Foreign Policy, 1920-1933.
Charles S. Maier, Recasting Bourgeois Europe.
Stephen A. Schuker, The End of French Predominance in Europe.
Robert H. Ferrell, Peace in Their Time: The Origins of the Kellogg-
      Briand Pact.
Piotr, Wandycz, France and Her Eastern Allies, 1919-1925.
Hans Gatzke, Stressemann and the Rearmament of Germany.
George Kennan, Russia and the West Under Lenin and Stalin.
Keith Eubank, The Origins of World War II.
Laurence Lafore, The End of Glory: An Interpretation of the Origins
      of World War II.
Pierre Renouvin, World War II and Its Origins: International
      Relations, 1929-1945.
Joachim Remak, The Origins of the Second World War.
Anthony Adamwaite, The Making of the Second World War.
Christopher Thorne, The Approach of War, 1938-1939.
Alan Bullock, Hitler: A Study in Tyranny.
Gerhart Weinberg, The Foreign Policy of Hitler's Germany, 2 vols.
Klaus Hildebrand, The Foreign Policy of the Third Reich.
Andreas Hillgruber, Germany and the Two World Wars.
Norman Rich, Hitler's War Aims, 2 vols.
Anthony Adamwaite, France and the Coming of the Second World War.
Martin Gilbert, The Roots of Appeasement.
William R. Rock, British Appeasement in the 1930s.

Keith Middlemas, Diplomacy of Illusion: The British Government
          and Germany, 1937-1939.
Sidney Aster, 1939: The Making of the Second World War.
Keith Eubank, Munich.
Elisabeth Wiskemann, The Rome-Berlin Axis.
Denis Mack Smith, Mussolini's Roman Empire.
John F. Cloverdale, Italian Intervention in the Spanish Civil War.
Arnold A. Offner, American Appeasement: United States Foreign
          Policy, 1933-1939.
Akira Iriye, The Origins of the Second World War in Asia and the
          Pacific.
          _____, After Imperialism: The Search for a New Order in the
          Far East, 1921-1931.
Gordon Martel (ed.), The Origins of the Second World War Reconsidered.

1939-1945

Basil H. Liddell-Hart, A History of the Second World War.
Peter Calvocoressi and Guy Wint, Causes and Courses of the Second
          World War.
A.J.P. Taylor, The Second World War: An Illustrated History
Basil Collier, The War in the Far East.
F.W. Winterbotham, The Ultra Secret.
Don W. Alexander, "Repercussions of the Breda Varient", French
          Historical Studies, v.8, no.3.
Marc Bloch, Strange Defeat.
Robert O. Paxton, Vichy France.
Henri Michel, The Shadow of War: The European Resistance, 1939-1945.
Herbert Feis, Churchill, Roosevelt, Stalin: The War They Fought
          and the Peace They Sought.
          _____, Between War and Peace: The Potsdam Conference.
Diane Shaver Clemens, Yalta.
T.R. Fehrenbach, FDR's Undeclared War, 1939-1941.
Robert A. Devine, Roosevelt and World War II.
Robert Beitzell, The Uneasy Alliance: America, Britain, and Russia,
          1941-1943.
Anne Armstrong, Unconditional Surrender: The Impact of Casablanca
          Policy Upon World War II.
Keith Eubank, Teheran.
Mark Stoler, The Politics of the Second Front.
Vojtech Mastny, Russia's Road to the Cold War: Diplomacy, Warfare,
          and The Politics of Communism, 1941-1945.
Martin Sherwin, A World Destroyed: The Atomic Bomb and the Grand
          Alliance.
Gar Alperovitz, Atomic Diplomacy: Hiroshima and Potsdam.
Herbert Feis, The Atomic Bomb and the End of World War II.
Gabriel Kolko, The Politics of War.
David Horowitz, The Free World Colossus.
Charles S. Maier, "Revisionism and Interpretation of Cold War
          Origins", Perspectives in American History, vol. 2 (1970).
John L. Gaddis, The United States and the Origins of the Cold War,
          1941-1947.
Keith Sainsbury, The Turning Point: Roosevelt, Stalin, Churchill,
          and Chaing-Kai-Shek.

David J. Lu, <u>From Marco Polo Bridge to Pearl: Japan's Entry into World War Two</u>.
Roberta Wohlstetter, <u>Pearl Harbor: Warning and Decision</u>.
Charles C. Tansill, <u>Back Door to War: The Roosevelt Foreign Policy, 1933-1941</u>.
Gordon Prang, <u>At Dawn We Slept</u>.
Akira Iriye, <u>Power and Culture: The Japanese-American War: 1941-1945</u>.
Christopher Thorne, <u>Allies of a Kind: The United States, Britain, and the War Against Japan, 1941-1945</u>.

1945-Present

Andre Fontaine, <u>History of the Cold War</u>, 2 vols.
Walter LaFeber, <u>America, Russia, and the Cold War</u>.
Louis Halle, <u>The Cold War as History</u>.
Colin Bown and Peter J. Mooney, <u>Cold War to Detente, 1945-1980</u>.
Lynn E. Davis, <u>The Cold War Begins: Soviet American Conflict over Eastern Europe</u>.
Daniel Yergin, <u>Shattered Peace: The Origins of the Cold War and the National Security State</u>.
A.W. DePorte, <u>Eurpe Between Superpowers</u>.
Warren F. Kimball, <u>Swords into Plowshares? The Morgenthau Plan for Defeated Nazi Germany, 1943-1946</u>.
Anthony Nichols, <u>The Semblance of Peace: The Political Settlement After the Second World War</u>.
Adam Ulam, <u>Expansion and Coexistence: The History of Soviet Foreign Policy, 1917-1967</u>.
Robert V. Daniels, <u>Russia: The Roots of Confrontation</u>.
Zbigniew Brzezinski, <u>The Soviet Bloc: Unity and Conflict</u>.
George Liska, <u>Russia and World Order</u>.
Charles B. McLane, <u>Soviet Strategies in Sooth East Asia</u>.
Hugh Seton-Watson, <u>The East European Revolution</u>.
Marshall Shulman, <u>Stalin's Foreign Policy Reappraised</u>.
David Dallin, <u>Soviet Foreign Policy After Stalin</u>.
Thomas Larson, <u>Soviet-American Rivalry</u>.
Nikolai V. Sivachev and Nikolai N. Yokovlev, <u>Russia and the United States: US-Soviet Relations from the Soviet Point of View</u>.
H. Stuart Hughes, <u>The United States and Italy</u>.
F. Roy Willis, <u>France, Germany, and the New Europe, 1945-1967</u>.
Wolfram Hanrieder, <u>The Stable Crisis: Two Decades of German Foreign Policy</u>.
Wladyslav K Kulski, <u>DeGaulle and the World: The Foreign Policy of the Fifth French Republic</u>.
John D. Hargreaves, <u>The End of Colonial Rule in West Africa</u>.
Marshall I. Goldman, <u>Soviet Foreign Aid</u>.
Geoffrey Jukes, <u>The Soviet Union in Asia</u>.
Hugh Thomas, <u>The Suez Affair</u>.
Arnold Kramner, <u>The Forgotten Friendship: Israel and the Soviet Bloc, 1947-1953</u>.
Nadav Safran, <u>From War to War: The Arab-Israeli Confrontation, 1948-1967</u>.

J.C. Hurewitz, Soviet-American Rivalry in the Middle East.
William F. Quant, Decade of Decision: American Policy Towards the Arab-Israeli Confrontation, 1948-1967.
Davud Green, The Containment of Latin America.
Samuel Baily, The United States and the Development of Latin America, 1945-1975.
C. Neal Ronning, Intervention in Latin America.
Walter M. Davis (ed.), Latin America and the Cold War.
Herbert Goldhamer, The Foreign Powers in Latin America.
Walter Laqueur, Terrorism.
James Nathan and James Oliver, United States Foreign Policy and World Order.
John K. Fairbank, The United States and China.
F.E.M. Irving, The First Indochina War: French and American Policy, 1945-1954.
James P. Harrison, Fifty Years of Struggle in Vietnam.
David Calleo, Beyond American Hegemony.

HISTORICAL STUDY A-12

International Conflict in the Modern World

Professor Stanley Hoffmann
Associate Professor Michael E. Mandelbaum.
Assistant Professors John S. Odell
and M. J. Peterson

Lectures will be given every Tuesday and some Thursdays at noon. Sections will meet once a week for two hours. Written requirements are a take-home midterm and regularly-scheduled three hour final examination.

All readings are on reserve at Lamont and Hilles. Books marked with an asterisk have been ordered at the Coop.

I. The Origins of Twentieth Century Conflict

1. 4 Feb (Th.) The Enduring Logic of Conflict
*Kenneth Waltz, Man, the State, and War, chs. 1, 2, 4, 6, and 8.

2. 9 Feb (T) The Peloponnesian War
Discussion: Athens, Sparta, and their Allies
*Thucydides, The Peloponnesian War (Penguin ed.) pp. 35-109 and 400-9.

3. 16 Feb (T) International Systems and War
18 Feb (Th) The Nineteenth Century Balance of Power
Discussion: Germany and the Balance of Power
A. J. P. Taylor, The Struggle for the Mastery of Europe, introduction.

* Edward V. Gulick, Europe's Classical Balance of Power, chs 1-3.
* Rene Albrecht-Carrie, A Diplomatic History of Europe Since the Congress of Vienna, pp. 3-31 and 121-8h.
* A. DePorte, Europe and the Superpower Balance, pp. 5-19.
R. B. Mowat, Europe, 1715-1815, pp. 65-75 and 91-104.

4. 23 Feb (T) Imperialism
Discussion: The Scramble for Africa

* Benjamin Cohen, The Question of Imperialism, ch 2
D. M. K. Fieldhouse, Economics and Empire, pp. 10-88, 260-311, and 340-61.

II. The World Wars

5. 2 Mar (T) Origins of World War I
4 Mar (Th) Versailles and Geneva
Discussion: World War I

* Barbara Tuchman, The Guns of August, pp. 1-157.
Rene Albrecht-Carrie, The Meaning of the First World War, pp. 1-46.

6. 9 Mar (T) Origins of World War II
   11 Mar (Th) The World in 1945.
   Discussion: Munich and Appeasement

   Arnold Wolfers, Discord and Collaboration, ch. 16.
   Martin Gilbert, The Roots of Appeasement, pp. 138-88.
   *Klaus Hildebrand, The Foreign Policy of the Third Reich,
   chs. 4-7 and conclusion.

7. 16 Mar (T) Midterm Questions Distributed

III. Conflicts since 1945

8. 23 Mar (T) The Cold War Debate
   Discussion: Origins of the Cold War

   *DePorte, pp. 20-76.
   *Walter LaFeber, America, Russia, and the Cold War, pp. 1-65.
   George Kennan "The Sources of Soviet Conduct," in Kennan, ed.,
   American Foreign Policy.
   Arthur Schlesinger, Jr., "The Origins of the Cold War,"
   Foreign Affairs, October 1967.
   Thomas G. Patterson, ed., The Origins of the Cold War, pp. 225-60.

Week of March 28 Spring Break

9. 6 Apr (T) Nuclear Weapons
   8 Apr (Th) Superpower Relations Today
   Discussion: Deterrence and the Question of Soviet Intentions

   *Michael Mandelbaum, The Nuclear Question, pp. 1-157.
   David Holloway, "Military Power and Purpose in Soviet Policy,"
   Daedelus, Fall 1980.
   Richard Pipes, "Militarism and the Soviet State," Daedelus,
   Fall 1980.
   George Kennan, "Reflections: The Soviet Union," The New Yorker,
   2 November 1981.

10. 12 Apr (T) The Mideast Conflict
    14 Apr (Th) The Role of International Law and Organization
    Discussion: The Arab-Israeli Wars

    Nadav Safran, From War to War, ch. 1.
    John Stoessinger, Why Nations go to War, ch 6.
    Institute for Strategic Studies, Strategic Survey, 1973, pp. 13-55.
    Inis L. Claude, Jr., "Collective Legitimization as a Function of the
    United Nations," International Organization, summer 1966.
    L. Scheinman and D. Wilkinson eds., International Law and
    Political Crisis, pp. 91-126.
    Donald Neff, Warriors at Suez, chs. 13-17.

11.   20 Apr (T) The International and Domestic Politics of Oil
       22 Apr (Th) International Inequality and Economic Conflict
       Discussion: Struggles over Oil

       *R. Keohane and J. Nye, Power and Interdependence, chs. 1 and 2.
       *R. Vernon, ed., The Oil Crisis. Essays by Vernon, Girvan,
       Stobaugh, Knorr, Smart, and Penrose.
       Joesph Nye, "Energy Nightmares," Foreign Policy, fall 1980.
       Robert Tucker, "Oil and American Power Five Years Later,"
       Commentary, September 1979.

12.   27 Apr (T) Responses to Dependency
       Discussion: North-South Conflict in the 1970's

       Stephen Krasner, "North-South Economic Relations," in
       K. Oye and others, eds., Eagle Entangled, pp. 153-203.
       Mahbub ul Haq, The Poverty Curtain: Choices for the Third World,
       pp. 153-203.
       *Cohen, ch. 5.
       *Joan Spero, The Politics of International Economic Relations
       (2d ed.), pp. 182-245.

13.   4 May (T) Ethics in International Relations
       6 May (Th) The Nation-State and the Future of International
                  Conflict
       Discussion: The US in Southeast Asia

       Arnold Wolfers, Discord and Collaboration, ch. 4.
       Stoessinger, Why Nations go to War, ch. 4
       Henry A. Kissinger, White House Years, pp. 457-521.
       *William Shawcross, Sideshow, chs. 1, 4-9, 19, 23, and 24.
       Irving Howe and Michael Walzer, "Were 'e 'rong about Vietnam?"
       The New Republic, 18 August 1979.
       Charles Horner, "America Five Years after Defeat,"
       Commentary, April 1980.

Information

1.   Sections will hold their first meeting during the week of February
9th. For course purposes the week begins on Tuesday and ends on the
following Monday. Since February 15th, which would otherwise be the
day for the first meeting of Monday sections, is a holiday, special times
for those groups' first meetings will be announced.

2.   Lists of sections, indicating hour and place of meeting and section
leader, will be posted in the hallway outside the Government Tutorial
Office (which is in Room G-2 in the basement of Littauer) at noon
on Friday the 5th. You will have to consult the list yourself or send
a friend to check. The Tutorial Office staff do not have time to take
phone calls asking them to look on your behalf.

3.   This course does section early, so we realize that there are a
number of reasons for having to change section.

4. Any student may change section through February 28th. No changes
will be allowed after that date. All changes must be done through the
head of sections.

5. Professor Peterson is head of sections for the course. Her phone
number is 5-2616, and her office at Coolidge (1737 Cambridge Street,
next to Gund Hall) Room 411. She takes care of all administrative matters,
including the signing of study cards.

6. Government concentrators may not take this course pass-fail. If
you think you will become a gov. concentrator, take the course for
a grade and avoid trouble later. (If you take the course pass-fail
and then decide to concentrate in Gov., you cannot count H.S. A-12
towards your concentration requirements. You would have to take Gov.
1720 or 1800 or Social Analysis 16 for a grade.) If you are taking the
course to fulfill Core/General Education requirements, the limits on
your ability to take courses pass-fail are set out on pages 12 and 14
of the Student Handbook. You will be responsible for keeping yourself
within the limits prescribed.

7. Grades are determined using the following formula: 20% for section
participation, 30% for the midterm, and 50% for the final examination.

8. The midterm will consist of two 5-page essays on topics to be
assigned. You will have a choice of questions. Questions will be
distributed in the lecture room at noon on March 16th, and completed
essays will be due the following Tuesday noon. Lectures and sections
are not held during this week, and you are not expected to read any
new material. You are expected to make effective use of what you have
heard and read up to that point.

9. As a consequence of this suspension, lectures and sections are
held during the first week of reading period.

10. The final is a regularly-scheduled three-hour exam. Copies of
last year's exam are printed in the CUE Guide and will be available
at Lamont. It is now scheduled for Thursday, May 27th at an hour to
be set by the Registrar.

"Psychodynamic Considerations on Crisis Management and Negotiations on the International, Political, and Interpersonal Systemic Levels"

This seminar will consider crisis management and negotiation on four systemic levels:

1. International
2. Group
3. Interpersonal
4. Intrapsychic

The task of the seminar is to explore what structural principles these levels have in common which may be applied from one level to another. Some instrumental structural principles of negotiation and crisis management abstracted from Alexander George's "Seven Operational 'Requirements'" are:

1. Principals must maintain control over their agents, instruments, or actors.

2. Timing should be slowed down rather than accelerated.

3. Communication must be co-ordinated with action.

4. Objectives must be focussed and limited.

5. Avoid the message that one is about to escalate.

6. Options should be chosen that signal a desire to negotiate rather than coerce.

7. Avoid "cornering" the opponent with no choice. Select options that vie the opponent an honorable ("face saving") way out of the crisis compatible with his fundamental interests

The seminar will include exposure to a number of different paradigms and levels of analysis: international diplomacy, terrorism, social psychology, economic game theory, litigation, labor mediation, and clinical intervention. A further seminar challenge is to inquire whether there may be mutually beneficial feedback and valuable insight in both directions: social to psychodynamic, and clinical to political.

Among guests who will present the seminar are:

1. Rita Rogers, M.D , American Academy of Child Psychiatry, Committee on Developmental Issues Related to Nuclear Issues; "Psychological Aspects of Diplomatic contacts in a Multi-Cultural Framework," January 29.

2. Professor Jack Hirschleifer, Department of Economics, UCLA; "Economic Game Theory and Conflict," February 12.

3. Paul Grossman, of Paul, Hastings, Janovsky, & Walker, "Litigation", February 26.

4. Professor Bertram H. Faven, Department of Psychology, UCLA: "The Social Psychology of Conflict and Power," March 5.

5. Walter Brackelmans, M.D., "Marital Conflict", March 19.

6. Professor Alexander L. George, Institute of Politics, Stanford University; "Soviet-American Crisis Management," date to be announced.

I do not regard the seminar format as rigid. Rather, it should be a living intellectual process; meaning that the structure and content will be altered and adapted to our needs as we move along.

Meetings: The seminar will meet in Professor Loewenberg's home: 449 Levering Avenue, Westwood (West of Veteran, South of Montana), Tel: 472-6809, on Wednesday evening at 7:30 pm. There will be no meeting on February 5.

Readings: Copies of all the articles are available in the Graduate Reserve Service of the University Research Library.

Presentations: Each member of the seminar will report and guide the discussion on several of the readings.

Paper: Each member of the seminar will give an oral presentation and write a 15 page research paper applying the ideas studied in the seminar to an historical case of your choice in consultation with the instructor. Some suggested international topics, not intended to be exclusive, are:

Europe in 1914.
Germany and England, 1890-1914.
Hitler's Attack on the Soviet Union, 1941.
Berlin Blockade.
Korean War.
Vietnam War.
Israeli-Palestinian Relations.
India and Pakistan.
Iraqi-Iranian War.
Cuban Missile Crisis.
Israeli-Egyptian Relations.
The Falkland Islands War.
Ulster.
Nicaragua.

You may also write on a domestic political, economic, or biographical conflict of your choice such as a parliamentary struggle, a labor dispute, or the decision of a leader.

Outlines for your papers will be due on 30 April. The final seven sessions will be reserved for oral presentations of the papers. Final papers are due on June 11.

Assignments: Members of the seminar are expected to do the reading and to be conscientious about attendance and reports. This is your work. If you do not fulfill your commitments you are letting the whole seminar down.

Readings:

I. The Intersystemic Problem Posed:

George Levinger, "Conflict and Compatibility: Comparing the Marital and International Spheres" (unpublished ms., 1984)

Dean G. Pruitt and Helena Syna, "Blame and Strategic Choice in Family and International Conflict" (unpublished ms., 1984)

II. Diplomatic Crisis Management:

Gordon A. Craig and Alexander L. George, Force and Statecraft: Diplomatic Problems of Our Time (N.Y.: Oxford, 1983), see especially pp. 157-219.

Alexander L. George, "Crisis Management: Lessons from Past U.S. - Soviet Crises" (unpublished ms., 1984).

Alexander L. George, "Political Crises," in Joseph S. Nye, jr., ed. The Making of America's Foreign Policy (Yale U.P., 1984), pp. 129-157.

G. Snyder and Paul Diesing, Conflict Among Nations (Princeton U.P., 1977).

III. Case Studies:

John G. Stoessigner, Way Nations Go to War, third edition (N.Y.: St. Martin's Press, 1982)

Richard N. Lebow, "Windows of Opportunity: Do States Jump Through Them?" International Security, 9:1 (Summer 1984), 147-186.

Richard N. Lebow, "Miscalculation in the South Atlantic: Origins of the Falkland War," Journal of Strategic Studies, 6 (March 1983), 5-35.

Phil Williams, "Crisis Management and the Falkland's Conflict" (unpublished ms., 1983).

Graham T. Allison, Essence of Decision: Explaining the Cuban Missile Crisis, (Boston: Little, Brown & Co., 1971).

Lloyd S. Etheredge, Can Governments Learn?: American Foreign Policy and Central American Revolutions (New York: Pergamon Press, 1985).

William C. Potter, "Nuclear Proliferation: U.S.-Soviet Cooperation," Washington Quarterly (Winter 1985), 141-154; Center for International and Strategic Affairs, UCLA, reprint No. 2. To be purchased from CISA, 11383 Ralph Bunche Hall for $2.00

IV. Group Dynamics and Leadership:

Wilfred Bion, Experiences in Groups (New York, Basic Books, 1961).

Manfred F.R. Kets de Vries & Danny Miller, The Neurotic Organization: Diagnosing and Changing Counterproductive Styles of Management (San Francisco: Jossey Bass, 1984).

Irving L. Janis and Leon Mann, <u>Decision Making: A Psychological Analysis of Conflict, Choice, and Commitment</u> (N.Y.: Free Press, 1977).

_____, _____, <u>Victims of Groupthink</u> (Boston: Houghton, Mifflin Co., 1972).

V. Game Theory:

Anatol Rapaport, <u>Fights, Games, and Debates</u> (Ann Arbor: Univ. of Michigan paperback, 1974).

Jack Hirschleifer, "On the Emotions as Guarantors of Threats and Promises," (unpublished ms.)

Jack Hirschleifer, "The Economic Approach to Conflict," (unpublished ms.).

P.G. Bennett & M.A. Dando, "Complex Strategic Analysis: A Hypergame Study of the fall of France," <u>Journal of the Operational Research Society</u> 30 (1979), 23-32.

Stephen W. SaPant, "Litigation of Questioned Settlement Claims: A Bayesian-Nash Equilibrium Approach" (Rand Publication P-6809, December 1982).

VI. Negotiations: The Interactional Model:

Herbert C. Kelman, "Creating the Conditions for Israeli-Palestinian Negotiation," <u>Journal of Conflict Resolution</u>, 26:1 (March 1982), 39-75.

_____, _____, "Overcoming the Psychological Bakrrier: An Analysis of the Egyptian-Israeli Peace Process".

_____, _____, "An Interactional Approach to Conflict Resolution and its Application to Israeli-Palestinian Relations," <u>International Interactions</u>, 6:2 (1979), 99-122.

Frederick J. Hacker, <u>Crusaders, Criminals, Crazies: Terror and Terrorism in Our Time</u> (N.Y.: Norton, 1976; Bantam, 1977).

UNIVERSITY OF TORONTO
Department of History

HISTORY 342Y

1985-1986

J. Kornberg

EUROPEAN INTELLECTUAL HISTORY, 1789-1914

Lectures: Tuesday, Thursday, 11:00 a.m.

This course in the intellectual history of modern Europe spans the period
from the French Revolution to World War I. No attempt is made to 'cover
the ground', instead we will focus on some major figures and trends. The
lectures will provide interpretations of the historic role and significance of these figures and movements. Small-group discussion classes will
be used for critical discussion of these interpretations.

There will be two lectures a week. Written work in the first term will involve either an exam or a book report. There will be a term paper in the
second term of about 3,000 words. There will also be a final exam. The
book report or exam will count for 10% of the final grade, the term paper
will count for 30%, class participation will count for 20%, and the final
exam for 40%. Students must complete each requirement to receive standing
in the course. This includes attending at least 75% of the discussion
classes.

PAPERBACK BOOKS ORDERED FOR TEXTBOOK STORE

Durkheim, Emile, On Morality and Society (University of Chicago Press)
Engels, Friedrich, Socialism: Utopian and Scientific (Progress Books)
Freud, Sigmund, Civilization and its Discontents (W.W. Norton)
_____, Totem and Taboo (Random)
Hall, Calvin, A Primer of Freudian Psychology (Mentor)
Hegel, Georg W.F., Reason in History (Bobbs-Merrill)
Kant, Immanuel, On History (Bobbs-Merrill)
Marx, Karl, Economic and Philosophic Manuscripts of 1844 (Progress Books)
_____, The Civil War in France (Progress Books)
Mill, John Stuart, On the Subjection of Women (Harlan Davidson)
Nietzsche, Friedrich, A Nietzsche Reader (Penguin)
Nisbet, Robert, The Sociological Tradition (Basic Books)

BOOKS ON RESERVE AT SIGMUND SAMUEL LIBRARY

Bowle, John, Politics and Opinion in the Nineteenth Century
Cole, G.D.H., A History of Socialist Thought, Vol. I, The Forerunners
    1789-1850
Comte, August, A General View of Positivism
_____, The Positive Philosophy of August Comte
_____, System of Positive Polity, Vol. I
Darwin, Charles, The Descent of Man
de Maistre, Joseph, On God and Society
A. Fried and R. Sanders, Socialist Thought: A Documentary History

BOOKS ON RESERVE AT SIGMUND SAMUEL LIBRARY - cont'd

Gooch, G.P., History and Historians in the Nineteenth Century
Hegel, Georg W.F., Philosophy of Right
Lively Jack, The Works of Joseph de Maistre
Mill, John Stuart, Essential Works
_____, Nature and Utility of Religion
_____, Three Essays on Religion
Randall, J.H. Jr., The Career of Philosophy, vol. II. From the German
    Enlightenment to the Age of Darwin
*Randall, J.H. Jr., The Making of the Modern Mind
Von Laue, Theodore, Leopold Von Ranke, The Formative Years
Von Ranke, Leopold, The Theory and Practice of History
*Sabine, G.H., A History of Political Theory
Sorel, Georges, Reflections on Violence

XEROX READINGS ON RESERVE AT NEW COLLEGE LIBRARY

Burckhardt, Jacob, The Letters of Jacob Burckhardt (selections)
Comte, August, System of Positive Polity (selections)
_____, The Positive Philosophy of August Comte (selections)

AVAILABILITY TO BE ANNOUNCED

Burckhardt, Jacob, Force and Freedom (selections)
The Doctrine of Saint Simon: An Exposition (selections)

* These works are available in several editions. Chapter sections will,
  therefore, be indicated by name.

Week	THEME I: SOCIAL THOUGHT IN POST REVOLUTIONARY FRANCE: THE REVOLT AGAINST EGOISTIC INDIVIDUALISM

September 9   THE REDISCOVERY OF COMMUNITY

                Nisbet, The Sociological Tradition, 1-16, 21-44, 47-55,
                    107-116, 221-231, 264-273

September 16   DE BONALD AND DE MAISTRE

                Randall, The Career of Philosophy, Vol. II, Book six,
                    Ch. I
                de Maistre, On God and Society OR Lively, The Works of
                    Joseph de Maistre, 147-181

September 23   ST. SIMON

                Cole, A History of Socialist Thought, Vol. I, Ch. IV
                Fried and Sanders, Socialist Thought, "Saint-Simon"

Week

September 3̄ THE ST. SIMONIANS
Cole, A History of Socialist Thought, Vol. I, Ch. V
The Doctrine of Saint-Simon: An Exposition (selections)

October   - COMTE
Randall, The Career of Philosophy, Vol. II, Book six, Ch. 4
Nisbet, The Sociological Tradition, 56-61
Comte, The Positive Philosophy of August Comte, 1858 ed.,
    "Existing State of Society", 401-412. (Vol. II,
    pp. 3-15 in the 1875 and 1893 editions)
System of Positive Polity, Vol. I, "The Social Aspect of
    Positivism," 73-86. (See also A General View of Posi-
    tivism, 2nd ed., tr. J.H. Bridges, 67-80. See also
    the 1972 Brown Reprint of the Bridges translation,
    97-116.)
System of Positive Polity, Vol. I, "The Influence of Posi-
    tivism upon Women," 164-219. (See also A General View
    of Positivism, 2nd ed., tr. J.H. Bridges, Ch. IV. See
    also the 1972 Brown Reprint of the Bridges translation
    Ch. IV.)

October   14 DURKHEIM
Nisbet, The Sociological Tradition, 82-97, 150-161, 243-
    251, 300-304
Durkheim, On Morality and Society, 43-57, 63-146

October   2̄ SOREL
Bowle, Politics and Opinions in the Nineteenth Century,
    Ch. X
Sorel, Reflections on Violence, Chs. 6-7

October   2̄ THE NEW ETHOS OF INSTINCTUAL FREEDOM

FOURIER
Cole, A History of Socialist Thought, Vol. I, Ch. VI
Fried and Sanders, Socialist Thought, "Fourier"

THEME II: THE POLITICS OF KULTUR: APOLITICAL
            INDIVIDUALISM IN GERMANY

November   - BURCKHARDT
"Jacob Burckhardt", The Encyclopedia of Philosophy, Vol. I
Nisbet, The Sociological Tradition, 266-270
Burckhardt, "On Fortune and Misfortune in History," Force
    and Freedom, 349-370
The Letters of Jacob Burckhardt, 73-75, 96-97, 118-123,
    139-142, 151-152, 206-208

Week

November 11   NIETZSCHE

A Nietzsche Reader, 7-11, 15-25, 29-70, 197-212
Bowle, Politics and Opinion in the Nineteenth Century,
     Ch. VIII, Part III

November 18   A Nietzsche Reader, 71-124, 149-193

November 25   A Nietzsche Reader, 215-262, 265-284

THEME III: THE IDEA OF THE STATE IN NINETEENTH
              CENTURY GERMANY

December 2   Kant, On History (Omit 27-84)

January 6   HEGEL

Sabine, A History of Political Theory, "Hegel: Dialectic
     and Nationalism"
Hegel, Reason in History

January 13   Hegel, Philosophy of Right, 105-216

January 20   VON RANKE

G.P. Gooch, History and Historians in Nineteenth Century,
     Ch. VI
Leopold von Ranke, The Theory and Practice of History,
     Part III, OR Theodore Von Laue, Leopold Ranke,
     152-218

THEME IV: REVOLUTIONARY PRAXIS - THE PROMETHEAN IMAGE
             OF MAN

January 27   Randall, The Career of Philosophy, Vol. II, Book five,
     Ch. 18
Marx, Economic and Philosophic Manuscripts of 1844

February 3   Marx, The Civil War in France

February 10   Engels, Socialism: Utopian and Scientific

February 17   READING WEEK

Week

THEME V: ELITIST INDIVIDUALISM - THE LIBERAL ENLIGHTENMENT

February 24   MILL

Randall, The Career of Philosophy, Vol. II, Book six,
       Ch. 10, Sections I-IV and Ch. 2, Sections IV-V
John Stuart Mill, On Liberty

March   3   John Stuart Mill, Nature
                       , The Utility of Religion

March   10   John Stuart Mill, The Subjection of Women

March   17   DARWIN

Randall, The Making of the Modern Mind, Ch. XVIII, "The
       World Conceived as a Process of Growth and Evolution",
       (omit section entitled "The newer concepts of physics")
       and Ch. XXI, "Philosophic Reactions to the Growing World
       of Mechanism and Naturalism", (up to and including
       section entitled "Faith in the inevitability of pro-
       gress")
Charles Darwin, The Descent of Man, Ch. XXI

THEME VI: THE EMERGENCE OF PSYCHOLOGICAL MAN: LIBERALISM
               TURNED INWARD

March   24   FREUD

Hall, A Primer of Freudian Psychology
Freud, Civilization and its Discontents

March   31   Freud, Totem and Taboo

April   7   THE SUMMING UP

No reading assignment

Lecture	Reading
August 25: Introduction to Intellectual History	
August 27: The Legacy of the Enlightenment	Norman Torrey, ed. Les Philosophes, intro., pp. 52-120 (In reader)
September 1 The Ambiguities of Jean-Jacques Rousseau	Torrey, pp. 121-167 (In reader)
September 3: Kant and the German Enlightenment	The Philosophy of Kant, ed. Carl Friedrich, intro., pp. 116-139
September 8: Kant and the Origins of German Idealism	The Philosophy of Kant, p. 24-115; 209-264
September 10: No class	
September 15: Mary Wollstonecraft and the Origins of Feminism	Mary Wollstonecraft, A Vindication of the Rights of Woman
September 17: Romanticism	
September 22: Goethe's Faust	Goethe, Faust, trans. Walter Kaufmann
September 24: Political Romanticism and the Rise of Conservative Thought	Edmund Burke, Reflections on the Revolution in France
September 29: Nationalism	J.G. Fichte, Addresses to the German Nation, pp. 1-129, 211-228. (In reader)
October 1: Hegel	The Philosophy of Hegel, ed., Carl Friedrich, intro., pp. 399-461
October 6: Hegel (cont.)	The Philosophy of Hegel, pp. 3-79, 85-94, 116-158, 221-227
October 8: Kierkegaard and the Critique of Idealism	Søren Kierkegaard, Fear and Trembling
October 13: Midterm	
October 15: English Liberalism: Classical Economics and Utilitarianism	

October 17: **The Crisis of English**
Liberalism: John Stuart Mill

J.S. Mill,
Autobiography

October 20 **French Liberalism: Alexis de**
Tocqueville

Alexis de Tocqueville,
The Old Regime and
French Revolution

October 22: **Utopian Socialism: Saint-Simon**
and Fourier

October 27: **The Life of Karl Marx**

The Marx-Engels
Reader, ed. Robert
Tucker, intro.

October 29: **Marx: The Early Writings**

The Marx-Engels
Reader, pp. 3-125

November 3: **Marx: The Mature Writings**

The Marx-Engels
Reader, pp. 143-145;
469-500; 294-361;
431-438.

November 5: **Anarchism from Godwin to**
Bakunin

Michael Bakunin,
"Revolutionary Cathe-
chism" and "Statism
and Anarchy" (in
reader)

November 10: **No class (papers due)**

November 12: **Baudelaire and the Crisis**
of Modernity

Charles Baudelaire,
"The Painter of Modern
Life" and selected
poems (In reader)

November 17: **Flaubert: Realism and**
Aestheticism

Gustave Flaubert,
The Sentimental
Education

November 19: **Jacob Burckhardt and**
the Aestheticization of History

November 24: **Richard Wagner and the**
Religion of Art

Listen to Wagner's
Tristan and Isolde

November 26: **Thanksgiving Holiday**

December 1-4: **Reading Week and summary**
Sections

For thsoe who want a general history background to the period,
Franklin Ford, Europe, 1780-1830 and H. Hearder, Europe in the
Nineteenth Century 1830/1880 are recommended.

January 20:	Introduction to Intellectual History	H. Stuart Hughes, Consciousness and Society, p.1-33.
January 22:	Positivism, Naturalism, and Impressionism	Alan Bowness, Modern European Art, p.9-46.
January 27:	The Degeneration of Marxism: Dialectical Materialism	Frederick L. Bender, ed., The Betrayal of Marx, p. 1-133.
January 29:	Aesthetic Reactions to Positivism: The Young Nietzsche	Friedrich Nietzsche, The Birth of Tragedy
February 3:	Aesthetic Reactions to Positivism: Decadence and the Symbolists	Joris-Karl Huysmans, Against the Grain
February 5:	Philosophical Reactions to Positivism: Nietzsche and Bergson	Nietzsche, The Genealogy of Morals: Hughes, p. 33-66, 105-125.
February 10:	Historical Reactions to Positivism: Dilthey and the Crisis of Historicism	Hughes, p. 183-249.
February 12:	Social Scientific Reactions to Positivism	Hans Gerth and From Max Weber, p.77-158, 180-196, 245-256; Hughes, p. 278-336.
February 17:	Psychological Reactions to Positivism: Freud	Hughes, p. 125-160.
February 19:	Revisionist Critiques of Dialectical Materialism: Bernstein and Sorel	Hughes, p. 67-95, 161-182; Bender, p. 135-184.
February 24:	The Realistic Novel as Recorder of Intellectual Currents: Martin du Gard and Mann	Georg Lukacs, Marxism and Human Liberation p. 109-131.
February 26:	The Intellectuals and the War	Hughes, p. 336-391.
March 3:	Midterm	
March 5:	Aesthetic Modernism	Bowness, p.47-165; Lukacs, p.277-307.
March 10:	Lukacs and the Rise of Western Marxism	Lukacs, p.3-60, 97-105; Bender, p.222-235.
March 12:	The Crisis of Liberalism: Pareto and Mosca	Hughes, p.249-277.
March 17:	The Intellectual Root of Fascism	Peter Gay, Weimar Culture Lukacs, p. 267-276.

March 19:	Weimar Culture	Gay, _Weimar Culture_
March 31:	The Intellectual Migration to America	Martin Jay, _The Dialectical Imagination_
April 2:	The Frankfurt School	Jay, _The Dialectical Imagination_
April 7:	Culture and Psychoanalysis	Sigmund Freud, _Civilization and its Discontents_
April 9:	Arnold Schoenberg and the Breakdown of Musical Tonality	Listen to _Moses and Aaron_
April 14:	The Crisis of the Intellectual Benda, Mannheim and Orwell	Hughes, p. 392-431.
April 16:	Existentialist Philosophy Heidegger	Martin Heidegger, _Basic Writings_, p.1-89, 189-242, 284-317; William Barrett, _Irrational Man_, p. 3-65, 206-238.
April 21:	Existentialist Philosophy:	Jean-Paul Sartre, "The Wall," "Self-Deception," "Portrait of an Anti-Semite" and "Existentialism is a Humanism" in Walter Kaufmann, ed., _Existentialism from Dostoyevsky to Sartre_; Barrett, p.239-263.
April 23:	French Feminism: From De Beauvoir to Irigaray	Elaine Marks and Isabelle de Courtivron, eds., _New French Feminisms_, selections to be announced.
April 28:	The Linguistic Turn in 20th-Century Philosophy: Wittgenstein, Saussure and Gadamer	
April 30:	Structuralism and Post-Structuralism	John Sturrock, ed., _Structuralism and Since_
May 5-7:	Reading Week	

*****

For those who want outside reading in the history of the period, the following books are recommended:

> J.M. Roberts, _Europe, 1880-1945_
> Robert O. Paxton, _Europe in the Twentieth Century_
> H. Stuart Hughes, _Contemporary Europe: A History_

Those who want an intellectual history textbook are encouraged to examine the following:

> Roland Stromberg, _An Intellectual History of Modern Europe_
> George L. Mosse, _The Culture of Western Europe_
> Willson H. Coates and Hayden V. White, _The Ordeal of Liberal Humanism_

Hofstra University   Pellegrino D'Acierno

Senior University Honors Seminar   Spring, 1986

The Problem of the Intellectual
in Contemporary Society

> It is the responsibility of intellectuals to speak
> the truth and to expose lies.
> Noam Chomsky

> The intellectual is thus someone who becomes aware
> of the opposition, both within himself and within
> society, between a search for practical truth
> (with all the norms it implies) and a ruling
> ideology (with its system of traditional values).
> Jean-Paul Sartre

The seminar will be centered around the problem of the intellectual and will examine the political, social, and cultural roles and the contradictory status of the intellectual in industrial and post-industrial society. What is an intellectual? How can we define the category of "intellectual" as a role type in social systems? Are intellectuals an autonomous ("free-floating") and independent social group, or does every social group have its own particular specialized category of intellectuals? What are the functions and responsibilities of the intellectuals? As producers of knowledge, what is their role in the creation and analysis of ideology, in the production of consciousness and the creation of conscience? Is the intellectual best defined completely in terms of a negative project, that is, as someone who speaks against his own group, class, or discipline thereby exposing the apparatus of power and the "regimes of truth" in place in a given society? Who is an intellectual? How much and what kind of knowledge does someone need to be an intellectual? Is the writer or artist an intellectual? Is the university student an intellectual?

Beginning with Gramsci's epochal framing of the problem in the Prison Notebooks and his distinction between organic and traditional intellectuals, the course will proceed to explore the major theoretical treatments of the intellectuals by such thinkers as Nietzsche, Weber, Benda, Mannheim, Lukacs, Adorno, Heidegger, Sartre, Hofstadter, Chomsky, Gouldner, and Foucault. After the formulation of working definitions of the intellectual and the intelligentsia based on these readings, the seminar will attempt to develop a historical analysis of the roles intellectuals have played in specific social contexts. An in-depth study of two historic situations will be undertaken under the following rubrics: "Consciousness, Conscience, and the Politics of Truth: European Intellectuals and the Confrontation with Fascism" and "From Dissent to Resistance: American Intellectuals and the Crisis of Democratic Values in the Age of Vietnam."

Each seminar meeting will be devoted to the discussion and detailed analysis of a set of texts organized into a thematic unit. Readings will be taken from a wide range of theoretical, practical, and artistic texts and an attempt will be made to construct dossiers or case studies dedicated to certain exemplary intellectuals and to the documentation of their projects. Furthermore, in order to situate the problematic of the intellectuals within the broad context of modern thought, a series of contiguous issues and topics will be studied: for example, the intellectual and mass society, the role of the woman intellectual, the representation of the intellectual in works of art, and the rationality of the sciences. (Consult the accompanying syllabus.)

The seminar is intended to give students the critical instruments and the knowledge necessary to situate the problem of the intellectual in an historical context and to define the specific position of the intellectual in a society like ours, a position that must be described with regard to social structure and class, to the actual conditions of life and work surrounding intellectual activity, and ultimately to what Foucault calls the "politics" or "regimes" of truth in place in a given society. One of the major pedagogic goals of the seminar is the production of independent research projects which students will develop into theses. At least three supplementary workshops will be held as a means of expediting the writing of the theses, and students will be required to give short expositions of their own work.

SYLLABUS

Class I.   The Situation of the Intellectual as a Double-bind: The Intellectual For and Against His Own Class.

        1. The Example of Socrates: Socrates and the Introduction of the Negative into the Polis.

        2. Gramsci's Double-bind: The Modern Intellectual caught between Organic and Traditional Roles.

Readings: Plato: The Apology
            A. Gramsci: "The Intellectuals" in the Prison Notebooks
            T. Parsons: "'The Intellectual': a Social Role Category" in On Intellectuals

---

Class II.   The Intellectual and Power: Hegemony, Counter-Hegemony and
             the Intellectual as Producer of Consciousness.

Readings: Machiavelli: The Prince
             A. Gramsci: "The Modern Prince" in the Prison Notebooks
             M. Foucault: Power and Truth
             E. Shils: The Intellectuals and the Powers and Other Essays

Class III.   The Intellectuals and Mass Society.

Readings: F. Nietzsche: Beyond Good and Evil
             Ortega y Gasset: The Revolt of the Masses
             M. Horkheimer and
             T. Adorno: "The Culture Industry" in the
                                Dialectic of Enlightenment

Class IV.   The Nationalization of Culture and the Task of the Intellectuals.

Readings: J. Benda: The Treason of the Intellectuals
             T. Mann: Reflections of an Unpolitical Man (selections)
             B. Russell: "Militant Pacifism" in My Political Ideas

Class V.   Autonomy and the Professionalization of the Intellectuals

Readings: M. Weber: "Science as a Profession" in Intellectual Work
                               as a Profession
             K. Mannheim: Ideology and Utopia (selections)
             C. Wright Mills: "The Intellectual and the Legitimization of
                               Power" in Power, Politics, and People.
             T. Adorno: "The Contradictions of the Intellectual"
                               in Minima Moralia.

Class VI.   Dissidence: The Intellectual between Commitment and Criticism

Readings: G. Lukács: History and Class Consciousness (selections)
             J. P. Sartre: "A Plea for the Intellectuals" in Between
                               Existentialism and Marxism
             S. Beauvoir: "The Problems of the Woman Intellectual" in
                               The Second Sex
             R. Aron: The Opium of the Intellectuals (selections)

Classes VII and VIII.   The Intellectual and Revolution

Class VII.   The Intellectuals and the Future

Readings: K. Marx and
              F. Engels: The Communist Manifesto
              V. Lenin: "The Intellectual as Elaborator of Ideologies for
                                 the Working Class" in What Is to Be Done?
              A. Gramsci: Selections from Prison Notebooks
              A. Gouldner: The Future of the Intellectuals and the Rise of
                                 The New Class (selections)
              G. Konrád and
              I. Szelényi: The Intellectuals on the Road to Class Power

Class VIII.   The Intellectual and the Third World

Screening: G. Pontecorvo: Battle of Algiers
Readings: F. Fanon: A Dying Colonialism
              E. Said: Orientalism

Class IX.   The Intellectual as Hero: The Representation of the Intellectual
                                          in the Modern Novel

Readings: A. Malraux: Man's Fate (references to Gide, Sartre, Camus,
                                 Joyce, Bellow, etc...)
              V. Brombert: The Intellectual Hero

Class X, XI, and XII.   Consciousness, Conscience, and the Politics of Truth:
                           European Intellectuals in Confrontation with Fascism

Class X.   Germany from Weimar to the Reich

Readings: T. Mann: "Mario and the Magician"
              B. Brecht: "The Criticism of the Economic Roots of Fascism"
              M. Heidegger: "Inaugural Address, 1933"
              A. Einstein: "The Scientist in Defense of Liberty"
              K. Jaspers: "The Guilt of the German Intellectuals with
                                 Regard to Fascism"

Class XI.   Italy: The Seizure of Power and Resistance

Readings: E. Gentile: "The Manifesto of the Fascist Intellectuals"
              B. Croce: "The Counter-Manifesto of the Liberal
                                 Intellectuals"
              F. T. Marinetti: Futurism and Fascism
              E. Pound: Jefferson and/or Mussolini
Screening: R. Rossellini: Rome, Open City

Class XII.   The Intellectuals and the Mass Psychology of Fascism

Screenings: Excerpts from L. Riefenstahl's Triumph of the Will
               B. Bertolucci: The Conformist
Reading: T. Adorno: "Freudian Theory and the Pattern of Fascist
                                 Propaganda"

Classes XIII and XIV.   From Dissent to Resistance: American Intellectuals
                          and the Crisis in Democratic Values in the Age of
                          Vietnam

Class XIII.   The Intellectual and Democratic Values

Readings: R. Hofstadter: Anti-intellectuals in American Life (selections)
               K. Galbraith: The Affluent Society (selections)
               D. Bell: The End of Ideology(selections)
               G. de Huszar,ed.: The Intellectuals: A Controversial Portrait

Class XIV.   Dissent

Readings: N. Chomsky: American Power and the New Mandarins
               S. Sayres et al.: The 60's Without Apology
Screening: F. Coppola: Apocalypse Now

Class XV.   The Crisis of Reason: The Intellectuals and the Rationality
                                      of the Sciences

Readings: E. Husserl: "The Apparent Failure of Rationalism"
               M. Heidegger: "Science as a Form of Domination'
               K. Popper: "Science as Critical Discussion"
               C. P. Snow: The Two Cultures (selections)
               H. Marcuse: "The Necessity of the Liberation of Science"
               R. Oppenheimer: "Science and Democratic Institutions"
               M. Foucault: "The Universal Intellectual and the Specific
                                 Intellectual"

History 12: HISTORY OF SCIENCE SINCE 1700

Dartmouth College   Richard Kremer
Fall 1985   Reed 305/MW 10-12

The purpose of this course is to explore the origins and impacts of three
major revolutions in science since 1700, and to compare scientific practice
in different political contexts.

Sept 23 Introduction; What is Science?
     25 Revolutions in Science and The Scientific Revolution
     27 Discussion; FIRST WRITING ASSIGNMENT DUE

     30 The Newtonian Style of Science
Oct   2 God, Gravity and Matter
      4 New Vessels for New Wine--Scientific Institutions; Discussion

      7 18th-Century Astronomy, Physiology, Chemistry--Newtonian Sciences?
      9 Newtonians, Anti-Newtonians and "World Politick" in the Enlightenment
     11 The Fate of "Nature" in a Newtonian World; Discussion

     14 Franklin and the "Electricians"
     16 Dartmouth Scientific Artifacts; SECOND WRITING ASSIGNMENT DUE
     18 HOLIDAY (In honor of Bohr's invention of quanta--18 October 1921)

     21 Species, Fossils and Transformism before Darwin
     23 MIDTERM EXAMINATION
     25 Genesis and Geological Change before Darwin; Discussion

     28 The Origin of Darwin's Theory
     30 Darwin's Theory: "Design without a Designer"; Discussion
X   31 "The Voyage of Charles Darwin" (Nova video)
Nov   1 No class meeting

      4 The Scientific Reception of Darwin's Theory
      6 Social Darwinism: The Uses of "Nature Red in Tooth and Claw"
      8 The Birth of a New Discipline--Biology; Discussion

     11 Successes and Failures of Newtonian Physics circa 1900
     13 1905--Einstein's Annus mirabilus
X   14 "The Clockwork Universe" (Bronowski film)
     15 Einstein's Style of Science; Discussion

     18 British, French and German Responses to Relativity
     20 Particles, Waves and Quanta: A Challenge to Realism?
· X 21 "Knowledge or Certainty" (Bronowski film)
     22 Modern Physics and Modern Culture; Discussion

     25 Science in the French Revolution
     27 Science under Hitler; THIRD WRITING ASSIGNMENT DUE

Dec   2 Soviet Science
      4 Thomas Kuhn and Scientific Revolutions; Discussion

         FINAL EXAMINATION

History 12: HISTORY OF SCIENCE SINCE 1700

Dartmouth College   Richard Kremer
Fall 1985   Reed 305/MW 10-12

Course Requirements

Written Assignments

1. Three analytical paragraphs (5%): Write three paragraphs (each less than
200 words) describing, respectively, the views of science presented by Dürrenmatt (playwright), Horton (anthropologist), and Feyerabend (philosopher) in
the assigned readings for the first week. Due 27 September in class.

2. Short essay and oral report on a Dartmouth artifact (10%): Select a
Dartmouth artifact (historical scientific instrument; significant text,
manuscript, or journal; contemporary tool of science), and write a three to
five-page essay describing its significance for the history of science. Be
prepared to report briefly to the class on your object. Clear your choice
of artifact with me by 7 October. Due 16 October in class.

3. Third essay (20%): Select some text in which ostensibly "Newtonian",
"Darwinian" or "Einsteinian" ideas are used to defend moral, religious,
political or social arguments. I will provide a list of possible texts.
Investigate the background of the text and its author, describe its uses of
scientific ideas, and try to infer the writer's fundamental beliefs or
world view from his/her arguments. Present your findings in a five to
seven-page essay. Due 27 November in class.

Class Participation

Read assigned materials critically, and participate in weekly class
discussions (15%).

Examinations

Midterm (15%); Final (35%)

Required Texts (available in Dartmouth Bookstore)

Thayer, H. S., ed. Newton's Philosophy of Nature. New York: Macmillan
    Publishing Co., 1953.

Ruse, Michael. The Darwinian Revolution. Chicago: University of Chicago
    Press, 1979.

Appleman, Philip, ed. Darwin. 2d ed. New York: Norton, 1979.

McCormmach, Russell. Night Thoughts of a Classical Physicist. New York:
    Avon Books, 1982.

/OVER/

Kuhn, Thomas S. <u>Structure</u> <u>of</u> <u>Scientific</u> <u>Revolutions</u>. 2d ed. Chicago: University of Chicago Press, 1970.

Frequently, additional primary materials will be assigned, which are on reserve in Baker Library. Total readings will average about 100-150 pages per week.

NB: No late papers or make-up examinations will be allowed without an official College excuse (health or family emergency). According to College policy (ORC, p. 77), there are no excused absences for participation in College-sponsored extracurricular events.

History 12: HISTORY OF SCIENCE SINCE 1700

Dartmouth College   Richard Kremer
Fall 1985   Reed 305/MW 10-12

Selected Bibliography of Secondary Works

I. REFERENCE WORKS

Dictionary of Scientific Biography. 16 vols. New York, 1970-80.

Elliott, Clark. Biographical Dictionary of American Science: The Seventeenth
    through the Nineteenth Centuries. Westport, CT, 1979.

Encyclopedia of Philosophy. 8 vols. New York, 1967.

Isis Cumulative Bibliography, 1913-1965. 6 vols. London, 1971-84.

Isis Cumulative Bibliography, 1965-1975. 2 vols. London, 1980-85.

Thackray, Arnold. "History of Science." In A Guide to the Culture of
    Science, Technology, and Medicine, pp. 3-69. Edited by Paul T.
    Durbin. New York, 1980.

II. GENERAL

Barnes, Barry and Edge, David, eds. Science in Context: Readings in the
    Sociology of Science. Cambridge, MA, 1982.

Ben-David, Joseph. The Scientist's Role in Society: A Comparative Study.
    Englewood Cliffs, NJ, 1971.

Cohen, I. Bernard. Album of Science: From Leonardo to Lavoisier, 1450-1800.
    New York, 1980.

_____. Revolution in Science. Cambridge, MA, 1985.

Crosland, Maurice, ed. The Emergence of Science in Western Europe. London,
    1975.

Graham, Loren. Between Science and Values. Cambridge, 1981.

Gutting, Gary, ed. Paradigms and Revolutions: Applications and Appraisals of
    Thomas Kuhn's Philosophy of Science. Notre Dame, 1980.

Lakatos, Irme and Musgrave, Alan, eds. Criticism and the Growth of
    Knowledge. Cambridge, 1970.

Marks, John. Science and the Making of the Modern World. London, 1983.

Mason, Stephen F. **A History of the Sciences.** New rev. ed. New York, 1962.

Mendelsohn, Everett. "The Emergence of Science as a Profession in Nineteenth Century Europe." In **Management of Scientists.** Edited by Karl Hill. Boston. 1963.

Russell, C. E. **Science and Social Change in Britain and Europe, 1700-1900.** New York, 1983.

Williams, L. Pearce. **Album of Science: The Nineteenth Century.** New York, 1978.

III. NEWTONIAN REVOLUTION

Buchdahl, Gert. **The Image of Locke and Newton in the Age of Reason.** London. 1961.

Burke, John G., ed. **The Uses of Science in the Age of Newton.** Berkeley, 1983.

Cassirer, Ernst. **The Philosophy of the Enlightenment.** Princeton, 1951.

Clark, G. N. **Science and Social Welfare in the Age of Newton.** Oxford, 1937.

Cohen, I. Bernard. **The Newtonian Revolution.** Cambridge, 1980.

Guerlac, Henry. **Newton on the Continent.** Ithaca, 1981.

Hahn, Roger. **The Anatomy of a Scientific Institution: The Paris Academy of Sciences. 1666-1803.** Berkeley, 1971.

Hankins, T. L. **Jean d'Alembert: Science and the Enlightenment.** Oxford, 1970.

Heilbron, John L. **Elements of Early Modern Physics.** Berkeley, 1982.

Jacob, Margaret C. **The Newtonians and the English Revolution, 1689-1720.** Ithaca. 1976.

Koyré, Alexander. **Newtonian Studies.** Chicago, 1965.

Porter, Roy and Teich, Mikulas, eds. **The Enlightenment in National Context.** Cambridge, 1981.

Rousseau, G. S. and Porter, Roy, eds. **The Ferment of Knowledge: Studies in the Historiography of Eighteenth-Century Science.** Cambridge, 1980.

Thackray, Arnold. **Atoms and Powers: An Essay on Newtonian Matter-Theory and the Development of Chemistry.** Cambridge, MA, 1970.

Westfall, Richard S. The Construction of Modern Science. New York, 1971.

_____. Never at Rest: A Biography of Isaac Newton. Cambridge, 1980.

Wolf, A. A History of Science, Technology, and Philosophy in the Eighteenth Century. Rev. ed. by D. McKie. London, 1952.

Yolton, John W. Thinking Mind: Materialism in Eighteenth-Century Britain. Minneapolis, 1983.

IV. DARWINIAN REVOLUTION

Bowler, Peter J. Fossils and Progress. New York, 1976.

_____. The Eclipse of Darwinism: Anti-Darwinian Evolution Theories in the Decades around 1900. Baltimore, 1983.

_____. Evolution: The History of an Idea. Berkeley, 1984.

Cannon, Walter F. "The Normative Role of Science in Early Victorian Thought." Journal of the History of Ideas, 25 (1964): 487-502.

Coleman, William. Biology in the Nineteenth Century. Cambridge, 1977.

Gasman, Daniel. The Scientific Origins of National Socialism. New York, 1971.

Gillispie, Charles G. Genesis and Geology. New York, 1951.

Glass, Bentley, et al., eds. Forerunners of Darwin: 1745-1859. Baltimore, 1959.

Gould, Stephen Jay. Ever since Darwin. New York, 1977.

Greene, John C. The Death of Adam: Evolution and its Impact on Western Thought. Ames, 1959.

Gruber, Howard E. Darwin on Man: A Psychological Study of Scientific Creativity. New York, 1974.

Hofstadter, Richard. Social Darwinism in American Thought. Rev. ed. Boston, 1955.

Hull, David L., ed. Darwin and his Critics. Cambridge, MA, 1973.

Kelly, Alfred. The Descent of Darwin: The Popularization of Darwinism in Germany, 1860-1914. Chapel Hill, 1981.

Kohn, David. "Theories to work by: Rejected Theories, Reproduction and Darwin's Path to Natural Selection." Studies in History of Biology, 4 (1980): 67-170.

Mayr, Ernst. The Growth of Biological Thought: Diversity, Evolution and Inheritance. Cambridge, MA, 1982.

Moore, James R. The Post-Darwinian Controversies: A Study of the Protestant Struggle to Come to Terms with Darwin in Great Britain and America, 1870-1900. Cambridge, 1979.

Oldroyd, R. David. Darwinian Impacts: An Introduction to the Darwinian Revolution. 2d rev. ed. New York, 1983.

Ospavat, Dov. The Development of Darwin's Theory. Cambridge, 1982.

Sulloway, Frank J. "Darwin's Conversion: The Beagle Voyage and its Aftermath." Journal of the History of Biology, 15 (1982): 325-96.

Wilson, L. G. Charles Lyell, The Years to 1841: The Revolution in Geology. New Haven, 1972.

V. EINSTEINIAN REVOLUTION

Aichelburg, Peter C. and Sexl, Roman U., eds. Albert Einstein: His Influence on Physics, Philosophy, and Politics. Braunschweig, 1979.

Bernstein, Jeremy. Einstein. New York, 1973.

Bunge, Mario and Shea, William R., eds. Rutherford and Physics at the Turn of the Century. New York, 1979.

Forman, Paul. "Weimar Culture, Causality, and Quantum Theory, 1918-1927: Adaptation by German Physicists and Mathematicians to a Hostile Intellectual Environment." Historical Studies in the Physical Sciences, 3 (1971): 1-115.

Goldberg, Stanley. Understanding Relativity: Origins and Impact of a Scientific Revolution. Boston, 1984.

Harman, P. M. Energy, Force and Matter: The Conceptual Development of Nineteenth-Century Physics. Cambridge, 1982.

Henderson, Linda D. The Fourth Dimension and Non-Euclidean Geometry in Modern Art. Princeton, 1983.

Hermann, Armin. The New Physics: The Route into the Atomic Age. Bonn-Bad Godesberg, 1979.

Holton, Gerald. "Einstein, Michelson and the 'Crucial' Experiment." _Isis_, 60 (1969): 133–97.

_____ and Elkana, Yehuda, eds. _Albert Einstein: Historical and Cultural Perspectives_. Princeton, 1982.

Kevles, Daniel J. _The Physicists: The History of a Scientific Community in Modern America_. New York, 1979.

Klein, Martin J. "Mechanical Explanation at the End of the Nineteenth Century." _Centaurus_, 17 (1972): 58–82.

Kuhn, Thomas S. _Black-Body Theory and the Quantum Discontinuity, 1894–1912_. Oxford, 1978.

Miller, Arthur I. _Albert Einstein's Special Theory of Relativity_. Reading, MA, 1981.

Pais, Abraham. _'Subtle is the Lord . . . .' The Science and Life of Albert Einstein_. Oxford, 1982.

Paul, Iain. _Science, Theology and Einstein_. New York, 1982.

Schilpp, Paul Arthur, ed. _Albert Einstein: Philosopher-Scientist_. 2 vols. Evanston, 1949.

Segré, Emilio. _From X-Rays to Quarks: Modern Physicists and their Discoveries_. Berkeley, 1980.

Swenson, Loyd S., Jr. _Genesis of Relativity: Einstein in Context_. New York, 1979.

Wheaton, Bruce C. _The Tiger and the Shark: Empirical Roots of the Wave-Particle Dualism_. Cambridge, 1983.

VI. SCIENCE UNDER BANNERS

Beyerchen, Alan D. _Scientists under Hitler_. New Haven, 1977.

Borkin, Joseph. _The Crime and Punishment of I. G. Farben_. New York, 1978.

Crosland, Maurice. _The Society of Arcueil: A View of French Science at the Time of Napoleon I_. Cambridge, MA, 1967.

Fayet, Joseph. _La Révolution Française et la Science 1789–1795_. Paris, 1960.

Graham, Loren. _Science and Philosophy in the Soviet Union_. New York, 1966.

Haberer, Joseph. _Politics and the Community of Science_. New York, 1969.

Lesch, John E. _Science and Medicine in France: The Emergence of Experimental Physiology, 1790–1855_. Cambridge, MA, 1984.

Lubrano, Linda L. _The Social Context of Soviet Science_. 1980.

Mehrtens, Herbert and Richter, Steffen, eds. _Naturwissenschaft, Technik und NS-Ideologie_. Frankfurt, 1980.

Smeaton, W. A. _Fourcroy: Chemist and Revolutionary, 1755–1809_. Cambridge, 1962.

History 12: HISTORY OF SCIENCE SINCE 1700

Dartmouth College

Richard Kremer
Reed 305/MW 10-12

Assigned Readings 1

Note: All readings are on reserve in Baker Library, except for the required textbooks, which may be purchased at the Dartmouth Bookstore.

<u>Week 1</u> What is Science?

Friedrich Dürrenmatt, "The Physicists" /1962/. In idem, <u>Four Plays</u> (New York, 1965), pp. 289-349.

Robin Horton, "African Traditional Thought and Western Science" /1967/. In <u>Rationality</u>, ed. B. R. Wilson (Oxford, 1979), pp. 131-71.

Paul Feyerabend, "'Science.' The Myth and its Role in Society." <u>Inquiry</u>, 18 (1975): 167-81.

<u>Week 2</u> Newton and the Scientific Revolution

Thayer, pp. 3-5, 9-26, 41-58, 159-79; "Rules of Reasoning," "Preface to the First Edition of the <u>Principia</u>," "Definitions and Axioms," "General Scholium", "God and Gravity," "Query 31 of the <u>Optics</u>."

I. Bernard Cohen, "Newton's Discovery of Gravity," <u>Scientific American</u>, March 1981.

Alan G. R. Smith, <u>Science and Society in the Sixteenth and Seventeenth Centuries</u> (London, 1972), skim pp. 67-123, read 123-34.

<u>Week 3</u> Newton in the Eighteenth Century

Richard Bentley, "A Confutation of Atheism from the Origin and Frame of the World, Part II" /1692 Boyle Lecture/. In idem, <u>The Works of Richard Bentley, D.D.</u> (London, 1838), iii: 146-72.

L. Pearce Williams and Henry John Steffens, eds, <u>The History of Science in Western Civilization</u> (Lanham, MD, 1978), iii: 1-21, 75-86; "The Enlightenment," Voltaire's "Philosophical Letters on the English" /1733/, Goethe's <u>Theory of Colors</u> /1810/.

Jean d'Alembert, <u>Preliminary Discourse to the Encyclopedia of Diderot</u> /1751/, transl. Richard N. Schwab (Indianapolis, 1963), pp. 16-36, 74-87, skim 129-39.

Albrecht von Haller, "A Dissertation on the Sensible and Irritable Parts of Animals" /1751/, Bulletin of the History of Medicine, 4 (1936): 651-99; read only pp. 657-60, 690-96.

Joseph Priestley, Disquisitions relating to Matter and Spirit /1777/ (New York, 1976), pp. 1-40.

Jonathan Swift, Gulliver's Travels /1726/, Part III, Chapts. 5-6.

Week 4 Instruments in the History of Science

Thomas S. Kuhn, "The Function of Measurement in Modern Physical Science" /1961/. In idem, The Essential Tension (Chicago, 1977), pp. 178-224.

Alan G. R. Smith, Science and Society in the Sixteenth and Seventeenth Centuries (London, 1972), skim pp. 153-98.

Dartmouth College

Richard Kremer
Reed 305/MW 10-12

Assigned Readings 2

Note: All readings are on reserve in Baker Library, except for the required textbooks, which may be purchased at the Dartmouth Bookstore.

Week 5 Evolution before Darwin

T. R. Malthus, Population: The First Essay /1798/ (London, 1926), Chapts. I-II, IV-V, XVIII-XIX.

Ruse, Chapts. 1-5.

Plus one of the following three selections:

Jean B. Lamarck, Zoological Philosophy /1809/, transl. Hugh Elliot (London, 1914), Chapt 7.

Georges Cuvier, Essay on the Theory of the Earth /1812/, transl. Robert Kerr (Edinburgh, 1815), Sections 1-6, 19-24, 27-30.

Charles Lyell, Principles of Geology (London, 1830-33), Chapt. 5.

Week 6 Charles Darwin

Charles Darwin, On the Origin of Species /1859/, selections in Appleman, pp. 35-131.

Ruse, Chapts. 6-7.

Week 7 Responses to Darwin

Appleman, scientific responses to Darwin, pp. 220-43; Social Darwinism, pp. 389-415; epilogue, pp. 529-51.

Ruse, Chapts. 8-10.

Dartmouth College

Richard Kremer
Reed 305/MW 10-11

Assigned Readings 3, with Queries

Note: All readings are on reserve in Baker Library, except for the required textbooks, which you purchased at the Dartmouth Bookstore.

Week 8 Einstein and the End of Classical Physics

McCormmach, Russell. Night Thoughts of a Classical Physicist. New York, 1982. You need not read the Notes.

Einstein, Albert. "On the Electrodynamics of Moving Bodies" [1905]. In L. Pearce Williams, ed., Relativity Theory: Its Origins and Impact on Modern Thought, pp. 49-55. New York, 1968.

_____. "Autobiographical Notes" [1949], in ibid., pp. 85-94.

1) What essential features of Victor Jakob's physics and worldview make them classical?
2) What challenges to this classical view had so disturbed Jakob by 1918?
3) What was the career of a classical physicist like? Where did he work, how did he get a job, how did he advance in his career, how were his contributions to physics evaluated and rewarded, for what was he paid, etc.?
4) How did World War I affect German physics and German universities?
5) Compare the roles of experimental data and hypotheses in Einstein's 1905 paper.

Week 9 Physics and Culture after Einstein

Holton, Gerald 1. "The Roots of Complementarity" [1970]. In idem, Thematic Origins of Scientific Thought, pp. 115-61. Cambridge, 1973.

Heisenberg, Werner. "The History of the Quantum Theory," and "The Role of Modern Physics in the Present Development of Human Thinking." In idem, Physics and Philosophy, Chaps. 2, 11. New York, 1958.

1) Compare and contrast Heisenberg's and Holton's approaches to the history of science.
2) What kind of improvements did Heisenberg think 20th-century physics represents over physics of the 19th century?
3) Why did Heisenberg think that ordinary language may at times be more adequate to describe natural phenomena than the precise, mathematical language of science?

History 12: HISTORY OF SCIENCE SINCE 1700

Dartmouth College   Richard Kremer
                                                        Reed 305/MW 10-12

Second Writing Assignment (due 16 October 1985)

Select a Dartmouth scientific "artifact," reporting your choice to me by 7
October, and write a three to five-page essay describing its significance
for the history of science, or the history of science at Dartmouth.
You may choose from among three types of artifacts, and should focus
your essay on different issues depending on your choice.

The following works, placed on closed reserve in Baker Library, may provide
information on your artifact. Start with them before you seek other materials.

Brown, Sanborn and Rieser, Leonard.- Natural Philosophy at Dartmouth.
     Hanover, 1974.
Dartmouth College Bicentennial Exhibit: Historical Philosophical Apparatus, A
     Pictorial Review. Hanover, 1979.
Daumas, Maurice. Scientific Instruments of the Seveenth and Eighteenth
     Centuries. Transl. Mary Holbrook. New York, 1972.
Latour, Bruno and Woolgar, Steven. Laboratory Life: The Social Construction
     of Scientific Facts. Beverly Hills, 1979.
Turner, Gerard L'Estrange. Nineteenth-Century Scientic Instruments.
     Berkeley, 1983.
Wheatland, David. The Apparatus of Science at Harvard, 1765-1800.
     Cambridge, MA, 1968.

Option 1: Scientific Instruments and Apparatus

A variety of historic scientific instruments and apparatus from Dartmouth's
excellent collection currently are being displayed at four sites on the
campus, arranged by Professor A. L. King. A glass case just beyond the
Hinman boxes in the Hop contains three items which came to the College
exactly two hundred years ago. Another case located at the head of the
front stairs in Wilder shows nearly a dozen instruments also from the
18th century. Nineteenth-century apparatus may be seen in several cases in
the Fairchild tower. You may view any of these whenever the buildings
are open. Several telescopes and other astronomical instruments from the
19th century are preserved in the Shattuck Observatory on the hill
behind Wilder. These may be examined only during public observing hours at
the observatory, on Tuesday and Thursday evenings when the skies are clear.
Call before you climb the hill (646-2310).

Read the Kuhn article (assigned readings for Week 4), and classify your
instrument (measurement, observation, experimentation, etc.). Using the
works placed on reserve, or others you may discover, try to determine how
the instrument might have been used at Dartmouth. In addition to its
explicit purposes, does the instrument reflect certain beliefs about nature
or about how to study nature? Summarize your findings in your essay.

Option 2: Scientific treatise, journal or textbook

Select a pre-19th-century scientific text (either from the list below, or
of your own choosing), and describe its function for science. Keep in mind
Kuhn's analysis (assigned readings Week 4) of textbooks. For what
audiences was the text intended? How often was it reprinted, revised in
new editions, or issued in translations? Were any annotations scribbled
into the margins which might indicate how the text was used? How did
Dartmouth acquire the text, or how was it used at Dartmouth? It is more
important to examine the use of the text than its specific contents.

Adams, George. Lectures on Natural and Experimental Philosophy. 4 vols.
    Philadelphia, 1806-07.
American Journal of Science. Early vols., 1818ff.
Darwin, Erasmus. Zoonomia; or the Laws of Organic Life. London, 1794-96.
Diderot, Denis. Encyclopèdie. 17 vols. Paris, 1751-65.
Ferguson, James. Astronomy Explained upon Sir Isaac Newton's Principles;
    Lectures on Select Subjects in Mechanics, Hydrostatics, Pneumatics, and
    Optics; An Introduction to Electricity; Select Mechanical Exercises. 4
    vols. London, 1790. [Text used at Dartmouth]
Franklin, Benjamin. Experiments and Observations on Electricity. 4th ed.
    London, 1769.
Kimball, Samuel A., '06 [1806, that is]. "A System of Plain Trigonometry by
    the Hon. Bezaleel Woodward, Professor of Mathematics and Natural
    Philosophy at Dartmouth University." Lectures notes. Dartmouth
    College Archives.
Newton, Isaac. Opticks. London, 1704.
Philosophical Transactions of the Royal Society of London. Early vols.,
    1666ff.
Smith, John. "My dear Class." Twelve letters to the junior class at
    Dartmouth, on astronomy and natural philosophy, 1778. Dartmouth
    College Archives.

Option 3: "Living" artifacts

Skim Latour and Woolgar on Laboratory Life. Find some Dartmouth
scientist (faculty or grad student) currently engaged in experimental
research who would be willing to be interviewed by you for no longer
than thirty minutes (please respect their busy schedules). Ask him/her
to tell you about the research being conducted, especially about how
instruments or apparatus are being used. Decide whether Latour's and
Woolgar's account does or does not elucidate the activity in the
laboratory you visit; focus your essay on this question.

Note: You may use this option only if you are NOT majoring in a science.

Oral Report: Be prepared to discuss your findings with the class on 16 October.

History 12: HISTORY OF SCIENCE SINCE 1700

Dartmouth College

Richard Kremer
Reed 305/MW 10-12

Third Writing Assignment (due 2 December 1985)

One of the themes of this course is that scientific ideas often are used to defend various religious, moral, social, or political views. Both scientists and non-scientists have linked science and values. For this assignment, you will examine a text which contains such a linkage, and will write a five to seven-page essay discussing your findings.

By Wednesday, 13 November, you should tell me which text you have selected from the list below or should propose one of your own. In your essay, you should i) describe the main argument or thesis of the text; ii) discuss the author's knowledge of scientific ideas, and his use of these to defend the central thesis; and iii) evaluate briefly the success of the author in convincing you of his argument. To achieve these goals, you may find it necessary to investigate the background of the text and its author. Such information, however, must support your treatment of the above three points; I will react critically to three pages of biography not connected to the arguments of your chosen text.

For general background, and a helpful scheme for analyzing science and values, you may want to read the first chapter of Loren Graham, Between Science and Values (New York, 1981), pp. 1-32, which is on closed reserve in Baker Library.

Suggested Texts

I include Dartmouth call numbers for the following texts; you may, however, be able to find a given essay in another edition or publication. See me if you cannot find a copy of your desired text. For books rather than shorter essays, I have indicated the chapters on which you should focus your attention.

Alexander, H. G., ed. The Leibniz-Clarke Correspondence [1715-16]. New York, 1956. [B 1365.L5 1956]

Bagehot, Walter. Physics and Politics; or, Thoughts on the Application of the Principles of 'Natural Selection' and 'Inheritance' to Political Society. New York, 1873, especially Chapt. 2, "The Use of Conflict." [JC 223.B14]

Bohr, Niels. "The Atomic Theory and the Fundamental Principles Underlying the Description of Nature" [1929]. In idem, Atomic Theory and the

Description of Nature, pp. 102-19. New York, 1934. [Phys Sci QC173.B633xa]

Condorcet, J. A. N. C. Sketch for a Historical Picture of the Progress of the Human Kind [1790]. London, 1955, especially Stages 7-10. [109 C754xe]

Derham, William. Physico-Theology; or, A Demonstration of the Being and Attributes of God, from His Works of Creation [1711-12]. London, 1732, especially Books 1-2. [BL 180.D4 1732—treat this old book very carefully]

Dewey, John. "The Influence of Darwin on Philosophy" [1909]. In idem, The Influence of Darwinism on Philosophy and Other Essays in Contemporary Thought, pp. 1-19. New York, 1910. [191.9 D515i]

Eddington, A. S. Science and the Unseen World. New York, 1929. [BL 241.E4 1929]

Fiske, John. "The Doctrine of Evolution: Its Scope and Purport." In idem, A Century of Science, and Other Essays, pp. 39-63. Boston, 1899. [816 F547 P3]

Gray, Asa. "Natural Selection not Inconsistent with Natural Theology" [1860]. In idem, Darwiniana, pp. 72-145. Ed. A. Hunter Dupree. Cambridge, 1963. [Dana 367.G77 1963]

Heisenberg, Werner. "Science as a Means of International Understanding" [1946]. In idem, Philosophical Problems of Nuclear Science, pp. 109-20. New York, 1952. [Phys Sci QC71.H3513]

_____. "Science and Religion." In idem, Physics and Beyond, pp. 82-92. New York, 1971. [Phys Sci QC173.H38613 1971, and on Baker reserve]

Hodge, Charles. What is Darwinism? New York, 1874. [Dana 579.1 H662w]

Huxley, Thomas H. "Evolution and Ethics" [1893]. In idem and Julian Huxley, Touchstone for Ethics, pp. 67-112. New York, 1947. [BJ 1311.H8]

La Mettrie, Julien Offray. Man a Machine [1749]. La Salle, Ill., 1912. [612 091 L183m]

O'Sullivan, John Louis. "Manifest Destiny." Harper's New Monthly Magazine, 70 (1885): 578-90. [AP 2.H32]

Roosevelt, Theodore. "Biological Analogies in History" [1910]. In idem, History as Literature and other Essays, pp. 39-93. New York, 1913. [816 R672 R5]

Ross, Edward Alsworth. Sin and Society. Boston, 1907, especially Chapt. 6, "The Rules of the Game." [174 R733 S]

Sumner, William Graham. "Sociology." In idem, <u>War and Other Essays</u>, pp. 167-92. New Haven, 1913. [304 S956w]

Symonds, John Addington. "On the Application of Evolutionary Principles to Art and Literature." In idem, <u>Essays, Speculative and Suggestive</u>, i: 42-83. London, 1890. [826 Sy6 M]

Vogt, Karl. <u>Lectures on Man; His Place in Creation and in the History of the Earth</u>. Ed. James Hunt. London, 1864. [Dana GN 23.V88]

Whiston, William. <u>A New Theory of the Earth</u> [1696]. London. 1725, especially Book IV, "Solutions." [BL 224.W57 1725]

White, Andrew D. <u>A History of the Warfare of Science with Theology</u> [1896]. New York, 1923, especially Chapt. 1, "From Creation to Evolution." [BL 245.W5 1923]

Newton's <u>Nut-Shell</u> Theory of Matter
(from A. Thackray, <u>Atoms and Powers</u>, pp. 19, 25)

Newton:

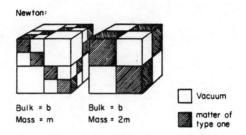

Bulk = b   Bulk = b
Mass = m   Mass = 2m

☐ Vacuum

▨ matter of
type one

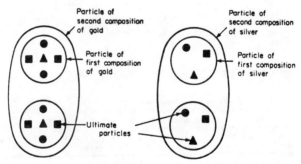

II. The possibility of transmutation.

85

Maxwell's Theory of the Ether
(From P. M. Harman, <u>Energy, Force, and Matter</u>, 1982, pp. 90-91)

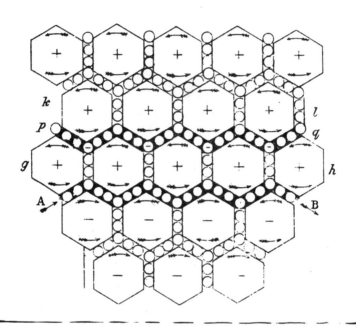

Fig. 4.4. Maxwell's physical model of molecular vortices and electric particles (1861). In this model of the ether Maxwell postulated a framework of vortices embedded in an incompressible fluid. Each vortex was separated from its neighbours by a layer of spherical particles, revolving in the opposite directions to the vortices. These 'idle-wheel' particles were identified with electricity. The electric current flowed from *A* to *B*, and the row of vortices *gh* above *AB* was set in motion in an anti-clockwise direction (+), engaging the layer of particles *pq*, which acted on the next row of vortices *kl*. The transmission of electric action was explained in terms of the process of communicating the rotatory velocity of the vortices from one part of the field to another. The idle-wheel particles (electricity) permitted adjacent vortices to rotate in the same direction. The figure contains a drafting error: The vortices below *AB* would rotate in a clockwise direction (−), despite the directions on some of the arrows.

Maxwell emphasised that this model of idle-wheel particles was provisional. Nevertheless, he continued to argue that magneto-optic rotation implied that the rotation of vortices represented physical reality. This 1861 representation of the mechanical structure of the field was intended as a heuristic illustration, not a working mechanical device of the kind later invented by Boltzmann (and also by Maxwell himself), which provided specific mechanical analogues for electromagnetic phenomena (see Figure 6.1). *Source: The scientific papers of James Clerk Maxwell*, ed. W. D. Niven, 2 vols. (Cambridge, 1890), 1:488, pl. VIII, fig. 2.

History 12
"Science under Hitler"

Intelligence tests devised in 1935 to determine who should be sterilized
in the Genetic Health Courts, from F. Dubitscher, "Die Bewährung Schwachsinniger
im täglichen Leben," Der Erbarzt, 4 (1935): 59. [Procter thesis, p. 487]

The "suitcase" test of organizational ability:

> In a box 60 x 30 x 30 cm are 20 different objects of different
> shapes, such as books, bottles, etc. which with careful packing
> exactly fill the box. Pack them all in such a way that the lid may
> be closed without force.

The "assignment" test:

> The testee is given the following map, and receives instructions
> to buy the following objects: a half a hundred weight of potatoes,
> $\frac{1}{2}$ lb. of coffee, $\frac{1}{2}$ lb of wurst, 50 pfennigs worth of fresh biscuits,
> and a lb of butter. He is further required to bring a pair of trousers
> to the tailor, and a pair of shoes to the shoeshop, as well as a 10-lb.
> package to the Post Office. He is also required to pay a certain amount
> of tax at City Hall, and to pick up a friend at the train station. The
> following rules are to be observed. The person leaves the house at
> 9:30. At 1:00 he should be back for lunch and have accomplished all
> his tasks. Now the tax office is open only from 8 to 10; fresh
> bread is only available after 11, and the friend arrives at the station
> at 12:30. . . .

The "carrying out orders" test:

> You are mayor of a city in time of war. Suddenly from high command
> comes an order that all windows are to be removed. How should this be
> done, and what should be used in place of glass for the windows?

Nazi mathematics textbook for 6th-graders, 1943:

> "The annual expense to the State for caring for a mentally ill patient
> is 766 RM; a deaf-mute and a blind patient costs 615 RM; a cripple 600 RM.
> State institutions hold 167,000 mentally ill, 8300 deaf-mutes and blind,
> and 20,600 cripples. How many genetically healthy families could be
> supported at 60 RM/month for the amount now spent on the genetically unfit?

History 12: HISTORY OF SCIENCE SINCE 1700

Dartmouth College

Richard Kremer
Reed 305/MW 10-12

Review Sheet for Midterm Examination

I. Terms whose meaning and significance you should be able to discuss:

revolvere	"warfare metaphor"	Lavoisier
Glorious Revolution	clockmaker God	nutshell theory
"saving the phenomena"	active principles	Boscovich
Tycho Brahe	voluntarist theology	chemical affinity
Johannes Kepler	secondary causes	vitalism
Descartes	natural theology	Albrecht von Haller
empiricism		irritability
mechanical philosophy	patronage	
inertia	Accademia del Cimento	"World Politik"
"geometrization of nature"	Royal Society	Latitudinarians
	Académie des Sciences	Boyle Lectures
refraction	Colbert	Hutchinson
vortex theory		d'Albert
Principia	perturbations	
centripetal force	Laplace	microcosm/macrocosm
"moon test"	nebular hypothesis	physical cabinet
Gilbert	système Nollet	voltaic pile
effluvia	Leyden jar	
von Guericke	Coulomb	

II. Important themes, issues, and questions:

1) Compare and contrast the role of hypotheses in the scientific thought of Newton and Descartes.

2) Discuss the path Newton followed in formulating the law of universal gravitation. What concepts did he take from predecessors, how did he transform these borrowed ideas, and what new ideas did he invent?

3) Discuss the various "Newtonianisms" and the influence of each in the eighteenth century, especially on politics, religion, and worldviews.

4) Compare and contrast the sciences of astronomy and electricity in the 18th century as examples of "Newtonian" sciences.

5) "The notions of the world's being a great machine, going on without the interposition of God, as a clock continues without the assistance of a clockmaker, is the notion of materialism." Would Newton have agreed with this claim? Why or why not? Discuss the role of God in Newton's science.

6) To what extent did distinct national "schools" (French, German, English) of natural philosophy exist in the 18th century? What factors might have contributed to such different traditions?

7) Compare and contrast Bentley's Boyle Lecture (1692) and Priestley's Disquisitions relating to Matter and Spirit (1777). Mention their respective views on the nature of matter, on God and Providence, and their goals or their intended audiences.

8) One of Newton's basic concepts was that of force. What did he mean by the term, and what roles did the concept play in 18th-century science?

9) Why did the Scientific Revolution require new institutions to support scientific activity? How did the new institutions, in turn, affect the type of science practiced after 1700, especially in France and England?

10) "When faced with new, puzzling phenomena, scientists usually attempt to squeeze them into old, familiar concepts or theories." Agree or disagree, referring to examples from the 18th century.

11) Discuss several roles played by instruments or apparatus in 18th-century science.

Dartmouth College

Richard Kremer
Reed 305/MW 10-12

Review Sheet for FINAL Examination (8 December, 1-3 p.m., Reed 104)

I. Terms whose meaning and significance you should be able to discuss:

Chain of Being
John Ray
Cuvier
Buffon
theory of degeneration
theory of organic progression

erratics
actualism
uniformitarianism
Werner
Hutton
primary/secondary rocks
scriptural geology
Elie de Beaumont

population thinking
Wallace
species competition
"struggle for existence"
Spencer
artificial/natural selection
Quetelet

sexual selection
principle of divergence

Jacobin science
Lycée des Arts
academician vs. artiste
second Scientific Revolution
Ecole polytechnique
Ecole de santé

X-Club
Eozoön canadense
Lord Kelvin
pangenesis
Weismann
Ancon sheep
biometry
hypothetical-deductive
          method
vera causa

Hofstadter
Galton
eugenics
ethical naturalism
Sumner
Haeckel

epistemology
Faraday
Maxwell's synthesis
Hertz
cathode ray tube
Zeeman effect
Röntgen
Becquerel
Lorentz
positivism

racial hygiene
Nuremberg laws
Gleichschaltung
"Aryan physics"
Lenard & Stark

heuristic
Brownian motion
aberration
Arago
Michelson & Morley
relativity of
          simultaneity
time dilation
twin paradox

Vermutung

Kaufmann
Society of German
    Scientists & Physicians
Poincaré
Tripos

complementarity
Planck
Bohr
stationary states
quantum mechanics
uncertainty principle

tactile space
Spengler

dialectical materialism
bourgeoise science
Deborinites
red specialists
Lysenko
vernalization
agrobiology

II. Important themes, issues and questions:

1) In formulating his theory of evolution, what did Darwin learn from his Beagle voyage, his reading of Malthus, and his study of plant and animal breeders in England?

-over-

2) In the _Origin_, what did Darwin describe as the major advantages of his theory? What major difficulties of the theory did he try to solve?

3) Compare and contrast the responses to Darwin's theory by the four leading scientists included in Appleman, pp. 220–43 (Sedgwick, Owen, Hooker, Huxley).

4) Compare and contrast the roles of speculative thinking and empirical data in the scientific work of Darwin and Einstein.

5) Why did Victor Jakob commit suicide in McCormmach's "novel?"

6) Compare and contrast the opinions of Heisenberg and Bronowski on the impact of modern physics on Western society and culture.

7) Compare and contrast the effects of politics on the practice of science in revolutionary France, Hitler's Germany, and the Soviet Union.

8) "Science is a unique type of knowledge because it is objective, morally neutral and totally apolitical." Agree or disagree with this claim, using examples from the course.

9) To what extent has science progressed since 1700? What does Kuhn think, and what do you think?

10) Describe Kuhn's theory of scientific change. Discuss the successes and failures of his theory as an explanation of the three major scientific revolutions studied in our course (Newtonian, Darwinian, Einsteinian).

University of PennsylvaniaMWF 11:00
                                                        Martin Wolfe

          SOCIETY AND ECONOMY IN WESTERN EUROPE

Fall term: Industrial Capitalism and the Western Social Conscience,
                1815-1914
(Spring term: Coping with Socioeconomic Crises during the First
                Postindustrial Era, 1914-1973)

The focus of this course is the enormous increases in wealth brought
to western Europe by 19th century industrialization and the fundamental changes in social relations that resulted. A second aim is
a better understanding of the British, French, Germans, and Italians
through a study of how they made their living during the transformation of their societies from agrarian to industrial. We use the
comparative approach--contrasting regions and groups as well as
countries--rather than treating western Europe as a unit.

This is a history course and not one in economics or social science.
It depends on description of concrete developments and relations
rather than on theories or models. To "learn Europe from the ground
up" we spend some time with historical geography. No previous work
in European history is needed. Chronologies and maps plus parts of
your instructor's presentations will help provide needed background.
If you want to use History 421A to acquire a knowledge of general
European history, you should buy a good text and read it not all at once
but in tandem with our own weekly readings. A highly recommended
general history is Gordon A. Craig, Europe since 1815, but there are
many fine texts covering 19th and 20th century Europe.

The separate terms of History 421 are taught as independent units;
it is not necessary to take both of them or to take them in
chronological order.

Students are asked to wrote two short papers, the first an evaluation
of some aspects of Zola's Germinal, the second a report on the industrial transformation of one region. Also required: three one-hour exams.

Topics and Assignments

Week

1. Sept. 8   The End of Agrarian Europe

   The price of industrialization
   "The world we have lost"

   Hobsbawm, Intro. and chs. 1 and 2

2. Sept. 13   The Social Impact of Industrialization

   The factory
   Standards of living: Up or Down?
   Speenhamland and All That

   Cipolla, ch. 3; Stearns, ch.s 1 and 2

3. Sept. 20   New Socioeconomic Landscapes

   Yorkshire and Lancashire
   The Massif Central
   The Ruhr

   Cipolla, ch. 1; Hobsbawm, chs. 3 and 4

4. Sept. 27   Toward a Market Economy

   Industrial capitalism formulates an ideology
   Social control vs. liberalism on the Continent
   "Backwash" in southern Italy

   Cipolla, pp. 76-115, 278-296; Stearns,
   ch. 3; Henderson, pp. 91-126

5. Oct. 4   The Bourgeois Triumph

   "Palace of Industry": the Exhibition of 1851
   Counter-industrial values and movements
   (1st exam)

   Stearns, pp. 116-143

6. Oct. 11   The Victorian Social Conscience

   The new Poor Laws
   The noble path: amelioration
   Charles Dickens: cynical sentimentalist or welfare hero?

   (1st paper due Oct. 15)

7. Oct. 18   High Tide of Industrial Capitalism

   Louis Napoleon and "social caesarism"
   Britain and France around 1900
   Germany and Italy around 1900

   Hobsbawm, ch. 6; Henderson, pp. 126-167

8. Oct. 25   Western Europe in the Age of "New Imperialism"

The profits and perils of imperialism
Beggaring neighbors
A banker's world

Cipolla, pp. 115-157

Nov. 1   Workers and Peasants under Industrial Capitalism

A new social structure: labor unions
Nobles and peasants: the agricultural scene around 1900
The dilemma of reformist socialism

Stearns, pp. 143-177

10. Nov. 8   "The Rise of the Masses"

The quality of life under mature industrial capitalism
New perceptions of social welfare
(2nd exam)

11. Nov. 15   Edwardian Britain

"Economic climacteric"
The Fabians and "collectivism"
Upstairs, Downstairs

Hobsbawm, chs. 7, 8, and 9

12. Nov. 22   Wilhelmine Germany

Class relations under paternal authoritarianism
A paradigm of finance capitalism
(Thanksgiving weekend)

Henderson, pp. 44-74

13. Nov. 29   Belle Epoque France

Backward-looking growth
French economic nationalism
Regional problems in prewar France

Stearns, ch. 5; Henderson, pp. 167-201

14. Dec. 6   United (?) Italy

Struggles over national economic policy
The economic centaur
Workers and peasants in pre-Fascist Italy

Cipolla, pp. 297-325
(Second paper due December 6)

TEXTS :   Carlo Cipolla, The Emergence of Industrial Societies (Vol. 4,
          part 1 of "The Fontana Economic History of Europe")
          Peter N. Stearns, European Society in Upheaval, 2nd ed.
          E. J. Hobsbawm, Industry and Empire
          Emile Zola, Germinal

          (In Rosengarten: W. O. Henderson, Industrial Revolution in Europe)

Required texts

> Carlo Cipolla, ed., The Fontana Economic History of Europe,
>> vol. 4 part 1: "The Emergence of Industrial Societies"
>
> Raymond F. Betts, Europe in Retrospect

You might want to buy (but these are in Rosengarten)

> E.J. Hobsbawm, Industry and Empire
>
> Peter N. Stearns, European Society in Upheaval, 2nd ed.

Also required: a chapter or so each (in Rosengarten)

> W.O. Henderson, The Industrial Revolution in Europe, 1815-1914
>
> E.J. Hobsbawm, The Age of Revolution, 1789-1848
>
> Jurgen Kuczynski, The Rise of the Working Class
>
> E.C. Midwinter, Victorian Social Reform

Good (and easy) reading: recommended for reports

> Duncan Bythell, The Handloom Weavers
>
> Friedrich Engels, The Condition of the Working Class in England
>
> Ross J.S. Hoffman, Great Britain and the German Trade Rivalry
>
> J.L. and Barbara Hammond, The Town Labourer
>
> David Landes, Bankers and Pashas
>
> Donald McKay, The National Workshops
>
> David Pinkney, Haussmann and the Rebuilding of Paris
>
> Ralph Samuel, Village Life and Labour
>
> Pierre-Jakez Helias, The Horse of Pride
>
> Val Lorwin, Labor and Working Conditions in Modern Europe
>
> Eugen Weber, Peasants into Frenchmen

History 421B
Spring 1983

MWF 11:00
Martin Wolfe

SOCIETY AND ECONOMY IN WESTERN EUROPE

Second term: Coping with Socioeconomic Crises during the Post-
industrial Era, 1914-1973

(First term: Industrial Capitalism and the Western Social
Conscience, 1815-1914)

The focus of this course during the spring term is the successes and
failures of western European governments in dealing with the vital problems
of twentieth century war, depression, monetary crisis, and class conflict.
A second aim is a better understanding of the British, French, Germans, and
Italians through a study of what they wanted from their material and social
affairs with the help of their governments. One of the main aims of the course
is to understand the relative performance of west European governments and the
connections between that performance and the presumed national personality
characteristics of each nation.

This is a history course and not one in economics or social science.
It depends on description of concrete events and developments and only
incidentally on theory or models. Its approach is comparative ("transnational")
rather than international, and it tends to deal with national differences
rather than similarities within western Europe. No previous work in European history is needed. Chronologies and other materials will be provided
for background. Students who want at the same time to improve their general
knowledge of 20th century European history should acquire a good text and read
it along with our week assignments. One good short text is Michael Richards,
Europe 1900-1980: A Brief History. The separate terms of this course are
taught as independent units; it is not necessary to take both of them or to
take them in chronological order.

Students are asked to take three one-hour exams. One short paper (about
7 pp.) will be required; it will be on relations between collective mentali-
ties and socioeconomic achievements (or the lack of them), andshould be
based in part on two of the works in our reading list.

Class Topics and Week Assignments

WEEK ONE   Socioeconomic Policy and European History

Course aims and procedures
Course themes: some examples from the literature of economics
Some examples from the literature of sociology

[For students who want background on the pre-1914 era:
Hobsbawm, 9-33 and 172-193; Stearns, 59-90, 109-133, and
152-177]

WEEK TWO   Total War and Heightened Expectations

Involving the "home front"
Release of new economic energies
Long-run implications of economic warfare

Stearns, 179-236; Marwick, 1-33 and 41-96; Aldcroft, Intro and
chapter 1

WEEK THREE   Recasting Bourgeois Europe

Reconstruction: "homes for heroes"
The war debts and reparations fiasco
"Normalcy"?

Stearns, 236-266; Aldcroft, ch. 2

WEEK FOUR   "Golden Twenties"?

Runaway inflation in Germany
Britain on the dole
Monetary stability and economic stagnation in France

Hobsbawm, 207-225; Cipolla, 128-148; Stearns, 276-288;
Wolfe, 73-104

WEEK FIVE   The Great Depression in Italy and Germany

The tragedy of the Weimar regime
Was there a Fascist economic system?
Fascism and modernization"

Cipolla, 266-290 and 180-200; Tannenbaum, 89-112 and 119-143

WEEK SIX   The Great Depression in France and Britain

The French Popular Front
Stanley Baldwin's England
[first exam]

Hobsbawm, 225-248; Aldcroft, ch. 3; Wolfe, 105-137 and 138-171

Class topics and week assignments, contd

WEEK SEVEN   The Nazi Socioeconomic Revolution

Nazi economic "miracles"
Class relations in Nazi Germany
Socioeconomic significance of the Nazi conquest of Europe

Schoenbaum, Intro, pp. 1-42, 113-151, and 275-288

WEEK EIGHT   World War II

New forms of economic mobilization
Social change in wartime Britain
Social change in wartime France

Marwick, pp. 98-123, 151-165, and 185-204

WEEK NINE   Laying the Groundwork for the Welfare State

The Liberation and Resistance mystique
The Keynesian Revolution
New social and economic structures

Cipolla, 91-100; Cipolla, vol 5, 366-399 (on Keynes)
Stearns, 289-330; Aldcroft, ch. 4

WEEK TEN   Britain after 1950: A New Society?

"Dukes and Dustmen": establishing welfare state values
Nationalized companies: some mixed results
[second exam]

Cipolla, 148-177; Hobsbawm, 249-293; Stearns, 331-336; Shonfield,
61-57 and 88-120

WEEK ELEVEN   France: New Values, New Structures

A long-delayed transformation
The Monnet Plan
"Embourgeoisement"

Cipolla, 100-124; Shonfield, 71-87 and 121-150; Hoffmann,
118-234; Aldcroft, ch. 5

WEEK TWELVE   The German Economic Miracle

The amazing 1948 currency reform
"Guided capitalism": Tucktigkeit and tycoons
"An economy in search of a nation"?

Cipolla, 208-259; Shonfield, 239-297

WEEK THIRTEEN The Italian Economic Centaur

An Italian economic miracle?
Southern Italian poverty: an uneradicable problem?
Economic failures and social turmoil

Cipolla, 290-318; Shonfield, 176-198; Grindrod, 120, 38-46, and
198-206

WEEK FOURTEEN   Conclusions

Prospects for better socioeconomic policy
1968: A turning point?

History 421B
Spring 1983

Texts

Derek H. Aldcroft, The European Economy, 1914-1980
Carlo Cipolla, ed., "Contemporary Economies," vol. 6, part 1 of the
    Fontana Economic History of Europe
E. J. Hobsbawm, Industry and Empire
David Schoenbaum, Hitler's Social Revolution
Peter N. Stearns, European Society in Upheaval

Required readings (in Rosengarten); a chapter or so in each

Carlo Cipolla, ed., "The Twentieth Century,", vol. 5, part 1 of the
    Fontana Economic History of Europe
Muriel Grindrod, The Rebuilding of Italy
Stanley Hoffmann, et el., In Search of France
Arthur Marwick, War and Social Change in the 20th Century
Andrew Shonfield, Modern Capitalism
Martin Wolfe, The French Franc between the Wars

For student papers

George Bailey, Germans
Luigi Barzini, The Italians
Ronald Blythe, Akenfield: Portrait of an English Village
Crane Brinton, The Americans and the French
Jacques Heliaz, A Horse of Pride [on Brittany]
Edwin Hartrich, The Fourth and Richest Reich: How the Germans Conquered
    the Postwar World
H. Stuart Hughes, The Americans and the Italians
Danilo Dolci, Sicilian Lives
Herbert Kubly, Stranger in Italy
Rudolf Leonhardt, This Germany: The Story since the Third Reich
Carlo Levi, Christ Stopped at Eboli
Edward Muir, Scottish Journey
Carlo Levi, Christ Stopped at Eboli
Peter Nichols, Italia, Italia
George Orwell, Down and Out in Paris and London
    ————————, The Road to Wigan Pier
    ————————, A Collection of Essays
Guido Piovene, In Searchof Europe
J. B. Priestley, English Journey
Laurence Wylie, Village in the Vauclause

HISTORY 1955

'The Wealth of Nations': Economic Problems and Policy since 1700

Alongside national security, economic well-being is deemed the major objective that any contemporary government must provide. Elected leaders are routinely assigned responsibility for reducing unemployment, lowering inflation, encouraging economic growth, minimizing government deficits and raising the welfare of the poor. But this was not always the case. Only from the seventeenth century do we find governments and writers learning to think about the economy as a coherent set of activities distinct from national power and subject to certain rules of behavior. Only since the world depression of the 1930's do we find national states made responsible for continued growth and welfare.

History 1955 follows the emergence of political economy, as this sphere of reasoning and policy was called. It looks at the successive economic problems that societies have had to face since the end of the seventeenth century. These included the challenge of national development and industrialization, the dilemmas of poverty and unemployment, major inflation, devastating unemployment. The course also examines the economic aspects of imperialist expansion. For each of these major challenges History 1955 covers both the nature of the problem, and the policy responses. The great economic writings were often conceived, not as abstract doctrines, but arguments for the pressing issues of the day.

This is not a course in economic theory or in economic history per se. The course does not presuppose prior formal instruction in economics. It will introduce any theory that is needed and devotes major attention to examination of ideas and institutions in their historical context. Lectures will concentrate on evolving economic institutions, the major crises, and the theoretical responses during two centuries of development. Weekly discussions (provisionally scheduled for Thursdays at 3 pm. or Mondays at 4 pm.) will focus on the issues raised by the reading, especially the selections from the economic theorists. The texts chosen represent some of the most vigorous theoretical and policy arguments in the history of economic literature.

Written requirements include a brief paper at midterm; a course essay of about 15 pages due in reading period; and a take-home final examination. Suggestions for course essays and for supplementary reading in each topic area will be distributed during the course.

Lecture Schedule and Assigned Reading

Sept. 21, 23. Course Introduction: States and Markets.
The Crisis of Feudal Europe and Early Modernization.

Required Reading (to be completed by October 2):
Jan De Vries, The Economy of Europe in an Age of Crisis, 1600-1750
(Cambridge UP, 1976: PB = Paperback), chapters 1-2, 4, 7-8.

Immanuel Wallerstein, The Modern World System, vol. I (Academic
Press, 1967: PB), chaps., 1-2, 7.

Douglass North and R. P. Thomas, The Rise of the Western World: A
New Economic History (Cambridge, 1973). pp. 1-24, 69-158.

Sept. 30, Oct. 2. Discovery of the Economic Realm and the Idea of
National Wealth: the Mercantilists, Whigs, Adam Smith.

Adam Smith, An Inquiry into the Nature and Causes of The Wealth of
Nations (Pelican PB, Modern Library or University of Chicago Press
[Edwin Cannon, ed.] edition): Book I, chaps., 1-5, 7-8; Book II,
chapter 3; Book III, chap. 4; Book IV, chap. 2 (not included in
the Pelican edition).

Oct. 7, 9. Commerce, Agriculture, and Industry: Smithian, Physiocratic
and Protectionist Strategies for Development.

Alexander Hamilton, "Report on Manufactures."

David S. Landes, The Unbound Prometheus (Cambridge UP, 1969: PB),
chaps. 1-2.

Oct. 14, 16. Classical Political Economy and the Problems of Income
Distribution, Class Conflict, and Poverty.

David Ricardo, The Principles of Political Economy and Taxation,
chaps. 1-2, 5. Any edition. The standard is now that of Piero
Sfraffa, ed., Works and Correspondence, vol. 1. There is also an
"Everyman" PB issued by J.M Dunt in London and E. P. Dutton in New
York.

Karl Polanyi, The Great Transformation (c.1944; Beacon 1957: PB),
chaps. 1, 3-10.

Oct. 21 only. Marx's Analysis of the Capitalist Economy.

Karl Marx, Capital (any edition), vol I: chapter I, sections 1-2, 4; chapter VII; chapter X; chapter XXV, sections 2-4; chapter XXVI.

William Reddy, The Rise of Market Culture: The Textile Trade and French Society (Cambridge UP, 1984), pp. 1-21, 40-47, 87-106, 134-204, 221-252, 326-336.

Oct. 28, 30. The Economics of Imperialism.

Joseph Schumpeter, "The Sociology of Imperialisms" in Imperialism and Social Classes (World Publishing Co. , 968), pp. 3-7, 64-98.

V. I. Lenin, Imperialism: The Highest Stage of Capitalism (any edition), chaps. I, IV-VIII, X.

Tony Smith, The Pattern of Imperialism (Cambridge UP, 1982: PB), chaps. 1-2.

Michael Doyle, Empires (Cornell UP, 1986: PB), 141-161, 257-305.

Nov. 4, 6. The Economics of Twentieth-Century War and Inflation.

Costantino Bresciani-Turroni, The Economics of Inflation (Allen & Unwin, 1937), chaps. I, II, VIII-IX, XI.

Charles S. Maier, "War Finance and Inflation, 1914-24." Xerox.

Fred Hirsch & John Goldthorpe, eds., The Political Economy of Inflation (Harvard UP, 1978: PB), chaps. 1-2, 7-8, conclusion.

Nov. 13, only. The Interwar Economy and the Sources of the World Depression.

Charles P. Kindleberger, The World in Depression, 1929-1939 (Univ. of California, 1976: PB), chaps. 3-8, 14.

Milton Friedman and Anna Schwartz, The Great Contraction (Princeton UP, 1965: PB), sections 2-5, 7. This is a separate edition of their Monetary History of the United States, 1867-1960 (Princeton UP: PB), chap. VII.

Harold James, The German Slump: Politics and Economics, 1924-1936 (Oxford: CLarendon Press, 1986), chap. VIII.

Nov. 18, 20. The Impact of the Depression: Mass Unemployment and
Comparative Policy Responses; Keynesian Theory.

John Maynard Keynes, The General Theory of Employment, Interest
and Money (c.1936, Macmillan PB), chaps. 1-3, 5, 11-13, 18, 24.

The Pilgrim Trust, Men Without Work (xeroxed selections).

Walter Greenwood, Love on the Dole (Penguin PB).

Nov. 25, only. Getting out of the Depression: What Worked?

Dec. 2, 4. Alternatives to the Market: Soviet Collectivization and Nazi
Economic Policies.

Alexander Erlich, The Soviet Industrialization Debate (Harvard UP,
1967), chaps. I-V, IX;
OR
Stephen F. Cohen, Bukharin and the Bolshevik Revolution (Vintage
1973: PB), chaps. V-IX.

Charles S. Maier, "Tne Economics of Nazism and Fascism: Premises
and Performance." Xerox on reserve.

Dec. 9, 11. The Rise and Decline of Postwar Dollar Leadership.

David P. Calleo, The Imperious Economy (Harvard UP, 1981), chaps.
1-7, conclusion.

Robert O. Keohane, After Hegemony: Cooperation and Discord in the
World Political Economy (Harvard UP, 1984: PB), chaps. 3, 8-9.

Dec. 16, 18. The Age of "Stagflation" and Revival of the Market.

Leon Lindberg and Charles S. Maier, The Politics of Inflation and
Economic Stagnation (Brookings, 1985: PB), chaps. 1-5, 8-9, 16.

Fred Hirsch, Social Limits of Growth (Harvard UP, 1978: PB),
Introduction, chaps. I, III-IV.

Mr. Moeller
History 299
Spring 1981

Columbia University

Colloquium in Modern European Social History

The purpose of this seminar is to provide students with a general
introduction to the recent literature in European social history. We will
begin with a discussion of the nature of social history and then proceed
to a consideration of individual topics. The readings are intended very
much as a "state of the art" survey of the variety of approaches currently
being employed and the sorts of topics being studied by social historians.
Since this is a new and in some senses still undefined field in which there
are still few "classic" works, we will attempt a broad survey primarily
of journal literature, rather than concentrating on a limited number of
monographs. Each student will be expected to prepare a presentation on
one or more of the week's readings, and in addition, to write a twenty
page paper, reviewing the literature on one of these topics. This paper
should include a review of the appropriate monographic literature and
other relevant articles as well. In order to facilitate an information
exchange in the seminar, each student will also prepare and distribute an
annotated bibliography on his or her topic.

.I. General Introduction -- What is Social History?

   Hobsbawm, E. J., "From Social History to the History of Society,"
       in: Felix Gilbert and Stephen R. Graubard, Historical Studies
       Today, 1-26.

   F. Braudel, "History and the Social Sciences," in P. Burke, ed.
       Economy and Society in Early Modern Europe, 11-42.

   Ann D. Gordon, Mari Jo Buhle, Nancy Schrom Dye, "The Problem of
       Women's History," in: Vernice, A. Carroll, Liberating Women's
       History, Urbana, 1976, 75-92.

   Elizabeth Fox-Genovese and Eugene Genovese, "The Political Crisis of
       Social History," JSH, X, 1976.

   Tony Judt, "A Clown in Regal Purple: Social History and the
       Historians," HWJ, VII, Spring, 1979, 66-94.

II. Rural Society and Economy Before the Industrial Revolution

   Jack Goody, Joan Thirsk, E. P. Thompson, eds., Family and Inheritance.
       Rural Society in Western Europe, Cambridge, 1976. articles by
       Goody, Sabean, Berkner.

   William N. Parker and Eric L. Jones, European Peasants and their
       Markets. Essays in Agrarian Economic History, Princeton, 1975,
       essays by Cohen and Weitzman, deVries, and Grantham.

III. Proto-Industrialization

Rudolf Braun, "The Impact of Cottage Industry on an Agricultural Population," in D. Landes, ed., The Rise of Capitalism, New York, 1964, 53-64.

Hermann Kellenbenz, "Rural Industries in the West from the end of the Middle Ages to the Eighteenth Century," in: Essays in European Economic History 1500-1800, ed. by Peter Earle, Oxford, 1974, 45-88.

Jan de Vries, Economy in Europe in an Age of Crisis, 1600-1750, Cambridge, 1976, 84-112.

Franklin F. Mendels, "Proto-industrialization: The First Phase of the Industrialization Process," JEH, XXXII, 1, 1972, 241-261.

Olwen Hufton, "Women and the Family Economy in Eighteenth Century France," French Historical Studies, 9, 1975, 1-22.

Hans Medick, "The Proto-industrial Family Economy: The Structural Function of Household and Family during the Transition from Peasant Society to Industrial Capitalism," Social History, 1, 3, 1976.

IV. Changing Patterns of Work

E. P. Thompson, "Time, Work-Discipline and Industrial Capitalism," Past and Present, 38, 1967.

E. P. Thompson, The Making of the English Working Class, New York, 1963, 189-313.

Joan Scott and Louise Tilly, "Women's Work and the Family in Nineteenth Century Europe," CSSH, 17, 1975, 36-64.

Ivy Pinchbeck, Women Workers and the Industrial Revolution, 1750-1850, London, 1969 (selections)

Raphael Samuel, ed., Village Life and Labour, London, Boston, 1975, editor's introduction.

Michelle Perrot, "Workers and Machines in France during the First Half of the 19th Century," (with comment). Proceedings of the Annual Meeting of the Western Society for French History, 1977, Santa Barbara, 1978, 198-217.

V. Fertility and Birth Control

Charles Tilly, ed. Historical Study of Changing Fertility, Princeton, 1975, 3-55.

Pierre Goubert, "Legitimate Fecundity and Infant Mortality in France during the Eighteenth Century: A Comparison," Dacdalus, Spring 1968, 593-603.

E. A. Wrigley, "Family Limitation in Pre-Industrial England," EcHR, 2nd series, 19, April 1966, 89-109.

Louise Tilly, Joan Scott and Miriam Cohen, "Women's Work and European Fertility Patterns," JIH, VI, 1976, 447-476.

Knodel, John, "Infant Mortality and Fertility in Three Bavarian Villages: An Analysis of Family Histories from the Nineteenth Century," Population Studies, 22, 1968, 293-318.

McLauren, Angus, "Abortion in France: Women and the Regulation of Family Size, 1800-1914," French Historical Studies, 10, 1978, 461-85.

Neuman, R. P., "Working Class Birth Control in Wilhelmine Germany," CSSH, 20, July 1978, 408-428.

VI. Family Structure

Peter Laslett, ed., Household and Family in Past Time, Cambridge, 1972, editor's introduction, 1-90.

Lawrence Stone, "The Rise of the Nuclear Family in Early Modern England: The Patriarchal Stage," in: C. Rosenberg, ed., The Family in History, Phila., 1975, 13-57.

John Knodel and Mary Jo Maynes, "Urban and Rural Marriage Patterns in Imperial Germany," Journal of Family History, 1, Winter, 1976.

Roderich Phillips, "Women and Family Breakdown in Eighteenth Century France: Rouen 1780-1800," Social History, 2, May 1976, 197-218.

Humphries, Jane, "The Working Class Family, Women's Liberation and Class Struggle: The Case of Nineteenth Century British History," Review of Radical Political Economy, 9, 1977, 25-41.

Peter Czap, Jr., "Marriage and the Peasant Joint Family in the Era of Serfdom," in: David L. Ransel, ed., The Family in Imperial Russia. New Lines of Historical Research, Urbana, Chicago, London, 1978, 103-123.

VII. Cities and Urbanization

E. A. Wrigley, "A Simple Model of London's Importance in Changing English Society and Economy 1650-1750," in P. Abrams, E. A. Wrigley, eds., Towns in Societies, Cambridge, London, New York, Melbourne, 1978, 215-243.

Asa Briggs, Victorian Cities, London, 1963, 55-82.

David Cannadine, "Victorian Cities; how different?" Social History, No. 4, Jan. 1977, 457-482.

J. J. Lee, "Aspects of Urbanization and Economic Development in Germany, 1815-1914," in: Abrams and Wrigley, eds., 279-293.

John Foster, "Nineteenth-Century Towns: A Class Dimension," in Flinn and Smout, eds., Essays in Social History, Oxford, 1974, 178-196.

Ronald Aminzade, "Breaking the Chains of Dependency: From Patronage to Class Politics, Toulouse, France, 1830-1872," Journal of Urban History, 3, no. 4, 1977, 485-506.

VIII. Forms of "Pre-industrial" Social Protest?

Michelle Perrot, "Delinquency and the Penitentiary System in Nineteenth-Century France," in: Robert Forster and Orest Ranum, ed., Deviants and the Abandoned in French Society, Baltimore and London, 1978, 213-245.

D. Hay, P. Linebaugh, J. Rule, E.P. Thompson, C. Winslow, Albion's Fatal Tree. Crime and Society in Eighteenth-Century England, New York, 1975 (selections).

Colin Jones, "Prostitution and the Ruling Class in 18th Century Montpelier," HWJ, Issue 6, Autumn. 1978, 7-29.

John K. Walton, "Lunacy in the Industrial Revolution: A Study of Asylum Admissions in Lancashire, 1848-50," JSH, 13, 1979, 1-22.

Neil B. Weissman, "Rural Crime in Tsarist Russia: The Question of Hooliganism, 1905-1914," Slavic Review, 37, 1978, 228-240.

H. Zehr, "The Modernization of Crime in Germany and France, 1830-1914," JSH, VIII, Summer 1975, 117-141.

IX. "Pre-Industrial" Forms of Collective Action

E.P. Thompson, "The Moral Economy of the English Crowd in the 18th Century," P&P, 1971.

Louise Tilly, "The Food Riot as a Form of Political Conflict in France," JIH, 2, Summer 1971, 24-57.

Charles Tilly, "Changing Nature of Collective Violence," in: Melvin Richter, ed., Essays in Theory and History: An Approach to the Social Sciences, Cambridge, MA, 1970, 139-164.

Charles A. Tamason, "From Mortuary to Cemetery:
Funeral Riots in Lille, 1779-1870," SSH,
4, 1, February 1980, 15-31.

Robert J. Bezucha, "The 'Preindustrial' Worker
Movement: The Canuts of Lyon," in Bezucha, ed.,
Modern European Social History, Lexington,
Toronto, London, 1972, 93-123.

Lüdtke, Alf, "The Role of State Violence in the
Period of Transition to Industrial Capitalism:
The Example of Prussia from 1815 to 1848,"
Social History, 4, 1979, 175-221.

Ted Margadant, "Modernisation and Insurgency in
December 1851: A Case Study of the Drome,"
in: Roger Price, ed., Revolution and Reaction.
1848 and the Second French Republic, London,
New York, 1975, 254-279.

X. Politics in the Countryside

Ian Farr, "Populism in the Countryside: The Peasant
Leagues in Bavaria in the 1890s," in: Richard
Evans, Society and Politics in Wilhelmine
Germany, New York, London, 1978, 136-159.

Teodor Shanin, The Awkward Class. Political Sociology
of the Peasantry in a Developing Society: Russia
1910-1925, Oxford, 1972 (selections).

Mark Harrison, "Resource Allocation and Agrarian
Class Formation: The Problem of Social Mobility
among Russian Peasant Households, 1880-1930,"
JPS, 4, 1977, 127-161.

Edward E. Malefakis, "Peasants, Politics, and Civil
War in Spain, 1931-1939," in: Bezucha, ed.,
Modern European Social History, 192-227.

Gavin Lewis, "The Peasantry, Rural Change and Con-
servative Agrarianism: Lower Austria at the
Turn of the Century," P&P, Nr. 81, 1978.

Tony Judt, "The Origins of Rural Socialism in Europe:
Economic Change and the Provencal Peasantry,
1870-1914," Social History, 1, January 1976,
45-65.

J. Harvey Smith, "Agricultural Workers and the French
Wine-Growers' Revolt of 1907," P&P, 1978, 101-125.

XI. <u>Changing Nature of Work in Industrial Societies</u>

Rose L. Glickman, "The Russian Factory Woman, 1880-1914," in: D. Atkinson, et al., <u>Women in Russia</u>, Stanford, 1977, 63-84.

Peter N. Stearns, "The Unskilled and Industrialization. A Transformation of Consciousness," <u>Archiv für Sozialgeschichte</u>, v. 16, 1976, 249-282.

Raphael Samuel, "The Workshop of the World: Steam Power and Hand Technology in mid-Victorian Britain," <u>HWJ</u>, 3, Spring 1977, 6-72.

Laura Owen, "The Welfare of Women in Labouring Families: England, 1860-1914," in: Hartmann and Banner, <u>Clio's Consciousness Raised. New Perspectives on the History of Women</u>, New York, Evanston, San Francisco, London, 1974.

Theresa McBride, <u>The Domestic Revolution: The Modernization of Household Service in England and France 1820-1920</u>, London, 1976 (selections).

XII. <u>Models for Understanding Labor Protest</u>

E.J. Hobsbawm, "Economic Fluctuations and Some Social Movements," in: <u>Labouring Men</u>, Garden City, 1967.

Peter Stearns, "Measuring the Evolution of Strike Movements," <u>IRSH</u>, 9, 1974, 1-27.

James E. Cronin, <u>Industrial Conflict in Modern Britain</u>, Totowa, 1979 (selections).

Charles Tilly and Edward Shorter, <u>Strikes in France, 1830-1968</u>, Cambridge, 1968 (selections).

XIII. <u>Community, Labor Organization, and Changing Forms of Labor Protest</u>

Stephen Hickey, "The Shaping of the German Labour Movement: Miners in the Ruhr," in Evans, ed., <u>Society and Politics in Wilhelmine Germany</u>.

Joan Scott, "The Glassworkers of Carmaux, 1850-1900," in: Sennett and Thernstrom, eds., <u>Nineteenth-Century Cities</u>, Yale, 1969, 3-42.

David Crew, <u>Town in the Ruhr. A Social History of Bochum, 1860-1914</u>, New York, 1979 (selections).

Lawrence Schofer, "Patterns of Labor Protest: Upper Silesia 1865-1914," <u>JSH</u>, 5, 1972.

Michael P. Hanagan, "The Logic of Solidarity. Social Structure in Le Chambon - Feugerolles," <u>Journal of Urban History</u>, 3, 4, 1977, 409-426.

William H. Sewell, Jr., "Social Change and the Rise of Working-Class Politics in Nineteenth-Century Marseille," <u>P&P</u>, 65, 1974, 75-109.

XIV. <u>Workers' Lives and Workers' Culture</u>

Gareth Stedman Jones, "Working-Class Culture and Working Class Politics in London, 1870-1900: Notes on the Remaking of a Working Class," <u>JSH</u>, 7, 1974, 460-507.

Gerhard A. Ritter, "Workers' Culture in Imperial Germany: Problems and Points of Departure for Research," <u>JCH</u>, 13, 1978.

Klaus Tenfelde, "Mining Festivals in the Nineteenth Century," <u>JCH</u>, 13, 1978, 377-412.

Reginald E. Zelnik, "Russian Bebels: An Introduction to the Memoirs of Semen Kanatchikov and Matrei Fisher," <u>Russian Review</u>, v. 35, 1976, 249-289, 417-447.

Guenther Roth, <u>The Social Democrats in Imperial Germany: A Study in Working Class Isolation and Negative Integration</u>, Totowa, 1963 (selections)

History 5710
Course Syllabus
Fall, 1984

Mary Jo Maynes
523 Social Sciences
373-4430

Introductory Proseminar in 18th and 19th-Century European History:
Social History

The aim of this course is to introduce students to the literature of modern
European social history, emphasizing France, Germany and Great Britain in the
18th and 19th centuries. Reading and discussion will center on selected topics,
and readings on this syllabus are all chosen from works available in English.
Students who can read European languages are encouraged to consult works in
these languages for their own more intensive readings. Class time will be
organized around discussions of the literature read each week. Students will
be required to write a series of evaluative papers on the works they read.

Course Requirements

The first requirement is to prepare for each week's discussion by a careful
reading of the required readings and of at least one selection from the list
of supplementary readings. In the course of the quarter, students should
select supplementary readings from among both books and articles on the
supplementary reading list. Students will then prepare a two-page "reaction paper"
addressing some of the week's discussion questions based on readings done
for that week. In addition, each student should at some point in the quarter write two two-page critiques of books drawn from the supplementary
reading list and present copies of these to all the participants in the
seminar on the day they are scheduled for discussion according to the syllabus.
Finally, each student will be required to write a 15-20 page bibliographic
or historiographic essay on a topic chosen after consultation with the
instructor.

List of Abbreviations used in the Reading List

AHR - American Historical Review
CEH - Central European History
CSSH - Comparative Studies in Society and History
FHS - French Historical Studies
HW - History Workshop
JCH - Journal of Contemporary History
JFH - Journal of Family History
JIH - Journal of Interdisciplinary History
JSH - Journal of Social History
P&P - Past and Present
SH - Social History

All items marked with a star are available on reserve in the Wilson Library
Reserve Reading Room.

1. Introduction to Social History - Terrain, Methods, Problems, Theories
October 2
Discussion Questions

How would you define the terrain of the social historian and distinguish social history from other approaches to the study of the past?(Take into account not only subject matter, but also methods, theoretical underpinnings, philosophy of history.) What have been the major areas of inquiry around which European social history has developed? What sources and methodological innovations have been important in the evolution of social history? Where (in terms of institutions, individuals or schools of thought) have innovations associated with the emergence of social history in Europe been based? What sorts of differences in orientation or disagreements seem to characterize social history as a field? What have been the major critiques of social-historical approaches developed to date?

Required Readings

✱ F.Braudel, "History and the Social Sciences: The Longue Durée," in F. Braudel, On History (Chicago, 1980).

✱ E.J.Hobsbawm, "From Social History to the History of Society," Daedalus (1971), 20-45.

✱ T. Judt, "A Clown in Regal Purple," HW, 7(1979), 66-94.

✱ L. Stone, "The Revival of the Narrative: Reflections on a New Old History," P&P, 85(1979), 3-24.

✱ E. Hobsbawm, "The Revival of Narrative: Some Comments," P&P, 86(1980), 3-8.

Supplementary Readings

P. Abrams,"History, Sociology, Historical Sociology" P&P, 87(1980), 3-16.

P. Anderson, Arguments Within English Marxism (London, 1980).

G. Eley, "Memories of Underdevelopment: Social History in Germany," SH, 7(1977), 785-791.

E.F. and E.D. Genovese, "The Political Crisis of Social History, " JSH, 10(1976). 205-220.

P. Goubert, "Historical Demography and the Reinterpretation of Early Modern French History," JIH, 1(1970), 37-48.

D. Herlihy, "Quantification in the 1980s: Numerical and Formal Analysis in European History," JIH, 12(1981), 115-135.

H.C.Johansen, "Trends in Modern and Early Modern Social History Writing in Denmark after 1970," SH, 8(1983), 375-381.

G.S.Jones, "From Historical Sociology to Theoretical History," British Journal of Sociology, 27(1976), 295-305.

S. Kinser,"Annaliste Paradigm? The Geohistorical Structure of Fernand Braudel," AHR, 86(1981), 63-105.

* W.R.Lee, "The German Family: A Critical Survey of the Current State of Historical Research," in R.J.Evans and W.R.Lee, eds., The German Family (London, 1982).

G.McLennan, Marxism and the Methodologies of History (London, 1981).

The New History: The 1980s and Beyond. Special Issue of JIH, 12:1-2(1981).

R.Samuels, "History and Theory," in R. Samuels, ed., People's History and Socialist Theory (London, 1981).

T. Stoianovitch, French Historical Method: The Annales Paradigm.

B.Strath, "Recent Development in Swedish Social History of the Period since 1800," SH, 9(1984), 77-86.

L.Stone, "Family History in the 1980s: Past Achievement and Future Trends," JIH, 12(1981), 51-87.

E.P.Thompson, The Poverty of Theory and Other Essays (London, 1978).

C.Tilly, As Sociology Meets History (New York, 1981).

L.Tilly and M. Cohen, "Does the Family Have a History? A Review of Theory and Practice in Family History," Social Science History, 6(1982), 131-180.

2. Agrarian Social Structure, Rural Communities and the Peasant Family Economy
October 9
Discussion Questions
What were the most significant changes between the 18th and 19th centuries in European land tenure patterns? What important regional distinctions have been noted? What are the postulated connections between land tenure and peasant household dynamics, family structure and familial relationships in rural communities? What are the major hypotheses about the connections between demographic change in rural Europe and landholding patterns? How would you classify European rural communities? According to what sorts of characteristics do social historians usually distinguish among types of communities? Are there major regional variations in community form or rural social structure? To what historical causes are such variations attributed?

Required Readings

* L.Berkner and F.Mendels, "Inheritance Systems, Family Structure and Demographic Patterns in Western Europe," in C. Tilly, ed., Historical Studies of Changing Fertility (Princeton, 1978).

History 5710, p. 4.

* L.Berkner, "The Stem Family and the Developmental Cycle of the Peasant Household," AHR, 77(1972), 398-418.

* P.M.Jones, "Parish, Seigneurie and the Community of Inhabitants in Southern Central France during the Eighteenth and Nineteenth Centuries," P&P, 91(1981) 74-108.

* S.D.Bowman, "Antebellum Planters and Vormärz Junkers in Comparative Perspective,: AHR, 85(1980), 779-808.

Supplementary Readings
K.Ågren et al, Aristocrats, Farmers,Proletarians: Essays in Swedish Demographic History (Uppsala, 1973).

R.Bell, Fate and Honor, Family and Village:Demographic and Cultural Change in Rural Italy Since 1800 (Chicago, 1979).

L.Berkner, "Inheritance, Land Tenure and Peasant Family Structure: A German Regional Comparison," in J.Goody, ed., Family and Inheritance in Rural Western Europe, 1200-1700(Cambridge, 1976).

L.Berkner and J. Shaffer, "The Joint Family in the Nivernais," JFH, 3(1978), 150-162.
J.Blum, The End of the Old Order in Rural Europe (Princeton, 1978).

R.Brenner, "Agrarian Class Structure and Economic Development in Pre-Industrial Europe: The Agrarain Roots of EUropean Capitalism," P&P, 97(1982) as well as the series of articles begun in issue 70 of P&P and indicated in notes of this latest contribution to the debate.

G.Dallas, The Imperfect Peasant Economy: The Loire Country, 1800-1914 (New York, 1982).

A.Goodwin, ed., The European Nobility in the Eighteenth Century

P. Goubert, "The French Peasantry of the Seventeenth Century," P&P, 10(1956), 55-77.

P. Horn, The Rural World, 1780-1850:SOcial Change in the English Countryside (New York, 1980).

* W.R.Lee, "Family and Modernisation: the Peasant Family and Social Change in Nineteenth-Century Bavaria," in R.J.Evan s and W.R.Lee, eds., The German Family (London, 1982).

* G. Lefebvre, "The Place of the Revolution in the Agrarian History of France," in R. Forsten and O. Ranum, eds., Rural Society in France (Baltimore, 1977).

J.Lehning, The Peasants of Marlhes (Chapel Hill, 1980).

E. Leroy Ladurie, The Peasants of Languedoc (Urbana, 1976).

R.R.Palmer, "Georges Lefebvre," JMH, 31[1959], 329-342.

A. Plakans, "Peasant Farmsteads in Baltic Littoral, 1797," CSSH 17(1975), 2-55.

D. Sabean, Household Formation and Geographic Mobility: A Family Register Study for a Württemberg Village, 1760-1900," Annales de Dempgraphie Historique (1970).

✱ D. Sabean, "Small Peasant Agriculture in Germany," Peasant Studies,7(1978), 218-224.

J.W.Shaffer, Family and Farm:Agrarian Change and Household Organization in the Loire Valley, 1500-1900 (Albany, 1982).

B. Singer, "Village Notables in Nineteenth-Century France: Priests, Mayors and Schoolmasters (Albany, 1983).

A. Soboul, "The French Rural Community in the Eighteenth and Nineteenth Centuries," P&P, 10(1956), 78-95.

D.Spring, ed., European Landed Elites in the Nineteenth Century (Baltimore, 1977).

D. Thorner, ed., The Theory of the Peasant Economy (Homewood, 1966).

E.Weber, Peasants into Frenchmen (Stanford, 1976).

3. Social Crisis and the Transition to Industrial Capitalism
October 16
Discussion Questions
Whar was the role of protoindustry in Western European economic development? What were the consequences of the introduction of wage labor into the rural community in terms of its impact on family and household dynamics, demographic patterns, community structure? What is meant by the term 'proletarianization'? What do you see as the main competing understandings of the historical process of proletarianization? What were the causes and consequences of rural prole-tarianization? of urban pre-industrial proletarianization?

Required Readings-

✱ C. Friedrichs, "Capitalism, Mobility and Class Formation in the Early Modern German City," P&P, 69(1975), 24-49.

✱ F.Mendels, "Proto-industrialization: the First Phase of the Process of Industrialization," Journal of Economic History, 32(1972), 241-261.

✱ H.Medick, "The Proto-industrial Family Economy: The Structural Function of Household and Family During the Transition from Peasant Society to Industrial Capitalism," SH, 3(1976), 291-315.

E.P.Thompson, "The Weavers," Chapter 9 of The Making of the English Working

History 5710, p. 6.

Class (London, 1963).

Supplementary Readings

✶ R.Braun, "Early Industrialization and Demographic Change in the Canton of
Zurich," in C. Tilly, ed., Historical Studies of Changing Fertility (Princeton,
1978).

W.Fischer, "Rural Industrialization and Population Change," CSSH, 15 (1973).

O. Hufton, The Poor of Eighteenth-Century France (Oxford, 1974).

✶ C.H.Johnson, "Patterns of Proletarianization: The Parisian Tailors and the
Lodeve Wollen Workers," in J. Merriman, ed., Consciousness and Class Experience
in Nineteenth-Century Europe (New York, 1979).

P. Kriedtke et al, Industrialization Before Industrialization: Rural Industry
Rural Industry in the Genesis of Capitalism (New York, 1981).

D. Levine, " The Demographic Conseque]nces of Rural Industrialization : A
Family Reconstitution Study of Shepshed, Leicestershire, 1600-1851," SH,
1(1976).

D.Levine, Family Formation in an Age of Nascent Capitalism (New York, 1979).

D. Levine, "Proletarianization, Economic Opportunity and Population Growth,"
in W. Conze, ed., Sozialgeschichte der Familie in der Neuzeit Europas
(Stuttgart, 1976).

C. Lis and H. Soly, Poverty and Capitalism in Pre-Industrial Europe

F. Mendels, "Agriculture and Peasant Industry in Eighteenth-Century Flanders,"
in E.L.Jones and N. Parker, eds., European Peasants and Their Markets (Princeton,
1976).

C. Tilly, "Proletarianization: Theory and Research," in C. Tilly, ed., As
Sociology Meets History (New Tork, 1981).

4. Urban Communities, Urban Social Structure and the Family Wage Economy
October 23
Discussion Questions
What types of urban communities have characterized European urban development
in the eighteenth and nineteenth centuries? Do you see a shift in the depiction
of urban structure, form, population, economic base during this period? What
were some of the important changes in urban class structure, family patterns,
residential patterns and demographic characteristics that occurred between the
early eighteenth and the late nineteenth century? What were the relationships
between the increasing urbanization associated with the development of industrial capitalism and the evolution of urban family life? What are the main
sources of variation in urban family form, family size, division of labor in
the family economy? How do patterns of social and geographic mobility in the
urban context compare with rural patterns?

Required Readings

G.Lefebvre, "Urban Society in the Orleannais in the Late Eighteenth Century," P&P, 19(1961), 46-65.

W. Sewell,"Social Mobility in a Nineteenth-Century European City,"JIH, 7(1976), 217-233.

L.A.Tilly, "The Family Wage Economy in a French Textile City," JFH, 4(1979), 381-394.

Supplementary Readings

M.Anderson, "Family and Household in the Industrial Revolution," in P. Laslett, ed., Household and Family in Past Time (Cambridge, 1972).

M.Anderson, Family Structure in Nineteenth Century Lancashire (Cambridge, 1971).

D. Cannadine and D. Reeder, eds., Exploring the Urban Past: Essays in Urban History by H.J.Dyos (Cambridge, 1982).

D. Crew, "Definitions of Modernity: Social Mobility in a German Town, 1880-1901," in P. Stearns and D. Walkowitz, eds., Workers and the Industrial Revolution

D. Crew, Town in the Ruhr: A Social History of Bochum, 1860-1914 (New York, 1979).

J.M.Diefendorf, Businessmen and Politics in the Rhineland, 1789-1834 (Princeton, 1980).

F. Ford, Strasbourg in Transition (New York, 1966).

R. Forster, Merchants, Landlords, Magistrates: The Depont Family on Eighteenth-Century France (Baltimore, 1981)

R. Forster, The Nobility of Toulouse in the Eighteenth Century (Baltimore, 1960).

O. Hufton, Bayeux in the Late Eighteenth Century

G.S.JOnes Outcast London (Oxford, 1971).

J. Kocka, "Family and Class Formation: Intergenerational Mobility and Marriage Patterns in NIneteenth-Century Westphalian Towns," JSH, 17(1984), 411-434.

W. Köllmann, "The Process of Urbanization in Germany," JCH, 4(1969), 59-76.

L.H.Lees, "Getting and Spending: The Family BUdgets of the English Industrial Workforce," in J. Merriman, ed., Consciousness and Class Experience in Nineteenth-Century Europe (New York, 1979).

H.Liang, "Lower-Class Migration in Wilhelmine Berlin," CEH, 3(1970), 94-111.

J. Merriman, ed., French Cities in the Nineteenth Century (London, 1982).

L.P.Moch, Paths to the City: Regional Migration in Nineteenth-Century France (Beverly Hills, 1982).H. Schomerus, "The Family Life Cycle: A Study of Factory Workers in Nineteenth-Century Württemberg," in R.J.Evans and W.R.Lee, eds., The German Family (London, 1981).
J. Scott, The Glassworkers of Carmaux(Cambridge, Mass., 1976).

N.Smelser, Social Change in the Industrial Revolution (Chicago, 1959).

J.K.J.Thomson, Clermont-de-Lodeve, 1633-1789: Fluctuations in the Prosperity of a Languedocien Clothmaking Town (Cambridge, 1982).

L. Tilly, "Individual LIves and Family Strategies in the French Proletariat," JFH, 3 (1979), 137-152.

M. Walker, German Home Towns (Ithaca, 1971).

5. Reproduction, Sexuality, Gender and the Sexual Division of Labor
October 30
Discussion Questions
What were the most significant regional variations and changes over time in European marriage and fertility patterns? To what sorts of causes do social and demographic historians attribute these broad patterns and changes? What are some of the postulated connections between women's roles in the family economy and their childbearing patterns? At what point and by what means did European women begin the limit family size? What are the significant differences along regional, class or gender lines concerning marital, extramarital, premarital sexuality and illegitimacy? What sorts of arguments have been put forward to explain changes in the perception and expression of sexuality? What do you see as the key changes in the definition in law, in prescription, in custom and in practice of 'woman's place'? Again, what are seen as ther dynamics of changes in gender ideology and the sexual division of labor?

Required Readings
✱ A.J.Coale, "The Decline of Fertility in Europe from the French Revolution to World War II," in S.J.Behrman, ed., Fertility and Family Planning (Ann Arbor, 1969).

✱ E. Shorter, "Female Emancipation, Birth Control and Fertility in European History," AHR, 78 (1973)

✱ L. Tilly, J. Scott and M. Cohen, "Women's Work and European Fertility Patterns," JIH, 6(1976), 447-476.

✱ L.Tilly, and J. Scott, "Women's Work and the Family in Nineteenth-Century Europe," CSSH, 17(1975), 36-64.

✱ K. Hausen, "Family and Role Division: The Polarization of Sexual Stereotypes in the Nineteenth Century - An Aspect of the Dissociation of Work and Family Life," in R.J.Evans and W.R.Lee, eds., The German Family (London,1981).

Supplementary Readings
J.C.Albisetti,"The Fight for Female Physicians in Imperial Germany," CEH, 15 (1982), 99-123.

L. Berlanstein, "Illegitimacy, Concubinage and Proletarianization in a Rural French Town, 1760-1914," JFH, 5(1980), 360-374.

M.J.Boxer, "Women in Industrial Homework: The Flowermakers of Paris in the Belle Epoque," FHS, 12(1982), 401-423.

G.Braybon, Women Workers in the First World War: The British Experience (Totowa, N.J., 1981).
✗ R. Dasey, "Women's Work and the Family: Women Garment Workers in Berlin and Hamburg before the First World War," in R.J.Evans and W.R.Lee, eds., The German Family (London, 1981).

L.Davidoff, "Class and Gender in Victorian England," in Sex and Class in Women's History , J.L.Newton, M. Ryan and J. Walkowitx, eds.,(Londom, 1983).

C. Dyhouse, Girls Growing Up in Late Victorian and Edwardian England (London, 1981).

R.J.Evans, "Prostitution, State and Society in Imperial Germany," P&P, 70(1976), 106-129.

C. Fairchilds, "Female Sexual Attitudes and the Rise of Illegitimacy: A Case Study," JIH, 8(1978).

J.-L.Flandrin, "Contraception, Marriage and Sexual Relations in the Christian West, in R. Forster and O. Ranum, eds., Biology of Man in History (Baltimore, 1975).

J.-L. Flandrin, Families in Former Times:Kinship, HOusehold and Sexuality (New York, 1979).

M.W.Flinn, The European Demographic System, 1500-1820 (Baltimore, 1981).

M. Foucault, The History of Sexuality, Vol.1(New York, 1978).

J. Gillis, "Servants, Sexuality and the Risk of Illegitimacy in London, 1801-1900," in J.L.Newton, M.Ryan and J. Walkowitz, eds., Sex and Class in Women's History (New York, 1983).

G.L.Gullichson, "The Sexual Division of Labor in Cottage INdustry and Agri-culture in the Pays de Caux, 1750-1850," FHS, 12(1981), 177-199.

J. Hajnal. "European Marriage Patterns in Historical Perspective," in D.V. Glass and D.E.C.Eversley. eds., Population in History (London, 1965).
✗ A. Imhof, "Women, Family and Death: Excess of Mortality of Women of Childbearing Age in Four Communities in Nineteenth-Century Germany," in R.J.Evans and W.R,Lee, eds., The German Family (London, 1981).

J. Knodel,"Natural Fertility in Pre-Industrial Germany," Population Studies 32 (1978).

P. Laslett, Family Life and Illicit Love in Earlier Generations (Cambridge, 1977).

W.R.Lee, "Bastardy and the Socio-economic Structure of Southern Germany," JIH 7(1977).

M. LiviBacci, "Fertility and NUptiality Changes in Spain from the Late 18th to the Early 20th Century," Population Studies, 22 (1968).
T. McBride, The Domestic Revolution (New York, 1976).

A. McLaren, Birth Control in Nineteenth-Century England(London, 1978).

A. McLaren, Sexuality and the Social Order:The Debate over the Fertility of Women and Workers in France, 1770-1920 (New York, 1983).

A. McLaren, "Some Secular Attitudes Toward Sexual Behavior in France, 1760-1860," FHS, 8(1973-4).
R.P.Neumann, "Industrialization and Sexual Behavior: Some Aspects of Working-Class Life in Imperial Germany," in R. Bezucha, ed., Modern European Social History.
M.J.Peterson, "No Angels in the House: The Victorian Myth and the Paget Women," AHR, 89(1984), 677-708.

P. Robertson, An Experience of Women:Patterns and Change in Nineteenth-Century Europe (Philadelphia, 1982).

J. Shaffer, "Family, Class and Young Women's Occupational Expectations," JFH, 3(1978), 62-77.

E. Shorter, A History of Women's Bodies (New York, 1982).

E. Shorter, The Making of the Modern Family (New York, 1976).

P. Smith, Ladies of the Leisure Class: The Bourgeoises of Northern France in the Nineteenth Century (Princeton, 1981).

L. Stone, The Family, Sex and Marriage inEngland, 1500-1800 (New York, 1977).

L.S.Strumingher. Women and the Making of the Working Class: Lyon, 1830-1870 (Montreal, 1979).

G.D.Sussmann, Selling Mother's Milk: The Wet Nursing Business in France, 1715-1914 (Champaign-Urbana, 1982).

L.Tilly and J. Scott, Women, Work and Family (New York, 1978).

M. Vicinus, ed., Suffer and Be Silent and A Widening Sphere.

J.R.Walkowitz, Prostitution and Victorian Society: Women, Class and tche State (New York, 1980).

J.Weeks, Sex, Politics and Society: The Regulation of Sexuality Since 1800 (London, 1981).

S, Wilson," The Myth of Motherhood a Myth: the Historical View of European Child-rearing, " SH, 9(1984), 181-198.

"Women in History"
 Early Modern, by O. Hufton
 Modern, by J. Scott
in P&P, 101 (1983), 125-157.

E.A.Wrigley, "Family Limitation in Pre-industrial England," Economic History Review, 19(1966).

6. Socialization, Education and Popular CUlture
November 6
Discussion Questions
What were the major shifts in child socialization occurring in Western Europe during the 18th and 19th century? How did the timing of life cycle transitions that defined 'childhood' and'youth' vary by region, class and over time? What institutions were most important in shaping the experiences and lifestyles of children and young adults? What are the major arguments about the causes of the increasing importance of formal education in the lives of children of the popular classes? What are regarded as the social agendas of the emergent schools systems of the late 18th through 19th centuries? What was the impact of increased formal schooling in terms of children's relationships with their family? access to jobs? social mobility? How would you describe the institutional bases of popular culture in the 18th century? the late 19th?

Required Readings
✱ R.Colls, "'Oh Happy English Children': Coal, Class and Education in the North-East," P&P, 73(1979), 75-99.

✱ M.J.Maynes, "Work or School? Youth and the Family Economy in the Midi in the Nineteenth Century," in D. Baker and P.J.Harrigan, eds., Making Frenchmen (Waterloo, Ont., 1980).

✱ T.W.Margadant, "Primary Schools and Youth Groups in Pre-War Paris: Les Petites A's," JCH, 13 (1978), 323-336.

✱ G.S.Jones, "Working Class Culture..." JSH, 7,(1974), 460-508.

Supplementary Readings

P. Aries, Centuries of Childhood (New York, 1962).

P. Burke, Popular Culture in Early Modern Europe (New York, 1978).

H.Chisick, The Limits of Reform in the Enlightenment: Attitudes Toward the Education of the Lower Classes in Eighteenth-Century France (Princeton, 1981).

R. Darnton, "The High Enlightenment and Low Life in Literature in Pre-Revolutionary France," P&P, 51 (1971), 81-115.

F.Furet and J. Ozouf, Reading and Writing: Literacy in France from Calvin to

History 5710, p. 12.

Jules Ferry (Cambridge, 1983).

J.Beaucroy, M.Bertrand and E. Gargan, eds., _Popular Culture in France_

R. Gildea, Education and the _Classes Moyennes_ in the Nineteenth Century," in P.J.Harrigan and D. Baker, eds., _The Making of Frenchmen_ (Waterloo, Ont., 1980).

J. Gillis, _Youth and History_ (New York, 1974).

R. HOuston, "Literacy and Society in the West," SH, 8(1983), 269-294.

R. Johnson, "Educational Policy and Social Control in Early Victorian Britain," P&P, 49(1970), 96-119.

R. Johnson, "'Really Useful Knowledge: Radical Education and Working-Class Culture, 1790-1848," in J. Clarke et al, eds., _Working-Class Culture_.

T. Laqueur, _Religion and Respectability_.

A.J.LaVopa, _Prussian Schoolteachers: Profession and Office_ (Chapel Hill, 1980)

D. Levine, "Education and Family Life in Early Industrial England," JFH, 4(1979), 368-380.

P.V.Meyers, "Professionalization and Societal Change: Rrual Teachers in Nineteenth Century France," JSH, 9(1976), 542-588.

M.Sanderson, "Literacy and Social Mobility in the Industrial Revolution in England," P&P, 56 (1972), 75-104 and reply by T. Laqueur in P&P, 64 (1974), 96-107.

M.Sanderson, "Social Change and Elementary Instruction in Industrial Lancashire," _Northern History_, 3(1968), 131-154.

J.W.Shaffer, "Family, Class and Young Women: Occupational Expectations in Nineteenth-Century Paris," JFH, 3(1978), 62-79).

T.Tackett, _Priest and Parish in Eighteenth-Century France_ (Princeton, 1977).

L. Stone, "Literacy and Education in England," P&P, 42(1969), 69-139.

L.Strumingher, _What Were LIttle Girls and Boys Made Of? Primary Schooling in Rural France_ (Albany, 1982).

R. Thabault, _Education and Change in a Village Community_

C. Tilly, "Population and Pedagogy in France," _HIstory of Education Quarterly_ 13 (1973), 113-129.

C.Truant, "Solidarity and Symbolism Among Journeymen Artisans: The Case of the Compagnonnage," CSSH, 21 (1979), 214-226.

7. Capitalism and Domination: The New Discipline
November 13
Discussion Questions
Why, according to the historical accounts you have read, did forms of regulation
such as legal systems, criminal systems, work regimens and welfare institutions
undergo change between the middle of the 18th and the middle of the 19th century?
What were the key institutions in the development of the attitudes, work
habits and personality traits deemed essential under the industrial capitalist
order? How well are the connections made by historians between the evolution
in the realm of social control and the actual demands of the new economic order?
To what extent do the new institutions seem to have accomplished their trans-
formative goals? In what realms were they unsuccessful?

Required Readings
✗ E.P.Thompson, "Time, Work Discipline and Industrial Capitalism," P&P,(1967),
56-96.

✱ M. Perrot, "The Three Ages of Industrial Discipline inNineteenth-Century France,"
in J. Merriman, Consciousness and Class Experience in Nineteenth-Century Europe
(New York, 1979).

✗ D. Hay, "Property, Authority and the Criminal Law," in D. Hay, ed., Albion's
Fatal Tree (New York, 1975).

✗ M. Foucault, "The BOdy of the Condemned," Ch. 1 of Discipline and Punish
(New York, 1975).

Supplementary Readings
V.A.C.Gatrell, ed., Crime and the Law: The Social History of Crime in Western
Europe Since 1500 (London, 1980).

P. Joyce, Work, Society and Politics: The Culture of the Factory in Later
Victorian England (New Brunswick, 1980).

A.J.KIDD,"Charity Organization and the Unemployed in Manchester ca. 1870-
1914," SH, 9(1984), 45-66.

A. Ludtke, "The Role of State Violence in the Period of Transistion to Industrial
Capitalism," SH, (1979), 175-221.

G.McLennan, "'The Labour aristocracy' and 'Incorporation': Notes on SOme Terms
in the Social History of the Working Class," SH, 6(1981), 71-82.

P.B.Munschke, Gentlemen and Poachers: The English Game Laws, 1671-1831 (New
York, 1980).

P. O'Brien, Promise of Punishment: Prisons in NIneteenth-Century France
(Princeton, 1982).

S.Pollard, "Factory Discipline in the Industrial Revolution," Economic History
Review, 16(1963) 254-271.

R. Price, "The Labour Process and Labour History," SH, 8(1983), 57-76. and reply
by P. Joyce in SH, 9(1984), 67-76.

D.A.Reid, "The Decline of Saint Monday, 1766-1876," P&P, 71(1976), 76-101.

H. Rosenberg, Bureaucracy, Aristocracy and Autocracy (Cambridge, Mass., 1958).

C. Tilly, "Food Supply and Public Order in Modern Europe," in C. Tilly, ed., The Formation of National States in Western Europe (princeton, 1975).

8. Changing Forms of Popular Protest and the Social History of Revolution
November 20
Discussion Questions
What were the common forms of popular protest in the 18th century? in the 19th? How were protests organized? Who participated in them? In what ways do changes in typical forms of protest reflect the changing character of social relations? changing political institutions? changing patterns of community and family life? What were the connections between routine protest actions and the numerous revolutionary movements that occurred in Western Europe in the late eighteenth and nineteenth centuries? Were there significant changes in the organizational bases, idealogical justification or class appeal of these revolutions between the late 18th and the late 19th century?

Required Readings
* L.Tilly, "The Food Riot as a Form of Political Protest," JIH, 2(1971), 23-59.

* J.Merriman, "The Demoiselles of the Ariège, 1829-1831," in J. Merriman, ed., 1830 in France (New York, 1975).

* T. Judt, "The Origins of Rural Socialism in Europe," SH. 1(1976), 45-65.

Supplementary Readings

R.Aminzade, Class, Politics and Early Industrial Capitalism (Albany, 1981).
R.Bezucha, The Lyon Uprising of 1834 (Princeton, 1966).

C.Calhoun, The Question of Class Struggle: Social Foundations of Popular Radicalism during the Industrial Revolution   (Chicago, 1982).

J.Epstein and D. Thompson, eds., The Chartist Experience: Studies in Working-Class Radicalism and CUlture (New York, 1982).

J.Foster, Class Struggle and the Industrial Revolution (London, 1974).

D.Geary, European Labour Protest, 1848-1939 (London. 1981).

D. Geary, "Radicalism and the Workers," in R.J.Evans, ed., Society and Politics in Wilhelmine Germany (London, 1978).

T.Hamerow, Restoration, Revolution and Reaction (Princeton, 1966).

E.J.Hobsbawm, Primitive Rebels
E.J.Hobsbawm and G.Rude, Captain Swing (London, 1969).

E.J.Hobsbawm and J.W.Scott, "Political Shoemakers,"P&P, 89(1980), 86-114.

L.Hunt, Revolution and Urban Politics in Urban France: Troyes and Reims, 1786-1790 (Stanford, 1980).

✗ C.Johnson, "The Revolution of 1830 in French Economic History," in J.Merriman, ed., 1830 in France (New York, 1975).

J. Kaplow, ed., New Perspectives on the French Revolution (New York, 1965).

G.Lefebvre, The Great Fear of 1789 (New York, 1973).

V.L.Lidtke, The OUtlawed Party: Social Democracy in Germany, 1878-1890 (Princeton, 1966).

C. Lucas, "Nobles, Bourgeois and the Origins of the French Revolution," P&P, 60(1973), 84-126.

T.Margadant, French Peasants in Revolt: The INsurrection of 1851 (Princeton, 1979).

J. Merriman, The Agony of the Republic(New Haven, 1978).

B. Moore, The Social Origins of Dictatorship and Democracy (Boston, 1967).

M.Nolan, Social Democracy and Society: Working-Class Radicalism in Düsseldorf, 1890-1920 (New York, 1980).

P.H.Noyes, Organization and Revolution (Princeton, 1966).

R.Price, Masters, Union and Men (Cambridge, 1980).

J.Quataert, "Unequal Partners in an Uneasy Alliance: Women and the Working-Class in Imperial Germany," in J.Quataert and M. Boxer, eds., Socialist Women (New York, 1978).

G. Rude, The Crowd in the French Revolution (Oxford, 19).

G.Rude, The Crowd in History (New York, 1964).

W. Reddy, "The Textile Trade and the Language of the Crowd at Rouen, 1752-1871," P&P, 74(1977), 62-89.

W.Sewell, Social Change and Working-Class Politics in 19th-Century Marseilles," P&P, 65 (1974), 75-109.

W. Sewell, Work and Revolution in France (Cambridge, 1980).

T.Scocpol, States and Social Revolutions(Cambridge, 1981).

A. Soboul, "Classes and Class Struggle During the French Revolution," in Science and Society

A. Soboul, _The French Revolution, 1787-1789_ (New York, 1975).

E. Shorter and C. Tilly, Strikes in France (New York, 1974).

✗ E.P.Thompson, The Making of the English Working Class (London, 1963).

E.P.Thompson, "The Moral Economy of the Crowd in the Eighteenth Century," P&P, 50(1971), 76-113.

C. Tilly, "The Changing Place of Collective Violence," in M. Richter, ed., Essays in Theory and History (Cambridge, Mass., 1970).

C. Tilly, The Vendée (New York, 1964).

C., L., and R. Tilly, The Rebellious Century (Cambridge, Mass., 1975).

B. Taylor, "The Men are as Bad as Their Masters: Socialism, Feminism and Sexual Antagonisms in the London Tailoring Trades in the 1830s," in J.L.Newton, M.P.Ryan and J.R.Walkowitzeds., Sex and Class in Women's History.

T. Tholfsen, Working-Class Radicalism in Mid-Victorian England (New York, 1977).

9. Last Meeting - Discussion of Individual Projects
November 27

Yale University

HISTORY 429b

Comparative American and Western European Social

History, 1770–1870

John Merriman
Paul Johnson

AGENDA

DATE	GENERAL TOPIC	READING
January 17	Introduction	
January 24	An Overview	Barrington Moore, Social Origins of Democracy and Dictatorship
January 31	Rural Society	Eugene Genovese, Roll Jordon, Roll E.J. Hobsbawm-George Rudé, Captain Swing
February 7	The State and Centralization	Charles Tilly, "Food Supply and Public Order in Modern Europe;" Charles Tilly, The Vendée; John Merriman, "The 'Demoiselles' of the Ariège, 1829-31"
February 14	Revolution, I: 1776, 1789	Robert Gross, Minutemen and Their World; Georges Lefebvre, The Coming of the French Revolution
February 21	Revolution, II: 1830 and 1848	Charles Tilly, "How Protest Modernized, 1845-55;" Tilly and Lynn Lees, "The People of June, 1848;" George Rudé, "Why was there no Revolution in England in 1830 or 1848?" and Karl Marx, The Eighteenth Brumaire of Louis Napoleon Bonaparte (Recommended: John Merriman, Agony of the Republic)
February 28	Urbanization	Lynn Lees and John Modell, "The Irish Countrymen Urbanized: A Comparative Perspective on the Famine Migration;" Charles Tilly, "The Chaos of the Living City;" S.B. Warner, The Private City
March 7	The Bourgeoisie	Philippe Aries, Centuries of Childhood, conclusion; Peter Gay, "On the Bourgeoisie: Towards a Psychological Interpretation" (Recommended: Paul Johnson, A Shopkeeper's Millennium)

DATE	GENERAL TOPIC	READING
March 28	Artisans	Joan W. Scott, "The Glassworkers of Carmaux;" Mack Walker, "Work and Community;" E.P. Thompson, Making of the English Working Class, Part I; Paul Faler, "Cultural Aspects of the Industrial Revolution: Lynn, Massachusetts Shoemakers and the Industrial Morality, 1826-1860"
April 4	Proletarianization	E. P. Thompson, Part 2; H. Gutman, "Work, Culture, and Society;" E.P. Thompson, "Time, Work Discipline and Industrial Capitalism;" Christopher Johnson, "Patterns of Proletarianization: Parisian Tailors & Lodève Woolens Workers;" Charles Tilly, "Did the Cake of Custom Break?"
April 11	Socialism	William Sewell, Jr., "Social Change and the Rise of Working-Class Politics in 19th Century Marseille;" Christopher Johnson, "Communism and the Working-Class before Marx: The Icarian Experience;" Alan Dawley, Class and Community, conclusion
April 18	Popular Religion	David Montgomery, "The Shuttle and the Cross;" Bruce Laurie, "Nothing on Compulsion: Life Styles of Philadelphia Artisans, 1820-1860;" Brian Harrison, "Religion and Recreation in Nineteenth Century England"
April 25	Women, Work, and the Family	Louise Tilly and Joan Scott, Women, Work, and Family; Thomas Dublin, "Women, Work, and the Family: Female Operatives in the Lowell Mills, 1830-1860;" Nancy Cott, The Bonds of Womanhood: 'Woman's Sphere in New England, 1780-1830,' chapter I.

History 333A/233A   Herrick Chapman
Spring Quarter 1984-85   Office Hours: Tu 3:15-5:15
                                     Phone: 497-4956

LABOR AND THE LEFT IN MODERN EUROPE

This course will explore how men and women responded to
economic and political change and in the process created
distinctive working-class cultures in Western Europe. The
first half of the course will explore on the emergence of trade
unions and leftwing parties between 1870 and 1914. The second
half will examine how the World Wars and Great Depression
transformed working-class politics after 1914. We will focus
primarily on Britain, Germany and France in an effort
to determine what is common to working-class experience in
several countries and what is unique to particular national
cultures.

The course assumes a familiarity with the political and
economic history of Europe since the French Revolution.
Students are strongly encouraged to consult the following
general surveys as the course proceeds:

     Charles Breunig, The Age of Revolution and Reaction, 1789-
          1850 (Norton, 1977).

     Eric J. Hobsbawm, The Age of Revolution, 1789-1848 (New
          American Library, 1962).

     Norman Rich, The Age of Nationalism and Reform, 1850-1890
          (Norton, 1977).

     Felix Gilbert, The End of the European Era, 1890 to the
          Present (Norton, 1979).

We will also proceed on the assumption that members of the
course have read two seminal works in the labor history,
namely, Edward Thompsons's The Making of the English Working
Class (1963) and William Sewell's Work and Revolution in
France: The Language of Labor from the Old Regime to 1848
(1980).   Anyone who has not read these books should do so
during the first two weeks of the course.

All required reading is on reserve in Green. The
following books are available for purchase at the Stanford
Bookstore:

     James E. Cronin and Carmen Siriani, eds., Work,
          Community and Power: The Experience of Labor in
          Europe and America, 1900-1925 (Temple, 1983).

Gareth Stedman Jones, <u>Languages</u> <u>of</u> <u>Class</u>: <u>Studies</u> <u>in</u>
<u>English</u> <u>Working</u> <u>Class</u> <u>History</u>, <u>1832-1982</u> (Cambridge,
1983).

Barrington Moore, Jr., <u>Injustice</u>: <u>The</u> <u>Social</u> <u>Bases</u> <u>of</u>
<u>Obedience</u> <u>and</u> <u>Revolt</u> (Sharpe, 1978).

Carl Schorske, <u>German</u> <u>Social</u> <u>Democracy</u>, <u>1905-1917</u>: <u>The</u>
<u>Development</u> <u>of</u> <u>the</u> <u>Great</u> <u>Schism</u> (Harvard, 1983).

Joan W. Scott, <u>Glassworkers</u> <u>of</u> <u>Carmaux</u>: <u>French</u> <u>Craftsmen</u>
<u>and</u> <u>Political</u> <u>Action</u> <u>in</u> <u>a</u> <u>Nineteenth-Century</u> <u>City</u>
(Harvard, 1974)

An essay of 15 to 20 pages is required and will be due on
June 7. Students will also be asked to make short oral
presentations as the course proceeds.

Class Schedule

Week 1 (Apr. 4) -- Registration

Week 2 (Apr. 11) -- **LABOR HISTORY IN COMPARATIVE PERSPECTIVE**

Required:

Adolf Sturmthal, <u>Unity</u> <u>and</u> <u>Diversity</u> <u>in</u> <u>European</u> <u>Labor</u>
(1953).

Peter Stearns, "National Character and European Labor
History," <u>Journal</u> <u>of</u> <u>Social</u> <u>History</u> 9, 2 (Winter
1970-1971).

Recommended:

Dick Geary, <u>European</u> <u>Labour</u> <u>Protest</u>, <u>1848-1939</u> (Croom
Helm, 1981).

Alexander Gershenkron, <u>Economic</u> <u>Backwardness</u> <u>in</u> <u>Historical</u>
<u>Perspective</u> (1966).

Arthur M. Ross and Paul T. Hartman, <u>Changing</u> <u>Patterns</u> <u>of</u>
<u>Industrial</u> <u>Conflict</u> (Wiley, 1960).

Edward Shorter and Charles Tilly, <u>Strikes</u> <u>in</u> <u>France</u>,<u>1830-</u>
<u>1968</u> (Harvard, 1974), chapter 12.

Charles, Louise and Richard Tilly, <u>The</u> <u>Rebellious</u> <u>Century</u>
(1975).

Week 3 (Apr. 18) -- **CLASS, CULTURE AND POLITICS IN BRITAIN**

Required:

Gareth Stedman Jones, Languages of Class: Studies in English Working Class History, 1832-1982 (1983).

Recommended:

Craig Calhoun, The Question of Class Struggle: Social Foundations of Popular Radicalism during the Industrial Revolution (Chicago, 1982).

K. F. Donnelly, "Ideology and Early English Working-Class History: Edward Thompson and His Critics," Social History (May 1976).

John Foster, Class Conflict in the Industrial Revolution: Early Industrial Capitalism in Three English Towns (Methuen, 1974).

Richard Johnson, "Thompson, Genovese, and Socialist-Humanist History," History Workshop 6 (Autumn 1978).

Patrick Joyce, Work, Society and Politics: The Culture of the Factory in Later Victorian Britain (Methuen, 1980).

Standish Meacham, A Life Apart: The English Working-Class, 1890-1914 (Harvard, 1977).

Henry Pelling, History of British Trade Unionism (1966).

Ioweth Prothero, Artisans and Politics in Early Nineteenth-Century London (1979).

Dorothy Thompson, The Chartists (1984).

Week 4 (Apr. 25) -- **WORKERS AND THE LEFT IN LATE NINETEENTH-CENTURY FRANCE**

Required:

Bernard Moss, The Origins of the French Labor Movement (California, 1976).

Joan W. Scott, The Glassmakers of Carmaux: French Craftsmen and Political Action in a Nineteenth-Century City (Harvard, 1974).

Recommended:

Lenard Berlanstein, The Working People of Paris, 1871-1914 (1984).

Madeline Guilbert, Les Femmes et l'organisation syndicale avant 1914 (CNRS, 1966).

Michael P. Hanagan, The Logic of Solidarity: Artisans and Industrial Workers in Three French Towns, 1871-1914 (Illinois, 1980)

Val R. Lorwin, The French Labor Movement (Harvard, 1954).

Michelle Perrot, Les Ouvriers en grève: France, 1871-1890 2 vols. (1974).

_____, "The Three Ages of Industrial Discipline in Nineteenth-Century France," in Consciousness and Class Experience in Nineteenth-Century Europe, edited by John M. Merriman (Holmes and Meier, 1979).

Denis Poulot, Le Sublime, ou le travailleur comme il est en 1870, et ce qu'il peut être (Maspero, 1980).

Jacques Rancière, La Nuit des prolétaires (Fayard, 1981).

William M. Reddy, "The Textile Trade and the Language of the Crowd at Rouen, 1752-1871," Past and Present (1977).

William Sewell, "Social Change and the Rise of Working-Class Politics in Nineteenth Century Marseilles," Past and Present (1974).

Peter N. Stearns, Revolutionary Syndicalism and French Labor: A Cause Without Rebels (Rutgers, 1971).

Charles Tilly, "The Changing Place of Collective Violence," in Essays in Theory and History: An Approach to the Social Sciences, edited by Melvin Richter (Harvard, 1970).

Rolande Trempé, Les Mineurs de Carmaux 2 vols. (1971).

Week 5 (May 2) --GERMAN SOCIAL DEMOCRACY

Required:

Carl Schorske, German Social Democracy, 1905-1917: The Development of the Great Schism (Harvard, 1983).

Recommended:

David Crew, <u>Town in the Ruhr</u>: <u>A Social History of Bochum,</u>
<u>1860-1914</u> (1979).

Dieter Groh, <u>Negative Integration und revolutionärer</u>
<u>Attentismus</u>: <u>Die deutsche sozialdemokratie am</u>
<u>Vorabend des Ersten Weltkrieg</u> (1973)

Peter Nettl, "The German Social Democratic Party, 1890-
1914, as a Political Model," <u>Past and Present</u> 30
(April 1965).

Guenther Roth, <u>The Social Democrats in Imperial German</u>: <u>A</u>
<u>Study in Working Class Isolation and National</u>
<u>Integration</u> (1963).

Lawrence Schofer, <u>The Formation of a Modern Labor Force,</u>
<u>Upper Silesia, 1865-1914</u> (1975).

Week 6 (May 9) -- WORKING-CLASS PROTEST IN GERMANY

Required:

Barrington Moore, Jr., <u>Injustice</u>: <u>The Social Basis of</u>
<u>Obedience and Revolt</u> (1978).

Recommended: ·

Dick Geary, "Radicalism and the German Worker:
Metalworkers and Revolution, 1914-1923," in <u>Society</u>
<u>and Politics in Wilhelmine Germany</u>, edited by
Richard J. Evans (1978).

_____, "The Ruhr: From Social Peace to Social
Revolution," <u>European Studies Review</u> 4 (1980).

Richard N. Hunt, <u>German Social Democracy, 1918-1933</u>
(1970).

Mary Nolan, <u>Social Democracy and Society</u>: <u>Working-Class</u>
<u>Radicalism in Dusseldorf, 1890-1920</u> (1981).

Eve Rosenhaft, "Organising the 'Lumpenproletariat':
Cliques and Communists in Berlin during the Weimar
Republic," in <u>The German Working Class, 1888-1933</u>,
edited by Richard J. Evans (1982).

Week 7 (May 16) -- **FROM SYNDICALISM TO COMMUNISM IN FRANCE**

Required:

Robert Wohl, French Communism in the Making, 1914-1924 (Stanford, 1966).

Recommended:

Bertrand Abhervé, "Les Origines de la grève des métallurgistes parisiens, juin 1919," Le Mouvement social 93 (October-December 1975).

Colette Chambelland and Jean Maitron, Syndicalisme révolutionnaire et communisme (1968).

Christian Gras, "La Fédération des Métaux en 1913-1914 et l'évolution du syndicalisme révolutionnaire française," Le Mouvement social 77(October-December 1971).

Annie Kriegel, Aux origines du communisme français (1964).

Roger Picard, Le Mouvement syndical durant la guerre (1928).

Week 8 (May 23) -- **WAR, REVOLUTION, DEFEAT, 1914-1929**

Required:

James E. Cronin and Carmen Sirianni, editors, Work, Community and Power: The Experience of Labor in Europe and America, 1900-1925 (Temple, 1983), selected essays.

Recommended:

Harry Braverman, Labor and Monopoly Capital: The Degradation of Work in the Twentieth Century (1974).

John M. Cammett, Antonio Gramsci and the Origins of Italian Communism (Stanford, 1967).

Paul Devinat, Scientific Management in Europe (1927).

Gerald D. Feldman, Army, Industry and Labor in Germany, 1914-1918 (Princeton, 1966).

Patrick Fridenson, ed., 1914-1918: L'Autre Front (1977).

Max Gallo, "Quelques aspects de la mentalité et du comportement ouvriers dans les usines de guerre,

1914-1918," Le Mouvement social 56 (1966).

Georges Haupt, Socialism and the Great War (Oxford, 1972).

James Hinton, The First Shop Stewards Movement, (Allen & Unwin, 1973).

Jurgen Kocka, Klassengesellschaft im Krieg (1973).

Annie Kriegel and Jean-Jacques Becker, 1914: La Guerre et le mouvement ouvrier francais (1964).

Adrian Lyttleton, "Revolution and Counter-revolution in Italy, 1918-1922," in Revolutionary Situations.

Charles S. Maier, "Between Taylorism and Technocracy," Journal of Contemporary History 5, 2 (1970).

Gerald Meaker, "Anarchists and Syndicalists: Conflicts with the CNT, 1917-23," in Politics and Society in Twentieth-Century Spain, edited by Stanley Payne.

Suzanne Miller, Burgfrieden und Klassenkampf (1974).

Branko Pribicevic, The Shop Stewards' Movement and Workers' Control, 1910-1922 (Basil Blackwell, 1959).

Paulo Spriano, The Occupation of the Factories: Italy, 1920 (Pluto Press, 1975).

S. A. Smith, Red Petrograd: Revolution in the Factories, 1917-1918 (Cambridge, 1983).

Robert Wheeler, "Revolutionary Socialist Internationalism: Rank-and-File Reaction in the USPD," International Review of Social History 22 (1977).

Week 9 (May 30) -- **WORKING-CLASS POLITICS IN TWENTIETH-CENTURY BRITAIN**

Required:

James E. Cronin, Labour and Society in Britain, 1918-1979 (1984).

Recommended:

James E. Cronin, Industrial Conflict in Modern Britain (Croom Helm, 1979)

John H. Goldthorpe, et al., The Affluent Worker: Industrial Attitudes and Behaviour (Cambridge,

1968).

_____, The Affluent Worker: Political Attitudes and Behaviour (Cambridge, 1968).

James Hinton, Labour and Socialism: A History of the British Labour Movement, 1867-1974 (1983).

_____, "Coventry Communism: A Study of Factory Politics in the Second World War," History Workshop 10 (Autumn 1980).

Richard Hoggart, The Uses of Literacy (Penguin, 1957).

Stuart Macintyre, "British Labor, Marxism and Working-Class Apathy in the Nineteen Twenties," The Historical Journal 20, 2 (June 1977).

Arthur Marwick, Class: Image and Reality in Britain, France and the USA Since 1930 (Oxford, 1980).

Keith Middlemas, Politics in Industrial Society: The Experience of the British System Since 1911 (A. Deutsch, 1979).

George Orwell, The Road to Wigan Pier (Harcourt Brace, 1958).

G. A. Phillips, The General Strike: The Politics of Industrial Conflict (Holmes and Meier, 1976).

Sidney Pollard, "Trade Union Reactions to the Economic Crisis," Journal of Contemporary History 4, 4 (October 1969).

Michael Young and Peter Willmott, The Symetrical Family: A Study of Work and Leisure in the London Region (Penguin, 1973).

Week 10 (June 6) -- WORKERS AND COMMUNISM IN ITALY AND FRANCE

Required:

George Ross, Workers and Communists in France: From Popular Front to Eurocommunism (California, 1982), selected chapters.

Donald L. M. Blackmer and Sidney Tarrow, eds., Communism in Italy and France (1975), selected essays.

Recommended:

Bertrand Badie, La Stratégie de la grève (1976).

Donald N. Baker, "The Socialist Party and the Workers of Paris: The Amicales Socialistes, 1936-40," International Research of Social History 24 (1979).

Daniel R. Brower, The New Jacobins (Cornell, 1968).

Michel Collinet, Esprit du syndicalisme (1951).

Colin Crouch and Alessandro Pizzorno, eds., The Resurgence of Class Conflict in Western Europe Since 1968 2 vols. (Holmes and Meier, 1978).

Henry W. Ehrmann, French Labor from Popular Front to the Liberation (Oxford, 1947).

Jacques Girault, Sur l'implantation du parti communiste français dans l'entre-deux-guerres (Editions Sociales, 1977).

Richard F. Hamilton, Affluence and the French Worker in the Fourth Republic (Princeton, 1967).

Annie Kriegel, The French Communists: Profile of a People (1972).

Peter Lange, George Ross and Maurizio Vannicelli, Unions, Change and Crisis: French and Italian Union Strategy and the Political Economy, 1945-1982 (Allen and Unwin, 1982).

Serge Mallet, La Nouvelle classe ouvrière (1963).

Arthur Mitzman, "The French Working Class and the Blum Government (1936-37)," in Contemporary France: Illusion, Conflict and Regeneration, edited by John C. Cairns (New Viewpoints, 1978).

Antoine Prost, La CGT à l'époque du front populaire (1964).

Michael Seidman, "The Birth of the Weekend and the Against Work: The Workers of the Paris Region During the Popular Front (1936-38)," French Historical Studies (Fall 1981).

Edward Shorter and Charles Tilly, Strikes in France, 1830-1968 (Harvard, 1974), chapter 12.

Adolf Sturmthal, Left of Center (Illinois, 1983).

Ronald Tiersky, <u>French Communism, 1920-1972</u> (Columbia, 1974).

Alain Touraine, <u>L'Evolution du travail ouvrier aux usines Renault</u> (1955).

Simone Weil, <u>La Condition ouvrière</u> (Gallimard, 1951).

Workers' Lives, Workers' Culture, the Working Class Movement:
Topics in European Labor History, 1780-1914

This seminar will present a general introduction to central
issues in modern European labor history. We will be examining
not only the historical development of the European working class,
but in addition, the variety of methodological approaches to the
study of this vast subject. Students will be expected to have
a general knowledge of European history in the period covered by
the seminar, and this background will be essential. Readings
will offer a comparative European perspective, drawing in particular
on examples from England, France and Germany, and will include
investigations of such important topics as the impact of the
industrial revolution on workers' lives and the working class
family, the problems of stratification within the working class,
the emergence of trade union organizations and political parties
representing labor's interests, the changing nature and function
of working class collective action and strike activity, and the
emergence of a uniquely working class culture. Requirements for
the course will include a short paper, due at midterm, one or two
brief oral presentations, and a term paper concentrating on one
of the topics covered in the seminar. All readings for the course
are on reserve in the College library, and in addition, I have
ordered one general text, John Gillis, The Development of European
Society which is available in the college bookstore. This text
provides a background to many of the topics which we will be
covering, and in addition, serves as an excellent introduction to
the study of social history in this period. You should complete
it by Week VI.

Please note that the reading for the first assignment should
be completed before the first class meeting.

Week I -- Why Study Labor History?

E.J. Hobsbawm, "From Social History and the History of Society,"
in: Felix Gilbert and Stephen R. Graubard, Historical Studies
Today, 1-26.

E.J. Hobsbawm, "Labor History and Ideology," Journal of Social
History, Vol. 7, #4, 1974

Elizabeth Fox-Genovese and Eugene Genovese, "The Political Crisis
of Social History," Journal of Social History, X, 1976.

Geoff Eley and Keith Nield, Social History, 1980 (currently at
bindery, will be available by 1/15/82)

<u>Week II</u> -- The Changing Nature of Work in Industrial Society

E.P. Thompson, "Time, Work Discipline and Industrial Capitalism,"
<u>Past and Present</u>, 38, 1967

E.J. Hobsbawm, "Custom, Wages and Workload," in <u>Labouring Men</u>

Michelle Perrot, "Workers and Machines in France during the First
Half of the Nineteenth Century," (with comment), <u>Proceedings
of the Western Society for French History</u>, 1977, Santa Barbara,
1978, 198-217

Ivy Pinchbeck, <u>Women Workers and the Industrial Revolution, 1750-
1850</u>, London, 1969 (selections)

<u>WeekIII</u> -- The Debate over the Standard of Living

Friedrich Engels,"The Conditions of the working class in England,"
selections in James J. Sheehan, ed., <u>Industrialization and
industrial Labor in Nineteenth Century Europe</u>, 13-32

E.J. Hobsbawm, "The British Standard of Living, 1790-1850,"
<u>Economic History Review</u>, August 1957 (also, <u>Labouring Men</u>, 64-
104)

R.M Hartwell, "The Rising Standard of Living in England, 1800-
1850," in: <u>The Industrial Revolution and Economic Growth</u>

E.J. Hobsbawm, "The Standard of Living during the Industrial
Revolution: A Discussion," <u>Economic History Review</u>, 2nd ser.,
vol. 16, 1963

R.M. Hartwell, "The Standard of Living: An Answer to the
Pessimists," in: <u>The Industrial Revolution and Economic Growth</u>

<u>Week IV</u> -- "Preindustrial" Forms fo Labor Protest

E.P. Thompson, "The Moral Economy of the English Crowd in the
18th Century," <u>Past and Present</u>, 1971

Alf Ludtke, "The Role of State Violence in the Period of Transition
to Industrial Capitalism,....," <u>Social History</u>, 4, 1, 1980, 15-31

Robert J. Bezucha, "The 'Preindustrial' Worker Movement: The <u>Canuts</u>
of Lyon," in Bezucha, ed., <u>Modern European Social History</u>, 93-123

George Rudé, <u>The Crowd in History</u>, Chapter Ten, "Captain Swing"
and "Rebecca's Daughters," pp. 149-163

<u>Week V</u> -- The Development of "Class Consciousness"

Christopher H. Johnson, "Patterns of Proleterianization: Parisian
Tailors and Lodève Woolen Workers," in John Merriman, ed.,
<u>Consciousness and Class Experience in Nineteenth-Century Europe</u>,
65-84

Frederick D. Marquardt, "A Working Class in Berlin in the 1840s?" in: H.-U. Wehler, ed., Sozialgeschichte Heute, 191-210

Laura S. Strumingher, Women and the Making of the Working Class: 1830-1870, selections

William H. Sewell, Jr., "Social Change and the Rise of Working-Class Politics in Nineteenth-Century Marseille," Past and Present, 65, 1974, 75-109

Week VI -- Work in "Advanced" Industrial Societies

Raphael Samuel, "The Workshop of the World: Steam Power and Hand Technology in mid-Victorian Britain," History Workshop, 3, spring 1977, 6-72

Peter N. Stearns, "The Unskilled and Industrialization. A Transformation of Consciousness," Archiv fur Sozialgeschichte, v. 16, 1976, 249-282

E.J. Hobsbawm, "The Labour Aristocracy in Nineteenth Century Britain," in Labouring Men

G. Stedman Jones, "Class Struggle and the Industrial Revolution," New Left Review, 90, 1975

Week VII -- Women in the Labor Force

Sally Alexander, "Women's Work in 19th Century London," in J. Mitchell and A. Oakley, The Rights and Wrongs of Women, 59-111

Joan W. Scott and Louise A. Tilly, "Women's Work and the Family in Nineteenth Century Europe," Comparative Studies in Society and History, 17, 1975, 36-64

Peter N. Stearns, "Working Class Women in Britain, 1890-1914," in Vicinus, ed., Suffer and be Still

Rose L. Glickman, "The Russian Factory Woman, 1880-1914," in D. Atkinson, et al., Women in Russia, 63-84

Laura Oren, "The Welfare of Women in Laboring Families: England, 1860-1950," Hartmann and Banner, ed., Clio's Consciousness Raised

Week VIII -- Trade Unions and Political Socialism, I -- An Overview

Peter N. Stearns and Harvey Mitchell, The European Labor Movement, the Working Classes and the Origins of Social Democracy 1890-1914

Marily J. Boxer and Jean H. Quataert, Socialist Women, 1-18

Week IX -- Trade Unions and Political Socialism, II -- Case Studies

Stephen Hickey, "The Shaping of the German Labour Movement: Miners in the Ruhr," in Richard Evans, ed., Society and Politics in Germany

Michael P. Hanagan, "The Logic of Solidarity, Social Structure in Le Chambon-Feugerolles," _Journal of Urban History_, 3, 4, 1977, 409-426

Donald H. Bell, "Worker Culture and Worker Politics: The Experience of an Italian Town, 1880-1915," _Social History_, 3, 1, 1978, 1-21

Victoria E. Bonnell, "Trade Unions, Parties, and the State in Tsarist Russia: A Study of Labor Politics in St. Petersburg and Moscow," _Politics and Society_, 9, 3, 1980, 299-322

Dorothy Thompson, "Women and Radical Politics: A Lost Dimension," in Mitchell and Oakley, _The Rights and Wrongs of Women_, 112-138

Week X -- Models for Understanding Labor Protest

Charles Tilly and Edward Shorter, "The Shape of Strikes in France," _Comparative Studies in Society and History_, 13, 1970, 60-86

E.J. Hobsbawm, "Economic Fluctuations and Some Social Movements," in _Labouring Men_, 126-157

James E. Cronin, "Theories of Strikes: Why Can't They Explain the British Experience?" _Journal of Social History_, Vol. 12, #2, 194-220

Dieter Groh, "Intensification of Work and Industrial Conflict in Germany, 1896-1914," _Politics and Society_, v. 8, nos. 3-4, 1978, 349-387

Week XI -- Presentations of Rough Drafts of Papers -- to be scheduled

Week XII -- Workers' Lives

John Burnett, ed., _The Annals of Labour_ (selections)

John Burnett, ed., _Useful Toil_ (selections)

Maud Pember-Reeves, ed., _Round About a Pound a Week_

Reginald E. Zelnik, "Russian Rebels: An Introduction to the Memoirs of Semen Kanatchikov and Matrei Fisher," _Russian Review_, 35, 1976, 249-289, 417-447

Peter N. Stearns, ed., _The Impact of the Industrial Revolution_ (selections)

Week XIII -- Workers' Culture

Gareth Stedman Jones, "Working-Class Culture and Working-Class Politics in London, 1870-1900: Notes on the Remaking of a Working-Class," _Journal of Social History_, 7, 1974, 460-507

Gerhard A. Ritter, "Workers' Culture in Imperial Germany: Problems and Points of Departure," _Journal of Contemporary History_, 13, 1978, 377-412

Klaus Tenfelde, "Mining Festivals in the Nineteenth Century," _Journal of Contemporary History_, 13, 1978, 377-412

Peter N. Stearns, "The Effort of continuity in Working-Class Culture," _Journal of Modern History_, 52, Dec. 1980, 626-55

Workers and   Social Change
   in twentieth Century Europe

History, V57.0146
Fall 1985
Nolan

    This course will examine the social and political history of
workers in Europe from 1900 to the present.   It will investigate
the composition of the working class, the changing nature of
work, types of working-class culture, forms of working-class
protest and the theory and practice of trade unions and working-
class political parties.   Readings and lectures will explore how
workers were influenced by technology and politics, peace and
war, revolution and fascism, economic depression and the welfare
state.   We will view the world of work and working-class lives
through the eyes of unskilled and skilled workers, of women and
men, of settled workers and migrants.   Britain, France, Germany
Italy and Russia will be discussed.

    There will be a mid-term, a ten page paper on a topic of
your choice (but which I need to approve) and a final exam.   The
readings consist primarily of books which you can purchase at the
bookstore or read in the reserve room.   In addition, there are
some articles which are on reserve in Bobst library and which are
also available in the History Dept.   The History Dept. copies
can be taken out to xerox but otherwise must remain in the Dept.
The articles on library reserve can be found under my name.

    My office hours are Monday, 2-3 and Wednesday, 3-5, and by
appointment.   . My office is 19 University Place, room 507. Tel.
598-2447 or 598-3323.

The following books have been ordered.

Cronin, James and Siriani, Carmen, ed. Work, Community and Power

Davies, Margaret, L. ed. Life As We Have Known It

Procacci, Giuliano. The Italian Working Class from Risorgimento
    to Fascism

Rosenberg, Wm. and Young, Marilyn. Transforming Russia and China

Orwell, George. The Road to Wigan Pier

Allen, William S. The Nazi Seizure of Power

Haraszti, Miklos. A Worker in a Worker's State

Gorz, Andre. Farewell to the Working Class

143

Part I: 1900-1914

I.   W.   Sept. 18   Introduction

II.   M.   Sept. 23   Working-class Culture and Politics in Britain
      W.   Sept. 25   Holiday

      Jones, Gareth S., "Working-class Culture and Working-class
          Politics in London," Journal of Social History 7
          (1973-4) 460-508.

      Ross, Ellen, "'Fierce Questions and Taunts': Married Life
      in   Working-Class London," Feminist Studies, 8, Nr. 3.

III, M.   Sept. 30   Varieties of Socialism: Germany
      W.   Oct. 2   Varieties of Socialism: Italy

      Procacci, G. The Italian Working Class, pp. 1-51.

      Hickey, Stephen, "The Shaping of the German Labor Move-
          ment: Miners in the Ruhr," in Evans, Richard, ed.,
          Society and Politics in Wilhelmine Germany

      Cross,G. "Redefining Workers' Control" in Cronin and
          Siriani, Work, Community and Power

IV.   M.   Oct. 7   Varieties of Socialism: France
      W.   Oct. 9   Women: Work, Family, and Politics

      Davies, Margaret L. Life As We Have Known It
      Alexander, Sally, From Hand to Mouth, Introduction.

Part II: War, Revolution and Counterrevolution

V.   M.   Oct. 14 Socialism, Internationalism and World War I
      W.   Oct. 16 Workers and Mobilization for Total War

      Montgomery, D. "New Tendencies in Union Struggles," in
          Cronin and Siriani, Work...

      Siriani, C., "Workers Control in Europe," in Cronin and
          Siriani, Work...

      Kaplan, Temma, "Quality of Life and Female Mass Move-
          movements in Barcelona, St. Petersberg and Turin"
          unpublished manuscript.

VI.   M. Oct. 21 Russian Revolution
      W. Oct. 23 Russian Revolution

Rosenberg, Wm. and Young, Marilyn, Transforming Russia and China, chapters 1-2.

VII. M. Oct.28 Revolution and Counterrevolution in Europe
     W. Oct.30 mid-term exam

Procacci, Italian Working Class, pp. 52-74.

Part III: The Twenties and Thirties

VIII.M. Nov. 4 New Technology and New Workers
     W. Nov. 6 Workers, Mass Culture and Americanism

Gramsci, Antonio, "Americanism and Fordism," in Gramsci, Prison Notebooks, pp. 277-320.

Maier, Charles, "Between Taylorism and Technocracy," Journal of Contemporary History, 5, 1970.

Bridenthal, Renata. "Beyond Kinder, Küche, Kirche: Working Women in Interwar Europe" in Bridenthal and Koonz, Becoming Visible.

IX. M. Nov. 11 Social Democracy and Communism in the 1920s
    W. Nov. 13 Workers and the Rise of Nazism

Allen, William S. The Nazi Seizure of Power: The Experience of a Single Town entire

X. M. Nov. 18 Workers in Fascist Italy
   W. Nov. 20 Workers in Nazi Germany

Mason, Tim, "National Socialism and the Working Class," New German Critique, 1977.

Mason, Tim. "The Workers' Opposition in Nazi Germany," History Workshop Journal, 11, Spring 1981.

De Grazia, Victoria. The Culture of Consent, Intro., Chapters 1, 3, 7 and 8.

XI. M. Nov.25 Economic Depression in Britain
    W. Nov.27 Popular Front in France

Orwell, George. The Road to Wigan Pier, pp. 1-118.

XII. M. Dec. 2 Spanish Civil War
     W. Dec. 4 Russia in the 1920s and 1930s

Rosenberg and Young, Transforming, pp. 120-35, 147-67.

Part IV: Post World War II Europe

XIII.   M. Dec. 9   Mobilization, Resistance and Collaboration
        W. Dec. 11   Postwar Settlements and the Working Class

        start Haraszti, M. Worker in a Workers' State

        Decide on your paper topic and consult with me.

XIV.   M. Dec. 16   Russia under Stalin and after
        W. Dec. 18   Workers in Eastern Europe

        finish Haraszti, Worker in a Workers' State

        Rosenberg and Young, Transforming, pp. 210-28,
           238-45, 267-74, 283-90.

XV.   M. Jan. 6   Social Democracy and Welfare Capitalism
        W. Jan. 8   The Underside of the Welfare State: Women
        and Migrants

        Kramer, Jane, Unsettling Europe, pp. 79-168.

        Campbell, Beatrix, Wigan Pier Revisited, pp. 1-
           19, 57-79, 116-28, 169-90.

XVI.   M. Jan. 13 The Resurgence of Class Conflict in the 1960s
        W. Jan. 15 Towards a Post Industrial Order?

        Gorz, Andre. Farewell to the Working Class.

History 27.8 EF
Room 3/4 Whitehead
12:15-1:30, Tues - Thurs. SYLLABUS
Fall, 1985

Prof. Bonnie Anderson
Office: 515 Whitehead
Hours: 9:50-10:50, 1:30-200
Phone: 780-5305 or 5303

Queens, Peasants, Housewives, and Rebels: Women in Modern European History

This course will explore recent findings in the new field of women's history.
Beginning with a background in the early modern period, we will examine
the traditions inherited from past ages by European women. The live
of women of privilege and women of the people will be studied and contrasted
as will the different national experiences of European women. The
focus will be both on what makes women's history unique and on women's
contributions to and participation in "regular" history. Questions dealt wi
with will include what differentiates the history of women, what makes
it similar to men's experience, and how women's participation can be viewed
and organized.

The following books have been ordered for the course and should be
purchased from the Brooklyn College Bookstore as soon as possible. They
will be read in the order listed.

> The Memoirs of Glückel of Hameln (Schocken, 1977)
>
> Ann Cornelison, Women of the Shadows: A Study of the Wives and
>   Mothers of Southern Italy (Vintage, 1977)
>
> Judith Murray, Strong-Minded Women and Other Lost Voices from
>   Nineteenth-Century England (Pantheon, 1982)
>
> Renate Bridenthal, Atina Grossman, and Marion Kaplan, eds.,
>   When Biology Became Destiny: Women in Weimar and Nazi
>   Germany (Monthly Review Press, 1984)

The course will consist primarily of lectures. Students are
expected to attend regularly and keep up with the reading. The class
work will be a short (8-10 page) research paper on a topic within the
subject of the student's choice, done with the instructor's guidance.
The final grade will be determined as follows:

Class Participation	20%
Term Paper	40%
Final Examination	40%

Recommended reading lists and the schedule of classes and
specific reading assignments will be distriubted on Tuesday. The
class will meet regularly on Tuesdays and Thursdays at 12:15. Note
that we do not meet on Tuesday, Sept. 17.

Recommended Reading for Modern European Women's History

Prof. Bonnie Anderson
Fall, 1983

General

Atkinson, Dorothy, Alexander Dallin and Gail Warshofsky Lapidus, eds., Women in Russia (1977)

Berkin, Carol R. and Clara M. Lovett, eds., Women, War and Revolution (1980

Bridenthal, Renate and Claudia Koonz, Becoming Visible: Women in European History (1977)

Faderman, Lillian, Surpassing the Love of Men: Romantic Friendship and Love between Women from the Renaissance to the Present (1981)

McMillan, James, Housewife or Harlot: The Place of Women in French Society 1870-1940 (1981)

Mitchell, Juliet, and Ann Oakley, eds., The Rights and Wrongs of Women (1976

Stock, Phyllis, Better than Rubies: A History of Woman's Education (1978)

Collections of Documents

Davies, Margaret Llewelyn, Life As We Have Known It: By Co-Operative Working Women (1931, 1975)

_____, Maternity: Letters from Working Women (1915,1978

Hellerstein, Erna O., Leslie P. Hume and Karen M. Offen, Victorian Women: A Documentary Account of Women's Lives in Nineteenth-Century England, France, and the United States (1981)

Murray, Janet Horowitz, Strong-Minded Women and Other Lost Voices from Nineteenth-Century England (1982)

Neuls-Bates, Carol, eds, Women in Music: An Anthology of Source Readings from the Middle Ages to the Present (1982)

Riemer, Eleanor and John Fout, eds., European Women: A Documentary History 1789-1945 (1980)

Schneir, Miriam, ed., Feminism: The Essential Historical Writings (1972)

Working Women

Adams, Carol, Ordinary Lives: A Hundred Years Ago (Eng, 1982)

Hufton, Olwen H., The Poor of Eighteenth-Century France: 1750-1789 (1974)

McBride, Theresa M., The Domestic Revolution: The Modernization of Household Service in England and France 1820-1920 (1976)

Pinchbeck, Ivy, Women Workers and the Industrial Revolution (Eng,1930,1977

Strumingher, Laura, Women and the Making of the Working Class: Lyon 1830-1870 (1979)

Tilly, Louise A. and Joan W. Scott, Women, Work, and Family (1978)

Walkowitz, Judith R., Prostitution and Victorian Society: Women, Class and the State (1980)

Women in Revolutions

Engel, Barbara and Clifford Rosenthal, Five Sisters: Women against the Tsar (1975)

Levy, Darline Gay, Harriet B. Applewhite and Mary D. Johnson, eds., Women in Revolutionary Paris: 1789-1795 (1979)

Rowbotham, Sheila, Women, Resistance and Revolution: A History of Women and Revolution in the Modern World (1974)

Thomas, Edith, The Women Incendiaries (Paris Commune) (1967)

Upper- and Middle-Class Women

Backer, Dorothy, Precious Women: A Feminist Phenomenon in the Age
    of Louis XIV (1974)
Basch, Françoise, Relative Creatures: Victorian Women in Society and
    the Novel (1974)
Crow, Duncan, The Victorian Woman (1972)
Greer, Germaine, The Obstacle Race: The Fortunes of Women Painters and
    Their Work (1979)
Harris, Ann Sutherland and Linda Nochlin, Women Artists: 1550-1950 (1981)
Hartman, Mary S. Victorian Murderesses: A True History of Thirteen
    Respectable French and English Women Accused of Unspeakable Crimes '(1
Holcombe, Lee, Victorian Ladies at Work: Middle-Class Working Women in
    England and Wales 1850-1914 (1973)
Lougee, Carolyn, Le Paradis des Femmes: Women, Salons, and Social
    Stratification in Seventeenth-Century France (1976)
Prochaska, F.K., Women and Philanthropy in Nineteenth- Century England (19
Smith, Bonnie G., Ladies of the Leisure Class: The Bourgeoises of
    of Northern France in the Nineteenth Century (1981)
Vicinus, Martha, Suffer and Be Still: Women in the Victorian Age (1972)
_____, A Widening Sphere: Changing Roles of Victorian Women (197

Feminism

Banks, Olive, Faces of Feminism: A Study of Feminism as a Social
    Movement (Eng & USA, 1981)
Evans, Richard, The Feminist Movement in Germany: 1894-1933 (1976)
    _____, The Feminists: Women's Emancipation Movements in
    Europe, America and Australasia 1840-1920 (1977)
Kaplan, Marion A., The Jewish Feminist Movement in Germany 1904-38 (1979)
Liddington, Jill and Jill Norris, One Hand Tied Behind Us: The Rise of
    the Women's Suffrage Movement (Eng, 1978)
Marks, Elaine and Isabelle de Courtivron, eds., New French Feminisms:
    An Anthology (1981)
Quataert, Jean H., Reluctant Feminists: Women in German Social Democracy,
    1885-1917 (1979)
Stites, Richard, The Women's Liberation Movement in Russia: Feminism,
    Nihilism, and Bolshevism, 1860-1930 (1978)
Thönnessen, Werner, The Emancipation of Women: Germany 1863-1933 (1969)

The Twentieth Century

Boxer, Marilyn J. and Jean H. Quataert, eds., Socialist Women:
    European Socialist Feminism in the Nineteenth and Twentieth
    Centuries (1978)
Jancar, Barbara Wolfe, Women Under Communism (1978)
Lapidus, Gail W., Women in Soviet Society: Equality, Development, and
    Social Change (1978)
Laska, Vera, Women in the Holocaust and Resistance (1983)
Lavenduski, Joni and Jill Hills, The Politics of the Second Electorate:
    Women and Public Participation (1981)
Rupp, LeilaJ, Mobilizing Women for War: German and American Propaganda,
    1939-1945 (1978)
Shaffer, Harry G., Women in the Two Germanies: A Comparative Study of a
    Socialist and a Non-Socialist Society (1981)
Sowerwine, Charles, Sisters or Citizens?: Women and Socialism in France
    since 1876 (1982)
Stephenson, Jill, Women in Nazi Society (1975)

Addenda to Recommended Reading for Modern European Women's History

Prof. Bonnie Anderson
Fall, 1985

Note: this list and its predecessor only contain books in English.
Biographies, articles, and books from fields other than history
have been excluded. Books assigned for required reading have not been
included.

General and Collections of Documents

Bell, Susan Groag and Karen M. Offen, Women, the Family, and Freedom:
The Debate in Documents, 2 vols. Vol I: 1750-1880, Vol. II: 1880-1950 (1983
Cambridge Women's Peace Collective, My Country is the Whole World:
An Anthology of Women's Work on Peace and War (1984)
Jane Lewis, Women in England: 1870-1950 (1984)
London Feminist History Group, The Sexual Dynamics of History (1983)

Working Women

Rose Glickman, The Russian Factory Woman: 1880-1917 (1985)
Charles Sowerwine, Sisters or Citizens?: Women and Socialism in France
since 1876 (1982)

Upper- and Middle-Class Women

Barbara Engel, Mothers and Daughters in Pre-Revolutionary Russia (1984)
Lee Holcombe, Wives and Property: Reform of the Married Women's Property
Law in Nineteenth-Century England (1983)
Elizabeth Longford, Eminent Victorian Women (1981)
Martha Vicinus, Independent Women: Work and Community for Single Women:
1850-1920 (1985)

Twentieth Century

Barbara Holland, ed., Soviet Sisterhood (1985)
Hilda Scott, Sweden's Right To Be Human: Sex-Role Equality, the Goal
and the Reality (1982)

Feminism

Patrick Bidelman, Pariahs Stand Up!: The Founding of the Liberal Feminist
Movement in France, 1858-1889 (1982)
Moira Ferguson, ed., First Feminists: British Women Writers, 1578-1799 (198
Tatyana Mamonova, ed., Women and Russia: Feminist Writings from the Soviet
Union (1984)

Women in Modern European Society and Politics

This course will explore the economic, social, cultural and political position of women in Britain, France and Germany from the late eighteenth century to the present. The course will explore the interaction of class and gender in different periods and national cultures. It will focus on women's work; sexuality, marriage and motherhood; and women's political activity.

The course meets Wednesday, 4:20-6:00. You are expected to do the reading before each class and to participate actively in class discussions. You will write either two 8-10 page analytic essays or one 18-20 page research paper.

All books are on reserve in Bobst. All articles are on reserve in Bobst and one copy is available in a box in the History Department 19 University Place, Rm. 400. (The material in the History Department

read only in the History Department.)

The following books have been ordered at the NYU Book Center:

Tilly, L. and Scott, J. Women, Work and Family

Taylor, Barbara. Eve and the New Jerusalem (Pantheon)

Davies, M. L. ed. Life As We Have Known It (Norton)

Weeks, Jeffrey. Sex, Politics and Society (Longman)

Walkowitz, Judith. Prostitution and Victorian Society (Cambridge)

Davies, M. L. ed. Maternity (Norton)

Smith, Bonnie. Ladies of the Leisure Class (Princeton)

Gissing, George. The Odd Women (Norton)

Fairbairns, Zoë. Benefits (Avon)

The Smith and Gissing books will not be in the bookstore until later in the term.

My office hours are Wednesday, 1:30 to 4:00 and by appointment. My office is 19 University Place, Rm. 409. 593-2447.

I. Jan. 25: Introduction

Part I: Women, Work and Family

II. Feb. 1: Women, Work and Industrial Capitalism

Tilly, L. and Scott, J. Women, Work and Family. entire.

Graves and White, "An Army of Redressers," International Labor and Working Class History, 1930.

III. Feb. 3: The Peculiarities of Women's Work and the Working-class Family

Davies, ed. Life As We Have Known It

Alexander, Sally, "Introduction" to Marianne Herzog, From Hand to Mouth

Davidoff, Leonore. "Mastered for Life: Servant and Wife in Victorian and Edwardian England," Journal of Social History, 7:4, Summer 1974.

Schlegel, Katharina, "Mistress and Servant in Nineteenth Century Hamburg," History Workshop Journal, Issue 15, Spring 1983, pp. 60-77.

Gamarnikow, Eva, "Sexual Division of Labour: the case of Nursing," in Kuhn, A. and Wolpe, A. Feminism and Materialism.

Bridenthal, Renata, "Beyond Kinder, Küche, Kirche: Weimar Women at Work," Central European History, 6, 1973, 148-66.

Part II: Women and Revolutionary Movements in the 19th Century

IV. Feb. 15 Women and Utopian Socialism

Taylor, Barbara. Eve and the New Jerusalem. entire.

V. Feb. 22 Women and French Revolutions

Hufton, Olwen, "Women in Revolution, 1789-96," Past and Present, 53, 1971.

Thomas, Edith. The Women Incendiaries, Chapters 1, 2, 4, 5, 7, 8, 10-12, and pp. 223-30. (The library has two copies on reserve and there will be 2-3 copies in the department.)

Part III: Sexuality, Marriage and Motherhood

VI. Feb. 29: Toward a History of Sexuality

Weeks, Jeffrey, Sex, Politics and Society. entire.

VII. Mar. 7: The Politics of Prostitution

Walkowitz, Judith. Prostitution and Victorian Society. entire.

March 14 Spring Vacation.

VIII. Mar. 21: Marriage and Motherhood in the English Working Class

Davies, ed. Maternity.

Davin, Anna. "Imperialism and Motherhood," History Workshop Journal, Issue 5, Spring 1978, pp. 9-88.

Ross, Ellen, "'Fierce Questions and TAunts': Married Life in Working-class London, 1870-1914," Feminist Studies, 8, nr. 3, Fall 1982, pp. 575-602.

McLaren, Angus, "Women's Work and the Regulation of Family Size," History Workshop Journal, Issue 7, 1977, pp. 70-81.

Part IV: Bourgeois Women

IX. Mar. 28: The Dilemmas of Single Women
Gissing, George. The Odd Women. entire.

X. Apr. 4: The Ambiguities of Domesticity

Smith, Bonnie. Ladies of the Leisure Class. entire.

Part V: Women and Twentieth Century Politics

XI. Apr. 11: Women and Socialism

Hartmann, Heidi. "The Unhappy Marriage of Marxism and Feminism:
Towards a More Progressive Union," in Lydia Sargent, ed. Women and
Revolution, pp. 1-42.

Liddington, Jill and Norris, Jill. One Hand Tied Behind Us. excerpts
to be selected.

Quartaert, Jean, "Feminist Tactics in German Social Democracy: A
Dilemma," Internationale wissenschaftliche Korrespondenz zur Geschichte
der deutschen Arbeiterbewegung, 13, 1977, pp. 48-65.

Kaplan, Temma. "Quality of Life and Female Mass Movements in Turin,
St. Petersburg, and Barcelona, 1917-18."

XII. April 18: Women and War

Gilbert, Sandra. "Soldier's Heart: Literary Men, Literary Women
and the Great War," Signs, vol, 8, no. 3, 1983, pp. 422-50.

Burnett, John, ed. Annals of Labour. autobiography of Rosina Whyatt,
munitions worker, pp. 125-32.

Rupp, Leila, "I don't Call that Volksgemeinschaft," in Berkin, C.R.
and Lovett, C. M., Women, War and Revolution, pp. 37-54.

Riley, Denise, "The Free Mothers: Pronatalism and Working
Mothers in Industry at the End of the Last War in Britain," History
Workshop Journal, nr. 11, Spring 1981, pp. 59-119.

XIII. April 25: Women and Fascism

Bridenthal, Renate, "Class Struggle around the Hearth: Women and
Domestic Service in the Weimar Republic," in Dobkowski and Walliman, ed.
Towards the Holocaust, pp. 243-64.

Mason, Tim. Women in Germany, 1925-40," History Workshop Journal,
Part I, Issue I, Spring 1976, pp. 74-133 and Part II, Issue 2, Autumn
1976, pp. 5-32.

Koonz, Claudia. "Mothers in the Fatherland: Women in Nazi
Germany," in Bridenthal and Koonz, Becoming Visible, pp. 445-73.

Bock, Gisela, "Racism and Sexism in Nazi Germany: Motherhood, Compulsory Sterilization and the State," Signs, 8, 3, 1983, pp. 400-21.

XIV. May 2 : Women, the State and Feminism

Fairbairns, Zoë. Benefits. entire.

History 67:   Women in Europe since 1750

Fall 1986   J.M. Bennett
Saunders 302   419 Hamilton
TuTh 9:30 a.m.   962-2155

   Office Hours: Tuesdays 2-4 p.m. (and by appointment)

     When the first factories opened in England in the late eighteenth
century, they inaugurated a process of economic change that has
radically transformed the human experience. In this class, we will
study how these changes altered the lives of European women. First,
we will trace the impact of industrialization on the working lives of
women. Second, we will consider women's personal lives and how they
balanced familial responsibilities with the new expectations of
Victorian society. Third, we will examine the emergence of women into
public life with the 'first wave' of feminism in the nineteenth and
early twentieth centuries.

REQUIRED READINGS FROM:

        Hellerstein, Erna, et al., VICTORIAN WOMEN.
        Zola, Emile, L'ASSOMOIR.
        Gissing, George, THE ODD WOMEN.
        Rossi, Alice, ed., THE FEMINIST PAPERS.
        Strunk & White, THE ELEMENTS OF STYLE.
        Coursepack of assorted readings.

     These books are available for purchase at the textbook store; the
coursepack can be purchased from Kinko's (114 West Franklin Street).
All readings are on reserve at the Undergraduate Library.

STUDENT RESPONSIBILITIES:

     Class meetings will mingle lecture and discussion. Because this
is a participatory course, it is essential that students complete
assigned readings on time and participate actively in class
discussions. Readings must be completed at the beginning of the
designated period. Final grades will be assessed as follows:

     (a) PARTICIPATION IN CLASS AND JOURNALS (20 per cent).
     The journal is designed as a study aid to help you integrate your
reading with lectures and discussions. Journals will be read, but not
graded. Average work (in both journals and class discussions) will
not affect your final grade, but particularly distinguished or
undistinguished performance will merit consideration.
     What should you put in your journal? The basic rule is to write
about whatever strikes you as the most interesting aspect of the
material covered in the past week. Some weeks you might compare the
experiences of women in the past to the experiences of women in 1986.
Some weeks you might react to a particular primary source. Suggested
topics will come out in class, but you should explore whatever
interests and excites you. A journal is a conversation with yourself:
keep it lively.

Most journal entries should run about 200-400 words. They may be handwritten or typed. Of the twelve main topics covered in class, you must complete entries for ten (this allows you to take off two weeks at your discretion). Journals must be submitted in class on 7 October and 2 December.

(b) ESSAYS (30 per cent).
Students must write three short essays on subjects covered in class. See the last page of this syllabus for further information.

(c) MID-TERM EXAMINATION (25 per cent): 2 October.

(d) FINAL EXAMINATION (25 per cent): 8 December.

TENTATIVE CLASS SCHEDULE:

Th 21 Aug   INTRODUCTION AND BACKGROUND
Tu 26 Aug   Reading: (a) McNeill, pp. 726-762.
Th 28 Aug   (b) Reiter, pp. 252-282.
                            (c) Hufton, pp. 1-22.

Tu 2 Sept   WORKING WOMEN TO 1870: INDUSTRIAL JOBS
Th 4 Sept   Reading: (a) Hellerstein, pp. 272-291
                            (b) McDougall, pp. 257-278.
                            (c) Pinchbeck. pp. 183-201.
                            (d) selections from Hellerstein:
                                (i) Cottage industries & workshops
                                        item 5 (pp. 39-44)
                                        item 67 (pp. 318-323)
                                        item 68i-iv (pp. 323-329)
                                (ii) Factories & mines
                                        item 6i (pp. 44-46)
                                        item 83 (pp. 386-392)
                                        item 85 (pp. 394-396)
                            (e) Strunk & White, pp. 1-33

Tu 9 Sept   WORKING WOMEN TO 1870: TRADITIONAL JOBS
Th 11 Sept   Reading: (a) Walkowitz, pp. 192-220.
                            (b) McBride, pp. 282-293.
                            (c) Gillis, pp. 114-145.
                            (d) selections from Hellerstein:
                                (i) Agriculture
                                        item 77 (pp. 359-365)
                                (ii) Domestic Service
                                        item 73 (pp. 346-350)
                                        item 74 (pp. 350-351)
                                (iii) Prostitution
                                        item 6ii (pp. 46-47)
                                        item 89i (pp. 410-414)
                                        item 90i-ii (pp. 418-423)
                                        item 91 (pp. 423-428)
                            (e) Strunk & White, pp. 35-65.

Tu 16 Sept   <u>CHANGES IN WOMEN'S WORK AFTER 1870: THE POPULAR CLASSES</u>
Th 18 Sept   Reading: (a) Stearns, pp. 100-120.
                          (b) Bridenthal, pp. 424-443.
                          (c) selections from Hellerstein:
                                    item 81 (pp. 373-377)
                                    item 82i (pp. 377-380)
                                    item 92 (pp. 428-429)
                          (d) Strunk & White, pp. 66-85.

Tu 23 Sept   <u>CHANGES IN WOMEN'S WORK AFTER 1870: THE MIDDLE CLASSES</u>
Th 25 Sept   Reading: (a) Vicinus, pp. 85-120
                          (b) excerpts from Patricia Hollis; WOMEN IN
                                PUBLIC on: Shops, Nursing,
                                and Clerical Work.
                          (c) selections from Hellerstein:
                                    item 13 (pp. 72-76)
                                    item 14 (pp. 76-80)
                                    item 19i-iv (pp. 96-98)
                                    item 72 (pp. 341-346)

Tu 30 Sept REVIEW
Th 2 Oct   MID-TERM EXAMINATION

Tu 7 Oct   <u>WOMEN AND THEIR FAMILIES: THE MIDDLE CLASSES</u>
Th 9 Oct   Reading: (a) Houghton, pp. 341-372
                          (b) Hellerstein, pp. 8-21, 118-133
                          (c) selections from Hellerstein:
                                    item 25i-ii (pp. 134-140)
                                    items 27-28 (pp. 143-149)
                                    item 33i-vi (pp. 161-164)
                                    item 48 (pp. 213-217)
                                    item 50 (pp. 221-224)
                                  item 60-61 (pp. 254-264)
                                  item 63i-iii (pp. 292-301)
                                  item 93i-iii (pp. 429-437)
                                  item 94i-iii (pp. 437-444)

Tu 14 Oct   <u>WOMEN AND THEIR FAMILIES: THE POPULAR CLASSES</u>
Th 16 Oct   Reading: (a) Zola (all)
Tu 21 Oct   (b) Oren, pp. 226-240

Th 23 Oct   FALL BREAK

Tu 28 Oct   <u>SINGLE WOMEN</u>
Th 30 Oct   Reading: (a) Gissing (all)
                          (b) Hammerton, pp. 52-71
                          (c) excerpts from Patricia Hollis, WOMEN IN
                                  PUBLIC on: Redundant Women
                        (d) selections from Hellerstein:
                                  item 30 (pp. 153-155)
                                  item 32 (pp. 157-160)
                                  items 38-39ii (pp. 182-189)
                                  item 47, (pp. 211-213)

Tu 4 Nov   WOMEN IN PUBLIC: ORIGINS OF NINETEENTH-CENTURY FEMINISM
Th 6 Nov   Reading: (a) Rossi, pp. 25-85

Tu 11 Nov   WOMEN IN PUBLIC: FEMINIST REFORMERS
Th 13 Nov   Reading: (a) Rossi, pp. 183-238

Tu 18 Nov   WOMEN IN PUBLIC: SOCIALISM & FEMINISM
Th 20 Nov   Reading: (a) Rossi, pp. 473-516
                            (b) selections from Hellerstein:
                                     item 86i-ii (pp. 396-400)
                                     item 87i-ii (pp. 400-408)

Tu 25 Nov: WOMEN IN PUBLIC: SUFFRAGE
                  Reading: (a) selections from Hellerstein:
                                     item 95i-ii (pp. 444-449)
                            (b) excerpts from Patricia Hollis, WOMEN IN
                                PUBLIC·on: The Right to Vote
Th 27 Nov: THANKSGIVING

Tu 2 Dec: REVIEW

Mo 8 Dec: FINAL EXAMINATION

                    LIST OF ITEMS CONTAINED IN COURSEPACK
                       (listed in order of scheduled use)

(1) McNeill: William H. McNeill, "The Rise of the West:
    Cosmopolitanism on a Global Scale 1850-1950 A.D." in THE RISE OF
    THE WEST (1963)., pp. 726-762.

(2) Reiter: Rayna Reiter, "Men and Women in the South of France:
    Public and Private Domains," in TOWARDS AN ANTHROPOLOGY OF WOMEN
    (1975), pp. 252-282.

(3) Hufton: Olwen Hufton, "Women and the Family Economy in
    Eighteenth-Century France," FRENCH HISTORICAL STUDIES, 9
    (1975), pp. 1-22.

(4) McDougall: Mary Lynn McDougall, "Working-Class Women During the
    Industrial Revolution, 1780-1914," in BECOMING VISIBLE: WOMEN IN
    EUROPEAN HISTORY, ed. Renate Bridenthal and Claudia Koonz (1977),
    pp. 257-278.

(5) Pinchbeck: Ivy Pinchbeck, "Textile Industries: Factory Workers,"
    in WOMEN WORKERS AND THE INDUSTRIAL REVOLUTION 1750-1850
    (1930), pp. 183-201.

(6) Walkowitz: Judith R. Walkowitz and Daniel J. Walkowitz, "'We are
    not Beasts of the Field': Prostitution and the Poor in Plymouth
    and Southampton under the Contagious Diseases Acts," in CLIO'S
    CONSCIOUSNESS RAISED: NEW PERSPECTIVES ON THE HISTORY OF WOMEN,
    ed. Mary Hartman & Lois Banner (1974), pp. 192-225.

(7) McBride: Theresa M. McBride, "The Long Road Home: Women's Work and Industrialization," in BECOMING VISIBLE: WOMEN IN EUROPEAN HISTORY, ed. Renate Bridenthal and Claudia Koonz (1977), pp. 282-295.

(8) Gillis: John Gillis, "Servants, Sexual Relations and the Risks of Illegitimacy in London, 1801-1900," in SEX AND CLASS IN WOMEN'S HISTORY, ed. Judith L. Newton, et al. (1983), pp. 114-145.

(9) Stearns: Peter Stearns, "Working-Class Women in Britain, 1890-1914," in SUFFER AND BE STILL: WOMEN IN THE VICTORIAN AGE, ed. Martha Vicinus (1973), pp. 100-120.

(10) Bridenthal: Renate Bridenthal, "Something Old, Something New: Women Between the Two World Wars," in BECOMING VISIBLE: WOMEN IN EUROPEAN HISTORY, ed. Renate Bridenthal and Claudia Koonz (1977), pp. 424-444.

(11) Vicinus: Martha Vicinus, "Reformed Hospital Nursing: Discipline and Cleanliness," in INDEPENDENT WOMEN: WORK AND COMMUNITY FOR SINGLE WOMEN 1850-1920 (1985), pp. 85-120.

(12) Hollis, Patricia Hollis, WOMEN IN PUBLIC (1979), excerpts on: Shops (3.7), Nursing (3.9), and Clerical Work (3.11).

(13) Houghton: Walter E. Houghton, THE VICTORIAN FRAME OF MIND (1957), pp. 341-372.

(14) Oren: Laura Oren, "The Welfare of Women in Laboring Families: England, 1860-1950," in CLIO'S CONSCIOUSNESS RAISED: NEW PERSPECTIVES ON THE HISTORY OF WOMEN, ed. Mary Hartman & Lois Banner (1974), pp. 226-244.

(15) Hammerton: A. James Hammerton, "Feminism & Female Emigration, 1861-1886," in A WIDENING SPHERE: CHANGING ROLES OF VICTORIAN WOMEN, ed. Martha Vicinus (1977), pp. 52- 71.

(16) Hollis, Patricia Hollis, WOMEN IN PUBLIC (1979), excerpt on: Redundant Women (2.3).

(17) Hollis, Patricia Hollis, WOMEN IN PUBLIC (1979), excerpts on: The Right to Vote (9.2).

INFORMATION ON REQUIRED ESSAYS

Students must write <u>three</u> short essays on subjects covered in class. These essays are <u>not</u> research papers; instead, they should be careful explorations of topics already discussed in the course.

The three essays can be selected from four possible topics. These topics (and due dates) are as follows:

(a) <u>Women's Work Before 1870</u>. This essay should compare the working experiences of either (a) married and single women or (b) women in industrial and traditional occupations. Due in class on 16 September.

(b) <u>Women's Work After 1870</u>. This essay should explore continuities and changes in women's work in the late nineteenth century. Due in class on 30 September.

(c) <u>The Personal Lives of Women.</u> This essay should either (a) explore the ways in which Gervaise, the heroine of Zola's <u>L'Assomoir</u>, did and did not conform to middle-class standards of feminine behavior or (b) consider now Gissing's <u>The Odd Women</u> reflects the advantages and disadvantages of being unmarried in late Victorian England. Due in class on 4 November.

(d) <u>Feminism</u>. This essay should (a) compare the feminist visions of Mary Wollstonecraft and John Stuart Mill or (b) define feminism and assess the writings of either Wollstonecraft or Mill against that definition. Due in class on 18 November.

Each essay should be four to six pages in typed length (1000-1500 words). Handwritten papers will be accepted <u>if</u> printed legibly with skipped lines. Estimated word length must be noted at the end of each essay--whether typed or handwritten. <u>Late papers and papers that do not meet the minimum length will not be accepted.</u>

--Do not use gender-specific words (e.g. 'man', 'he', or 'mankind') to refer generically to both sexes.

--Beware of plagiarism. Plagiarism is the representation of another person's words, thoughts or ideas as your own. All uncited words, thoughts and ideas are assumed to be the sole product of the author. The only exceptions are items considered to be common knowledge. You may, for the purposes of your essays, consider all material covered in class to be common knowledge. But you should footnote relevant parts of course readings.

--Remember that the essential elements of an essay are:
    THESIS: The above topics are themes; a thesis is the
        argument that you must develop from a theme.
    ORGANIZATION: An essay needs an introduction stating thesis,
        a coherent proof of thesis, and a conclusion.
    ANALYSIS: A good essayist doesn't simply <u>describe</u> material,
        he or she <u>analyzes</u> that material in order to establish
        convincing proofs of thesis.

GENDER AND CLASS

Instructors:

Mary Jo Maynes   Barbara Laslett
Department of History   Department of Sociology
Office: Soc. Sci. 523   Office: 1014B Soc.Sci.
Phone: 373-4430 or   Phone: 376-7659
        373-2705 (message)
Office hours: T,Th. 11-12:00   Office hours: T,Th 2-3:00
        and by appointment   and by appointment

This course, designed for graduate students and advanced
undergraduates, will examine the intersection of gender and class
and the social organization of reproduction in modern Western
societies. The approach will be interdisciplinary, with an
emphasis on sociological and historical studies.

The following books have been ordered at the West Bank Bookstore:

(Entire book is required reading)

> Newton, Judith L., Mary P. Ryan and Judith R. Walkowitz,
> (eds.): Sex and Class in Women's History Routledge and
> Kegan Paul, 1983.

> Willis, Paul: Learning to Labor. Columbia University
> Press, 1977.

> Luxton, Meg: More Than a Labor of Love. Toronto, The
> Women's Press, 1980.

(Part of book is required reading)

> Ostrander, Susan: Women of the Upper Class. Temple
> University Press, 1984.

> Sacks, Karen and Dorothy Remy, eds.: My Troubles are Going
> to Have Trouble With Me. New Brunswick, N.J., Rutgers
> University Press, 1984.

All of the books listed above, and the additional required readings,
are available on Reserve in Wilson library and also can be copied at
the West Bank Kinko's. The supplementary readings marked with an
asterisk are also available at these two locations.

Week 1 (Apr. 2-4): SOCIAL REPRODUCTION, GENDER, CLASS AND HISTORY

Required Reading:

B. Laslett: "Production, Reproduction and Social Change: The
                  Family in Historical Perspective." Pp. 239-258 in
                  James F. Short (ed.): The State of Sociology.
                  Beverly Hills, Sage Publications, 1981.
                  ONE COPY ON RESERVE UNDER SHORT;ONE UNDER LASLETT.

Week 2 (Apr. 9-11): SOCIAL REPRODUCTION, THE FAMILY AND THE
                  DEVELOPMENT OF INDUSTRIAL CAPITALISM

Required Reading:

Luxton, Meg: More Than a Labor of Love

Supplementary Reading:

*Medick, Hans.   "The Proto-Industrial Family," in Kriedte, Peter
                  et al, Industrialization Before Industrialization
                  Cambridge University Press, 1981.

Week 3 (Apr. 16-18): SOCIAL REPRODUCTION IN MIDDLE AND UPPER
                  CLASS FAMILIES

Required Reading:

Hausen, Karin.   "Family and Role-division: The Polarisation of
                  Sexual Stereotypes in the Nineteenth Century —
                  an Aspect of the Dissociation of Work and
                  Family life." Pp. 51-83 in Evans, Richard J.
                  and W.R. Lee (eds.), The German Family.
                  Barnes and Noble, 1981.

Palmer, Phyllis. "Housework and Domestic Labor: Racial and
                  Technological Change." In Sacks and Remy.

Ostrander, Susan. Upper Class Woman. Temple University Press,
                  1984. Chaps. 1-4, 7; skim chaps. 5-6.

Supplementary Reading:

*Welter, Barbara. "The Cult of True Womanhood." Pp. 224-249 in
                  M. Gordon (ed.),The American Family in
                  Social Historical Perspective. St. Martin's
                  Press.

Bloch, Ruth H. "Untangling the Roots of Modern Sex Roles: A Survey of Four Centuries of Change" *Signs* 4, Winter, 1978:237-252.

Branca, Patricia. *Silent Sisterhood.Middle-Class Women in the Victorian Home*. Carnegie-Mellon, 1975.

Davidoff, Leonore. *The Best Circles. Women and Society in Victorian England*. Rowman and Littlefield, 1973.

Smith, Bonnie. *Ladies of the Leisure Class. The Bourgeoise of Northern France in the Nineteenth Century*. Princeton, 1981.

Week 4 (Apr. 23-25): SEXUALITY, GENDER AND SOCIAL REPRODUCTION

Required Reading:

Davidoff, Lenore. "Class and Gender in Victorian England." In Newton, Ryan and Walkowitz.

Ramas, Maria. "Freud's Dora, Dora's Hysteria." In Newton, Ryan and Walkowitz.

Gillis, John R. "Servants, Sexual Relations and the Risks of Illegitimacy in London, 1801-1900." In Newton, Ryan and Walkowitz.

Rich, Adrienne. "Compulsory Heterosexuality and Lesbian Existence." *Signs* 5, 1980. Also in Snitow et al.

Carothers, Suzanne C. and Peggy Crull. "Contrasting Sexual Harassment in Female- and Male-Dominated Occupations." In Sacks and Remy.

Ehrenreich, Barbara. *The Hearts of Men*, Anchor Press, Doubleday, New York,1983. Chapter 4. "Playboy Joins the Battle of the Sexes".

Supplementary Reading:

Cott, Nancy F. "Passionlessness: An Interpretation of Victorian Sexuality, 1790-1850. *Signs* 4, Winter, 1978: 219-236.

*Barker-Benfield, Ben. "The Spermatic Economy: A Nineteenth Century View of Sexuality." In Michael Gordon (ed.), *The American Family in Social-Historical*

<u>Perspective.</u> St. Martin's Press.

*Trimberger, Kay Ellen. "Feminism, Men and Modern Love: Greenwich
                        Village, 1900-1925." Pp. 131-152 in Ann
                        Snitow, Christine Stansell and Sharon
                        Thompson (eds.), <u>Powers of Desire: The
                        Politics of Sexuality.</u> NY, Monthly Review
                        Press, 1983.

*Benjamin, Jessica. "Master and Slave: The Fantasy of Erotic
                     Domination," in Snitow et al (eds.),
                     <u>Powers of Desire.</u>

Chodorow, Nancy. "Oedipal Asymmetries and Heterosexual Knots, "
                  in <u>The Reproduction of Mothering</u>. University of
                  California Press,1978.

<u>Signs,</u> vol. 10, Autumn, 1984, pp. 102-134: section on the
               Feminist Sexuality Debates.

McLaren, Angus. <u>Sexuality and the Social Order</u>. Holmes and Meier,
                1983.

Walkowitz, Judith, <u>Prostitution and Victorian Society. Women,
                   Class and the State</u>.1980.

<u>Week 5 (Apr. 30 - May 2):</u> THE GENDERED LABOR FORCE: HISTORICAL
                                 PERSPECTIVES

Required Reading:

Hartmann, Heidi. "Capitalism, Patriarchy and Job Segregation by
                  Sex," in Z.R. Eisenstein, ed., <u>Capitalist
                  Patriarchy and the Case for Socialist
                  Feminism</u>, Monthly Review Press, 1979.

Tilly, Louise A. "Paths of Proletarianization: Organization of
                  Production, Sexual Divison of Labor and
                  Women's Collective Action." <u>Signs</u> 7 (1981-2),
                  400-417.

Quataert, Jean H. "Teamwork in Saxon Homeweaving Families in the
                   Ninteenth Century: A Preliminary
                   Investigation into the Issue of Gender Work
                   Roles." Joeres, R.E.B. and Mary Jo Maynes
                   (eds.), <u>German Women in the 18th and 19th
                   Centuries</u> (forthcoming, 1985). manuscript.

Frankel, Linda: "Southern Textile Women: Generations of Survival
                 and Struggle." In Sacks and Remy.

Jensen, Joan M. "Cloth, Butter and Boarders: Women's Household

164

Production for the Market." <u>Review</u> <u>of</u>
<u>Radical Political Economics</u> 12(2): 14-24, 1980.

Supplementary:

Tilly, Louise and Joan Scott, <u>Women. Work and Family</u>
Holt, Rinehart and Winston, 1978.

Kessler Harris, Alice. <u>Out to Work. A History of Wage-earning</u>
<u>Women in the United States.</u> 1982.

Amsden, Alice, ed. <u>The Economics of Women and Work</u>

<u>Week 6 (May 7-9):</u> SOCIAL REPRODUCTION AND THE SCHOOLS

Required Reading:

Willis, Paul: <u>Learning to Labor</u>

Supplementary:

Bowles, Sam and Herbert Gintis, <u>Schooling in Capitalist America</u>
Basic Books, 1975.

Delamont, Sara and Lorna Duffin, eds. <u>The Nineteenth-Century</u>
<u>Woman. Her Physical and Cultural World. 1978.</u>

<u>Struminqher, Laura.</u> What Were Little Girls and Boys Made Of?
Elementary Schooling in Rural France, 1830-
1880. S.U.N.Y. Press, 1983.

<u>Week 7 (May 14-16):</u> GENDER AND THE LEFT

Required Reading:

Maynes, Mary Jo. "Feminism in Working Class Autobiographies."
In Joeres and Maynes. manuscript.

Evans, Sara. <u>Personal Politics.</u> Vintage Books, 1980.Chapters 4-7.

Taylor, Barbara. "'The Men are as Bad as Their Masters..."
Socialism, Feminism and Sexual Antagonism in
the London Tailoring Trades in the 1830s." in
Newton, Ryan and Walkowitz.

Supplementary:

Boxer, Marilyn and Jean Quataert. <u>Socialist Women.</u> Elsevier,1978.

Buhle, Mary Jo. <u>Women and American Socialism</u> . University of
Illinois, 1981.

Engel, Barbara. "Women as Revolutionaries: The Case of the Russian Populists," in R.Bridenthal and C, Koonz, eds. Becoming Visible. Houghton Mifflin, 1974.

Honeycutt, Karen, "Clara Zetkin: A Socialist Approach to the Problem of Women's Oppression," Feminist Studies, 3(1976),131-141.

Taylor, Barbara, Eve and the New Jerusalem. Pantheon, 1983.

Week 9 (May 21-23): GENDER, THE STATE AND SOCIALIZING THE COSTS OF REPRODUCTION

Required Reading:

Evans, Richard J. "Prostitution, State and Society in Imperial Germany." Past and Present no. 70 (1976)

Zaretsky, Eli. "The Place of the Family in the Origins of the Welfare State. Pp. 188-224 in Barrie Thorne (ed.) Rethinking the Family: Some Feminist Questions. Longman, 1982.

Nelson, Barbara. "Women's Poverty and Women's Citizenship: Some Political Consequences of Economic Marginality." Signs 10, Winter 1984.

Praeger, Susan. "Shifting Perspectives on Marital Property Law." In Thorne, Rethinking the Family.

Orloff, Ann and Theda Skocpol. "Why Not Equal Protection? Explaining the Politics of Social Spending in Britain, 1900-1911, and the United States, 1880s-1920." American Sociological Review 49, Dec. 1984.

Supplementary :

Nelson, Barbara. "Family Politics and Policy in the United States and Western Europe." Comparative Politics 17, Jan. 1985.

Barker, Diana Leonard. "The Regulation of Marriage: Repressive Benevolence." In Littlejohn, Gary et al (eds.): Power and the State. St. Martin's Press, 1978.

Donzelot, Jacques. The Policing of Families. Pantheon Books, 1979

Petchesky, Rosalind P. Abortion and Women's Choice. Longman,
                        1984

Quadagno, Jill S.   "Welfare Capitalism and the Social Security
                    Act of 1935." American Sociological
                    Review 49, Oct. 1984.

Week 9 (May 28-30): WOMEN, MEN AND UNIONS

Required reading:

Clawson, Mary Ann. "Early Modern Fraternalism and the Patriarchal
                    Family, Feminist Studies, 6(1980),368-391.

Milkman,   Ruth.   "Organizing the Sexual Division of Labor:
                    Historical Perspectives on 'Women's Work'
                    and the American Labor Movement,"
                    Socialist Review (1979), 95-150.

Brenner,   Johanna and Maria Ramas.   "Rethinking Women's
                    Oppression." New Left Review, No. 144,
                    Mar.-Apr., 1984.

Kelly, Maria Patricia Fernandez.   "Maquiladoras: The View from
                    the Inside." in Sacks and Remy.

Shapiro-Perl, Nina. "Resistance Strategies: The Routine Struggle
                    for Bread and Roses." In Sacks and Remy.

Week 10 (June 4-6): FEMINISM

Required Reading:

Ryan, Mary P. "The Power of Women's Networks." In Newton, Ryan
                and Walkowitz.

Cook, Blanche Wiesen: "Female Support Networks and Political
                    Activism." Pp. 412-444 in Cott, Nancy
                    F. and Elizabeth H. Pleck (eds.): A
                    Heritage of Her Own: Towards a New
                    Social History of American Women. New
                    York, Simon and Schuster, 1979.

Gordon, Linda. "The Struggle for Reproductive Freedom: Three
                    Stages of Feminism." Pp. 107-135 in Zillah R.
                    Eisenstein (eds.); Capitalist Patriarchy and
                    the Case for Socialist Feminism. Monthly
                    Review Press, 1979.

Dye, Nancy Schrom. "Creating a Feminist Alliance: Sisterhood and

Class Conflict in the New York Women's Trade
Union League." Pp. 225-245 in Cantor, Milton
and Bruce Laurie (eds.): Class, Sex and the
Woman Worker. Greenwood Press, 1977.

Kelly, Joan. "The Double Vision of Feminist Theory." In Newton,
Ryan and Walkowitz.

Stansell, Christine. "One Hand Tied Behind Us: A Review Essay."
in Newton, Ryan and Walkowitz

Freeman, Jo. "The Women's Liberation Movement: It's Origins,
Structure, Activities and Ideas." In Freeman,
Jo, ed. Women: A Feminist Perspective.
Mayfield Publishing Co., 1975.

Supplementary:

Jacoby, Robin Miller. "The Women's Trade Union League and
American Feminism." In Cantor and Laurie.

Freeman, Jo. The Politics of Women's Liberation.
David McKay, 1975.

Marshall, Susan E. "Keep Us on the Pedestal: Women Against
Feminism in Twentieth-Century America," In
Freeman, Jo, ed. Women: A Feminist
Perspective. 3rd edition.

Dubois, Ellen. Women and Suffrage: The Emergence of an
Independent Women's Movement in the United
States, 1848-1869. 1978.

Hackett, Amy. "The German Women's Movement and Suffrage, 1890-
1914," in R>J>Bezucha, ed. Modern European
Social History. 1972.

Evans, Richard. The Feminist Movement in Germany, 1894 -1933.
Sage, 1976.

Rosen, Andrew. Rise Up Women! The Militant Campaign of the
Women's Social and Political Union, 1903-
1914.1974.

Course Requirements

In addition to attending class, doing all the required readings and participating in class discussion, the following written assignments are expected to fulfill the requirements of the course:

Undergraduates:

1. Two "reaction papers" of around two typed pages for each of two chosen discussion sections. (Sign-up sheet will be passed around in class.) For the week that you have written a reaction paper, you will be expected to help lead off the general discussion. Reaction papers are based on required readings for the week.

2. Two longer essays on the required readings, one due on April 18 an one due on May 16. Specific assignments will be distributed in advance. Each paper will be around four typed pages.

3. A take-home final exam covering all aspects of the course.

Graduate students:

Two options are available for graduate students. You may either choose to do a variation of the above requirements (that is, two "reaction papers", two essays and a take-home final) or, you may substitute for the two longer essays a single research paper based on some project that is connected to themes we will explore in the course. You should consult with the instructors if you wish to choose this option. If you do the research paper, you will still have to contribute "reaction papers" and write a take-home final.

History 383: Modern Jewish History to 1880
Professor Endelman
Fall Term 1987

Students should purchase the following books:

Paul R. Mendes-Flohr and Jehuda Reinharz, eds., The Jew in the Modern World: A Documentary History

Marvin Lowenthal, trans., The Memoirs of Gluckel of Hameln

Todd M. Endelman, The Jews of Georgian England

Michael A. Meyer, The Origins of the Modern Jew

Michael Stanislawski, Tsar Nicholas I and the Jews

Lectures

Sep. 11   Introduction: Out of the Ghetto

Sep. 14   Symposium on Jewish Political Ideas and Institutions
           Rackham Amphitheater

Sep. 16   European Jewry on the Eve of the Modern Era
           Reading: Gluckel of Hameln

Sep. 18   The Sephardi Community of Amsterdam
           Reading: Mendes-Flohr and Reinharz, I: 3

Sep. 21   Harbingers of Intellectual and Cultural Revolution
           Reading: Mendes-Flohr and Reinharz, II: 1-3

Sep. 23   The Sephardim of Southwestern France

Sep. 25   No Class (Rosh Ha-Shanah)

Sep. 28   The Return of the Jews to England
           Reading: Mendes-Flohr and Reinharz, I: 1

Examination #1 (take-home, to be distributed in class)

Sep. 30   The Jews of Georgian England (slide lecture)

Reading: Endelman

Take-home examination due at the beginning of class

Oct. 2   Jewish Settlement in the New World

Oct. 5   The Age of the Court Jew in Central Europe

Reading: Mendes-Flohr and Reinharz, I: 4, 6

Oct. 7   New European Attitudes toward the Jews

Reading: Mendes-Flohr and Reinharz, I: 8, 9, 13; II: 4, 5

Oct. 9   Moses Mendelssohn and the Haskalah

Reading: Mendes-Flohr and Reinharz, II: 7-19
Meyer, chaps. 1, 2

Oct. 12   The Radicalization of the Haskalah in Germany

Reading: Mendes-Flohr and Reinharz, II: 20-22
Meyer, chaps. 3, 4

Oct. 14   The French Revolution and the Emancipation of the Jews

Reading: Mendes-Flohr and Reinharz, III: 1-9

Oct. 16   No Class (Simhat Torah)

Oct. 19   Napoleon and the Assembly of Jewish Notables

Reading: Mendes-Flohr and Reinharz, III: 10-16

Oct. 21   The Struggle for Emancipation in Germany, 1806-1870

Reading: Mendes-Flohr and Reinharz, III: 18-25; VII: 4-11

Oct. 23   The Origins of Reform Judaism

           Reading: Mendes-Flohr and Reinharz, IV: 1-10
                     Meyer, chap. 5

Oct. 26   The Spread of Reform Judaism in Europe

Oct. 28   The Transformation of the Synagogue (slide lecture)

Oct. 30   Wissenschaft des Judentums

           Reading: Mendes-Flohr and Reinharz, V: 1-7
                     Meyer, chap. 6

Nov. 2   Conference on Jewish Intellectuals
           Wayne State University, Detroit

Nov. 4   Zecharias Frankel's Positive-Historical Judaism

           Reading: Mendes-Flohr and Reinharz, IV: 11

Nov. 6   Samson Raphael Hirsch's Neo-Orthodoxy

           Reading: Mendes-Flohr and Reinharz, IV: 12

Nov. 9   Examination #2

Nov. 11   The Flight from Jewishness

           Reading: Mendes-Flohr and Reinharz, VI: 1-9

Nov. 13   German Jews in America, 1830-1880

Nov. 16   The Americanization of Judaism

Nov. 18   Polish Jewry before the Partitions

Nov. 20   The Origins of Hasidism

Nov. 23   Hasidim and Mitnagdim

172

Nov. 25   The Religious Culture of Eastern European Jewry in the Early Nineteenth Century

Nov. 27   No Class (Thanksgiving)

Nov. 30   The Political and Economic Status of Russian Jewry to 1881

Reading: Stanislawski, intro., chaps. 1, 2

Dec. 2   The Beginnings of the Haskalah in Russia

Reading: Mendes-Flohr and Reinharz, VIII: 6-9, 13-15
Stanislawski, chaps. 3, 4

Dec. 4   The Haskalah at its Zenith

Reading: Stanislawski, chaps. 5, 6, conclusion

Dec. 7   The Jews of North Africa and the Middle East

Dec. 9   Rich Jews, Poor Jews: The Jews and Capitalism

Dec. 11   Conclusion: Ancient Loyalties and New Identities

Final Examination: Wednesday, December 16, 1:30 - 3:30

The final grade for the course will be weighted in the following way:

examination #1	25%
examination #2	35%
final examination	40%

Office Hours

Mondays   11-12   Department of History
3625 Haven Hall
764-7308

Wednesdays   2-3   Program in Judaic Studies
206 Angell Hall
763-9047

History 384: Modern Jewish History, 1880-1948
Professor Endelman
Winter Term 1986
MWF 10-11

Students should purchase the following books:

Paul R. Mendes-Flohr and Jehuda Reinharz, eds., The Jew in the
Modern World: A Documentary History

Michael R. Marrus, The Politics of Assimilation: A Study of the
French Jewish Community at the Time of the Dreyfus Affair

Walter Laqueur, A History of Zionism

Lucy S. Dawidowicz, On Equal Terms: Jews in America, 1881-1981

Abraham Cahan, The Rise of David Levinsky

Primo Levi, Survival in Auschwitz

Lectures

Jan. 8   Introduction

Jan. 10   Western European Jewry in the Late-Nineteenth Century

              Reading: Marrus, chaps. 2-4
                        Laqueur, chap. 1
                        Mendes-Flohr and Reinharz, VI: 3, 10

Jan. 13   Eastern European Jewry in the Late-Nineteenth Century

              Reading: Mendes-Flohr and Reinharz, VIII: 1

Jan. 15   The Emergence of the Jewish Question in Germany

              Reading: Mendes-Flohr and Reinharz, VII: 12, 13, 16-20

Jan. 17   Antisemitism in the Austro-Hungarian Empire

Jan. 20   The Dreyfus Affair

              Reading: Mendes-Flohr and Reinharz, VII: 14, 15

Jan. 22   Antisemitism and British Society, 1870-1914

Jan. 24   Pogroms and Repression in Tsarist Russia

              Reading: Mendes-Flohr and Reinharz, VIII: 5, 19-22

Jan. 27   Communal Responses to Antisemitism in Western Europe

        Reading: Marrus, chaps. 5, 6, 8

Jan. 29   The Flight from Jewishness

        Reading: Mendes-Flohr and Reinharz, VI: 8, 12-14

Jan. 31   Russifiers and Modernizers in Tsarist Russia

        Reading: Mendes-Flohr and Reinharz, VIII: 12

Feb. 3   Emigration from Eastern Europe

        Reading: Dawidowicz, chap. 1
                 Mendes-Flohr and Reinharz, VIII: 23-25

Feb. 5   Class Conflict and Revolutionary Socialism

        Reading: Mendes-Flohr and Reinharz, VIII: 27

Feb. 7   Jewish Nationalism before Herzl

        Reading: Laqueur, chap. 2
                 Mendes-Flohr and Reinharz, VI: 15;
                   VIII: 16, 26; X: 1

Feb. 10   Theodor Herzl and Political Zionism

        Reading: Laqueur, chaps. 3, 4
                 Marrus, chaps. 7, 9
                 Mendes-Flohr and Reinharz, X: 2-5, 9-11, 13

Feb. 12   Varieties of Zionist Ideology

        Reading: Mendes-Flohr and Reinharz, X: 8, 12, 14, 17

Feb. 14   The Zionist Revolution

Feb. 17   Zionism and Its Critics

        Reading: Laqueur, chap. 8
                 Mendes-Flohr, X: 6, 15, 16, 18

Feb. 19   The Impact of World War I on European Jewry

        Reading: Mendes-Flohr and Reinharz, X: 19, 20

Feb. 21   The Bolshevik Revolution and the Fate of Soviet Jewry

        Reading: Mendes-Flohr and Reinharz, VIII: 24, 30-32

Mar. 3   Midterm Examination

Mar. 5   **Eastern European Immigrants in America**

> **Reading:** Dawidowicz, chaps. 2, 3
> Mendes-Flohr and Reinharz, IX: 15-20

Mar. 7   **Problems of Immigrant Adjustment**

> **Reading:** Cahan

Mar. 10   Uptown Jews and Downtown Jews

> **Reading:** Dawidowicz, chap. 4
> Mendes-Flohr and Reinharz, IX: 11-14, 21-24

Mar. 12   Second Generation American Jews

> **Reading:** Mendes-Flohr and Reinharz, IX: 26-31

Mar. 14   Judaism and Jewish Identity in Interwar America

Mar. 17   American Jewish Responses to Antisemitism

> **Reading:** Dawidowicz, chaps. 5, 6
> Mendes-Flohr and Reinharz, IX: 32-35

Mar. 19   The Resurgence of Antisemitism in Europe

> **Reading:** Mendes-Flohr and Reinharz, VII: 21-22

Mar. 21   Polish Jewry between the Wars

> **Videotape:** "Image before My Eyes"

Mar. 24   Jewish Politics in East Central Europe

Mar. 26   Judaism and Jewish Identity in Western and Central
Europe between the Wars

Mar. 28   German Jewish Renaissance

Mar. 31   Jewish Politics in Western Europe

Apr. 2   Jews in European Cultural and Intellectual Life

Apr. 4   Zionism and the British Mandate

> **Reading:** Laqueur, chaps. 7, 9
> Mendes-Flohr and Reinharz, X: 21-24

Apr. 7   The Growth of the Yishuv

> **Reading:** Laqueur, chaps. 5, 6

Apr. 9   **The Jews of North Africa and the Middle East, 1880-1918**

Apr. 11   The Jews of North Africa and the Middle East, 1918-1948

Apr. 14   The Origins of the "Final Solution"

           Reading: Mendes-Flohr and Reinharz, XI: 1-20

Apr. 16   Ghettoization, Deportation, Mass Murder

           Reading: Mendes-Flohr and Reinharz, XI: 21-28

Apr. 18   Jewish Behavior in Crisis and Extremity

           Reading: Levi

Apr. 21   The Struggle for the State of Israel

           Reading: Laqueur, chaps. 10, 11, conclusion
                    Mendes-Flohr and Reinharz, X: 25-31

Apr. 23   Jewish Life in Postwar America

           Reading: Dawidowicz, chaps. 7, 8

Final Examination: Wednesday, April 30, 1:30-3:30

Office Hours: 3625 Haven Hall   Wednesdays 11-12
               764-7308   Fridays   9-10

Marion Kaplan

Princeton University
Fall 1988

Office Hours: before class and
 by appointment

Jewish Women in the Modern World

This course will approach Jewish women's history from the
perspective of social history. After an introduction which looks
at the normative role of women in Judaism, we will briefly survey
women in the Middle Ages and Early Modern Europe. The body of
the course will focus on women in Modern Europe and the U.S.,
analyzing their history through primary and secondary sources.

BOOKS to be Purchased: (available at book store)

The Memoirs of Gluckl of Hameln, NY, 1977

Charlotte Baum, Paula Hyman, Sonya Michel, The Jewish Woman in
America, NY, 1977

Rachel Biale, Women and Jewish Law, NY, 1984

Elizabeth Ewen, Immigrant Women in the Land of Dollars: Life and
Culture on the Lower East Side, 1890-1925, NY, 1985

Since there are few books on this subject, a large part of the
reading is from ARTICLES culled from many sources. These articles
are on reserve at the library. They may also be purchased in a
xerox packet.

Since some of you may not have a background in modern Jewish
history or in women's history, I would suggest glancing through
one or two of the following books when you feel the need. I have
asked that they be placed on reserve at the library, but you may
want to purchase one or two.

H. H. Ben-Sasson, ed., A History of the Jewish People (paper)

Howard Morley Sachar, The Course of Modern Jewish History (paper)

Bonnie S. Anderson & Judith P. Zinsser, A History of their Own:
Women in Europe from Prehistory to the Present

Renate Bridenthal, Claudia Koonz, Susan Stuard, Becoming Visible:
Women in European History, (paper)

Nancy Woloch, Women and the American Experience (paper)

The course consists of two papers and a final. Class
discussion is an essential part of your responsibility. There
will be few lectures; class members will be responsible for

introducing the discussion (based on the readings) each week; everyone is expected to participate fully and critically.

Reading Assignments -- according to class meetings

Class # 1   INTRODUCTION to Course: Gender and
               Modern Jewish History

                    Paula Hyman, "Gender and Jewish
                    History," Tikkun, Jan. 1988 (on reserve and in
                    xerox packet. Hereafter, assume that any article
                    on reserve has also been included in the xerox
                    packet.)

                    Carol Meyers, "The Roots of Restrictionism:
                    Women in Early Israel, Biblical
                    Archaeologist, 41, no 3 (Sept. 1978) (on
                    reserve)

Class #2   ORIGINS:The Normative Role of Women in
               Traditional Judaism

                    Judith Hauptman, "Images of Women in the
                    Talmud," in Religion and Sexism, ed. by R.R.
                    Reuther (on reserve)

                    Paula Hyman, "The Other Half: Women in the
                    Jewish Tradition," Response, 1973 (on
                    reserve)

                    Biale, Women and Jewish Law, chaps. 1- 4
                    Recommended (not required): David Feldman, Marital
                    Relations, Birth Control and Abortion in Jewish
                    Law (on reserve and at book store)

Class #3   WOMEN IN TRADITIONAL JEWISH SOCIETIES

                    Isadore Epstein, "The Jewish Woman in the
                    Responsa," Response, 1973 (on reserve)

                    Franz Kobler, Letters of the Jews through the Ages
                    pp. 147-50; 233-34; 289-90 (on reserve)

                    Biale, Women and Jewish Law, chaps. 5 - 10

Class #4   S.D. Goitein, A Mediterranean Society, vol. 3, The
               Family, pp. 47-65; 160-205; 223-48; 312-359 (on
               reserve)

               The Memoirs of Gluckl of Hameln (entire)

               Jacob Katz, "Family, Kinship and Marriage among

Ashkenazim in the 16th to 18th Centuries,"
<u>Journal of Jewish Sociology</u>, 1959 (on reserve)

Chava Weissler, "The Traditional Piety of Ash-
kenazic Women," <u>Jewish Spirituality</u>, (reserve)

Class #5   EMANCIPATION AND ASSIMILATION: MODERN WESTERN
            EUROPEAN JEWRY

Michael Meyer, "Rationalism and Romanticism: Two
Roads to Conversion," <u>The Origins of the Modern
Jew</u>, pp. 85-114 (on reserve)

Deborah Hertz, "Intermarriage in the Berlin
Salons," <u>Central European History</u>, XVI (on
reserve)

Marion Kaplan, "Tradition and Transition: The
Acculturation, Assimilation and Integration of
Jews in Imperial Germany," <u>Leo Baeck Inst.
Year Book</u>, 1982 (on reserve)

Kaplan, "Priestess and Hausfrau: Women and
Tradition in the German-Jewish Family," <u>The
Jewish Family</u>, ed. by S. Cohen and P. Hyman (on
reserve)

Kaplan, "For Love or Money: The
Marriage Strategies of Jews in Imperial
Germany," <u>LBIYB,</u> 1983 (on reserve)

Class # 6   JEWISH WOMEN IN EASTERN EUROPE

Elizabeth Ewen, <u>Immigrant Women in the Land of
Dollars</u>, chap. 2 (Read on all immigrant women,
not just Jewish women.)

Baum, et.al., <u>The Jewish Woman in America</u>,
chap. 3

Lucy Dawidowicz, ed., <u>The Golden Tradition,</u>
pp. 160-68; 388-93 (on reserve)

Zborowski and Herzog, <u>Life is With People</u>, pp.
124-41 (on reserve)

Film: Image before My Eyes

Recommended: Sydney Weinberg, <u>The World of our
Mothers</u>, chaps. 1-4 (reserve and bookstore)

Class #7   THE AMERICAN EXPERIENCE
            <u>The First Generation Immigrants</u>

Baum, et. al., <u>Jewish Woman in America</u>,
chaps. 2, 4-5

Ewen, <u>Immigrant Women</u>, chaps. 1, 3 - 10

Recommended: Weinberg, <u>World of Our</u>
<u>Mothers</u>, chaps. 5 -9 (on reserve); Judith Smith,
<u>Family Ties</u>; Thomas Kessner, <u>The Golden Door</u>

Class #8 and 9   <u>The Second Generation in America</u>

Baum, et. al., <u>Jewish Woman in America,</u>
chap. 6

Ewen, <u>Immigrant Women,</u> chaps. 11-14

PAPER DUE (for class #9): Choose <u>one</u> of the
following memoirs or novels and compare it, in
a 9 - 10 page paper, with the secondary
source material you have read (for class) on
Eastern Europe and/or the immigrant
experience. Use at least one other book on the
subject (from recommended readings or of your
own choice). Be ready to discuss your paper
in class. It is possible to choose another
book after a discussion with the instructor.

Choices:
Kim Chernin, <u>In My Mother's House</u>, (available
       at book store and on reserve)
Vivian Gornick, <u>Fierce Attachments</u> (reserve)
Marie Jastrow, <u>A Time to Remember</u> or <u>Looking</u>
       <u>Back:The American Dream through</u>
       <u>Immigrant Eyes</u> (reserve)
Kate Simon, <u>Bronx Primitive</u>, (available at
       book store and on reserve)
Meredith Tax, <u>Rivington Street</u> (reserve)
Anzia Yezierska, <u>The Bread Givers</u> (at book
       store and on reserve)

Class # 10   JEWISH FEMINISTS, REBELS, AND FEMALE LEADERS

PAPER DUE: Choose <u>one</u> of the following and
write a paper about the woman (women)
and her (their) times. The report should be
about 10 pages long and should refer to your
previous readings as well as to one other
book on the subject. (For example, you might
choose to read about Emma Goldman and then
pick a book about anarchism or women

anarchists. Or, you might read about Mamie
and a general book in the
topic of prostitution. Discuss the
possibilities with me. You may also choose a
book which is not on this list after
discussion with the instructor. Be ready to
report on your topic in class.

Richard Drinnon, Rebel in Paradise: A
Biography of Emma Goldman (at book store
and on reserve)

Vivian Gornick, The Romance of American
Communism (on reserve)

Marion Kaplan, The Jewish Feminist Movement
in Germany: The Campaigns of the Juedischer
Frauenbund, 1904-1938 (at book store and
on reserve)

Ruth Rosen, ed., The Mamie Papers (on
reserve)

Ellen Umansky, Lily Montagu and the Advancement of Liberal Judaism (at book store and
on reserve)

Class #11   WOMEN IN THE HOLOCAUST

Claudia Koonz, "Jewish Women between Survival
and Death" from her book, Mothers in the
Fatherland: Women, the Family and Nazi
Politics (on reserve)

Vera Laska, Women in the Resistance and the
Holocaust, selections (on reserve)

Sybil Milton, "Women and the Holocaust,"
When Biology became Destiny: Women in
Weimar and Nazi Germany, ed. by Renate
Bridenthal, et. al. (on reserve)

Recommended: Ilona Karmel, An Estate of
Memory (a novel)

Class # 12   JEWISH WOMEN IN THE US AND ISRAEL

Lesley Hazleton, "Israeli Women: Three
Myths," On Being a Jewish Feminist, ed. by
Susannah Heschel (on reserve)

Film: Anou Banou:The Daughters of Utopia
(about the pioneer generation of women in
Israe))

Baum, et.al., The Jewish Woman in America,
chaps. 7-8

Susannah Heschel, "Introduction," to On
Being a Jewish Feminist (on reserve)

Biale, Women and Jewish Law, epilogue

Evelyn Torton Beck, "Why is this Book
different from all other Books?" Nice
Jewish Girls:A Lesbian Anthology, ed. by
E.T. Beck (on reserve)

Recommended: E.M.Broner, A Weave of Women
(a novel); Carol Ascher, The Flood (a
novel); Barbara Meyerhof, Number Our Days;
(interviews with elderly Jewish immigrants)
Natalie Rein, Daughters of Rachel (about
women in Israel)

UNIVERSITY OF TORONTO
Department of History

HIS 398Y
1987-88

THE HOLOCAUST: THE NAZIS, OCCUPIED EUROPE, AND THE JEWS

TR2   M.R. Marrus

This course surveys the destruction of two-thirds of European Jewry by the
Nazis during the Second World War. The first term explores Nazi policy
toward the Jews in the context of anti-Jewish ideology, bureaucratic
structures, and the varying conditions of occupation and domination in
Europe under the Third Reich. The second term continues the latter theme,
but emphasizes the world outside -- reactions of Jews, European populations
and governments, the Allies, churches, and political movements.

Students will attend bi-weekly tutorial groups to discuss issues raised in
lectures, assigned readings, and, occasionally, films presented in conjunction
with the course. These tutorials are an integral part of the course and
satisfactory attendance at them is essential in order to obtain standing.
There will be a term test at the end of the first term, an essay due at the end
of the second, and a final examination.

The final grade in the course will be computed as follows: A tentative grade
will be determined by allowing 25% for the term test and 75% for the
average of the essay and final examination. Each student's tutorial
participation will then be assessed, and the tentative grade previously
calculated may then be adjusted upwards or downwards by a maximum of
five percentage points.

Weekly readings, marked with an asterisk (*), address specific themes, but
are not necessarily intended to cover material discussed in lectures. As
noted above, there will also be some effort to show a number of films in
conjunction with the course. Students should make every effort to see these
at the times and places to be announced. For most weeks there is an

assigned reading from book(s) purchased as texts in the course. In addition, there is a list of alternate readings which follow these works, from which students should make choices according to their own time and interest. When there is no specifically assigned reading, students are asked to choose from among the alternate selections. These lists of alternate readings will also be the basis for the essays in the second term. The Sigmund Samuel Library should have copies of much of the syllabus material, including photocopied articles, on short-term loan.

Students should purchase copies of the following, which are available in the Textbook Store:

Raul Hilberg, Destruction of the European Jews. Student Edition (Holmes & Meir)
Lucy Dawidowicz, A Holocaust Reader (Behrman House)
Eberhard Jackel, Hitler's World View (Harvard)
Primo Levi, Survival in Auschwitz (Macmillan)
David Wyman. The Abandonment of the Jews (Pantheon)

Students may also wish to consult the following, which will be available in late October or early November:

Michael Marrus, The Holocaust in History (Lester & Orpen Dennys)

FIRST TERM: THE DESTRUCTION PROCESS

WEEK   LECTURES. ASSIGNED READING. AND FURTHER SUGGESTIONS

Sept. 14   ANTECEDENTS (1): THE JEWS AND MODERN EUROPEANS

Salo Baron, "European Jewry Before and After Hitler," American Jewish Yearbook, 63 (1962), 3-49.
Yehuda Bauer, "The Place of the Holocaust in Contemporary History," Studies in Contemporary Jewry, I (1984), 201-24.
Shmuel Ettinger, "The Origins of Modern Anti-Semitism," in Yisrael Gutman and Livia Rothkirchaen. eds., The Catastrophe of European Jewry (1976), 3-39.

Jacob Katz, From Prejudice to Destruction: Anti-Semitism, 1700-1933 (1980)
_____, "Was the Holocaust Predictable?" Commentary, May 1975, 41-8.
Michael Marrus, "The Theory and Practice of Antisemitism," Commentary, August 1982, 38-42.
George Mosse, Toward the Final Solution: A Study of European Racism (1978)
J. L. Talmon, "European History: The Seedbed of the Holocaust," Midstream, May 1973, 3-25.
Shulamit Volkov, "Antisemitism as a Cultural Code -- Reflections on the History and Historiography of Antisemitism in Imperial Germany," Leo Baeck Institute Year Book, XXIII (1978), 25-46.
Meyer Weinberg, Because They Were Jews: A History of Antisemitism (1986)

Sept. 21   ANTECEDENTS (2): THE JEWS AND THE GERMANS

*Raul Hilberg, Destruction of the European Jews, Ch. 1.
*Lucy Dawidowicz, Holocaust Reader, Introduction, plus 28-9.

Werner Angress, "The German Jews, 1933-1939," in Henry Friedlander and Sybil Milton, eds., The Holocaust: Ideology, Bureaucracy, and Genocide (1980)
Sarah Gordon, Hitler, Germans, and the "Jewish Question" (1984)
Michael Kater, "Everyday Anti-Semitism in Pre-War Nazi Germany: The Popular Basis," Yad Vashem Studies, XVI (1984), 129-59.
George Kren and Leon Rappoport, The Holocaust and the Crisis of Human Behavior (1980)
George L. Mosse, The Crisis of German Ideology (1971)
_____, Germans and Jews (1970)
_____, German Jews Beyond Judaism (1980)
Donald Niewyk, The Jews in Weimar Germany (1980)
Peter Pulzer, "Why Was There a Jewish Question in Imperial Germany?" Leo Baeck Institute Year Book, 25 (1980), 133-46.

Sept. 28   ANTECEDENTS (3): THE JEWS AND THE NAZIS

*Eberhard Jackel, Hitler's World View (entire book)
*Lucy Dawidowicz, Holocaust Reader, 30-3.

Yehuda Bauer, "Genocide: Was it the Nazis Original Plan?"
        Annals of the American Academy of Political and Social
        Science, 450 (July 1980), 35-45.
Sarah Gordon, Hitler, Germans, and the "Jewish Question" (1984)
Adolf Hitler, Mein Kampf
Peter Merkl, Political Violence Under the Swastika (1975)
George Mosse, Germans and Jews (1970)
Ernst Nolte, Three Faces of Fascism (1966)
Karl Schleunes, The Twisted Road to Auschwitz (1970)

Oct. 5   PERSECUTION OF THE JEWS IN GERMANY, 1933-1941

*Raul Hilberg, Destruction of the European Jews, 27-64.
*Lucy Dawidowicz, Holocaust Reader, Chs. 2, 5.

Helmut Krausnick, "The Persecution of the Jews," in Helmut
        Krausnick and Martin Broszat, Anatomy of the SS State
        (1968)
Michael Marrus, The Unwanted: European Refugees in the
        Twentieth Century (1985)
Karl Schleunes, The Twisted Road to Auschwitz (1970)
Herbert A. Strauss, "Jewish Emigration from Germany: Nazi
        Policies and Jewish Response," Leo Baeck Institute Year
        Book, 25 (1980), 313-63, and ibid, 26 (1981)

Oct. 12   THE JEWS AND THE EAST EUROPEANS

*Lucy Dawidowicz, Holocaust Reader, Ch. 3 (in preparation for
    the next week)

Stanislav Andreski, "An Economic Interpretation of
Antisemitism in Eastern Europe," Jewish Journal of
Sociology, December 1963, 201-13.
Celia Heller, On the Edge of Destruction: Jews of Poland Between
the Two World Wars (1977)
Pawel Korzec, Juifs en Pologne (1980)
Ezra Mendelsohn, The Jews of East Central Europe Between the
World Wars (1983)
_____. "Interwar Poland: Good For the Jews or Bad
for the Jews?" in Chimen Abramsky, Maciej Jachimczyk,
and Antony Polonsky, eds., The Jews in Poland (1986)
Hugh Seton-Watson, "Government Policies Towards the Jews in
Pre-Communist Eastern Europe," Soviet Jewish Affairs,
December 1969, 20-5.

Oct. 19   EVOLUTION OF THE "FINAL SOLUTION"

*Raul Hilberg, Destruction of the European Jews, Ch. 4, 157-86.

Martin Broszat, "Hitler and the Genesis of the 'Final Solution': An
Assessment of David Irving's Theses," Yad Vashem
Studies, XIII (1979), 73-125.
Christopher Browning, The Final Solution and the German
Foreign Office (1978)
_____. Fateful Months: Essays on the Emergence
of the Final Solution (1985)
Gerald Fleming, Hitler and the Final Solution (1984)
Saul Friedlander, "From Anti-Semitism to Extermination: A
Historiographical Study of Nazi Polices Toward the Jews
and an Essay in Interpretation," Yad Vashem Studies,
XVI (1984), 1-50.
Eberhard Jackel, Hitler in History (1984)
Lothar Kettenacker, Hitler's Final Solution and its
Rationalization," in Gerhard Hirschfeld, ed., The Policies of
Genocide (1986), 73-92.
Michael Marrus, The Unwanted, European Refugees in the
Twentieth Century (1985)

_____, "The History of the Holocaust: A Survey of
Recent Literature." Journal of Modern History, 59 (1987),
114-60.
Hans Mommsen, "The Realization of the Unthinkable: The Final
Solution of the Jewish Question' in the Third Reich," in
Gerhard Hirschfeld, ed., The Policies of Genocide (1986),
93-144.
Norman Rich, Hitler's War Aims, 2 vols. (1973-4)
Karl Schleunes, The Twisted Road to Auschwitz (1970)

Oct. 26   THE MACHINERY OF DESTRUCTION: PARTY, SS, BUREAUCRACY

            *Raul Hilberg, Destruction of the European Jews, 187-221, 263-
            93.
            *Lucy Dawidowicz, Holocaust Reader, Ch. 4.

            Uwe Dietrich Adam, "Persecution of the Jews, Bureaucracy and
            Authority in the Totalitarian State," Leo Baeck Institute
            Year Book, XXIII (1978), 139-48.
            Heinz Hohne, The Order of the Death's Head (1970)
            Fred Katz, "Implementation of the Holocaust: The Behavior of
            Nazi Officials," Comparative Studies in Society and
            History, 24 (1982), 510-29.
            Robert Koehl, RKFDV: German Resettlement and Population
            Policy (1957)
            _____, The Black Corps: The Structure and Power
            Struggles of the SS (1983)
            Helmut Krausnick and Martin Broszat, Anatomy of the SS State
            (1968)
            Jochen von Lang, ed., Eichmann Interrogated: Transcripts from
            the Archives of the Israeli Police (1984)
            Robert Jay Lifton, The Nazi Doctors: Medical Killing and the
            Psychology of Genocide (1986)

Nov. 2   GHETTOIZATION IN THE EAST (1): CONCENTRATION

            *Raul Hilberg, Destruction of the European Jews, 64-96.

Yitzhak Arad, Ghetto in Flames: The Struggle and Destruction of
the Jews in Vilna in the Holocaust (1980)
Solomon Bloom, "Dictator of the Lodz Ghetto: the Strange
History of Mordechai Chaim Rumkowski," Commentary, 7
(1949), 111-22.
Lucjan Dobroszycki, ed., The Chronicle of the Lodz Ghetto (1984)
Philip Friedman, "Two 'Saviors' Who Failed: Moses Merin of
Sosnowiec and Jacob Gens of Vilna," Commentary, 26
(1958), 479-91.
Yisrael Gutman, The Jews of Warsaw, 1939-1943: Ghetto,
Underground, Revolt (1982)
Yisrael Gutman and Cynthia J. Haft, eds., Patterns of Jewish
Leadership in Nazi Europe, 1933-1945 (1979)
Raul Hilberg, "The Ghetto as a Form of Government: An
Analysis of Isaiah Trunk's Judenrat," in Yehuda Bauer
and Nathan Rotenstreich, eds., The Holocaust as a
Historical Experience (1981), 155-71.
Raul Hilberg, Stanislaw Staron, and Josef Kermisz, eds., The
Warsaw Diary of Adam Czerniakow (1979)
Shmuel Huppert, "KIng of the Ghetto -- Mordechai Haim
Rumkowski, the Elder of the Lodz Ghetto," Yad Vashem
Studies, XV (1983), 125-57.
Chaim Kaplan, The Warsaw Diary of Chaim A. Kaplan (1965)
Emanuel Ringelblum, Notes from the Warsaw Ghetto (1958)
Isaiah Trunk, Judenrat: the Jewish Councils in Eastern Europe
under Nazi Occupation (1972)
Leonard Tushnet, Pavement of Hell (1972)

Nov. 9   GHETTOIZATION IN THE EAST (2): DEPORTATION

*Lucy Dawidowicz, Holocaust Reader, Chs. 6-8.

Yitzhak Arad, "'Operation Reinhard': Extermination Camps of
Belzec, Sobibor and Treblinka, Yad Vashem Studies, XVI
(1984), 205-39.
_____, Belzec, Sobibor, Treblinka: The Operation
Reinhard Death Camps (1987)

Jurgen Forster, The Wehrmacht and the War of Extermination:
against the Soviet Union," Yad Vashem Studies, XIV
(1981), 7-34 and Gerhard Hirschfeld, ed., The Policies of
Genocide (1986).

Heinz Hohne, The Order of the Death's Head (1972)

Jochen von Lang, ed., Eichmann Interrogated: Transcripts from
the Archives of the Israeli Police (1984)

Nov. 16   JEWISH RESISTANCE IN EASTERN EUROPE

*Lucy Dawidowicz, Holocaust Reader, Ch. 9.
*Raul Hilberg, Destruction of the European Jews, 293-305.

Reuben Ainsztein, Jewish Resistance in Nazi Occupied Europe
(1974)

Yitzhak Arad, Ghetto in Flames: the Struggle and Destruction of
the Jews in Vilna in the Holocaust (1980)

Yehuda Bauer, They Chose Life: Jewish Resistance in the
Holocaust (1973)

Yisrael Gutman, The Jews of Warsaw, 1939-1943: Ghetto,
Underground, Revolt (1982)

_____, "Polish Responses to the Liquidation of Warsaw
Jewry," Jerusalem Quarterly, 17 (Fall 1980), 40-55.

Oscar Handlin, "Jewish Resistance to the Nazis," Commentary, 34
(1962), 398-405.

Richard Lukas, Forgotten Holocaust: The Poles Under German
Occupation (1986)

Shmuel Krakowski, The War of the Doomed: Jewish Armed
Resistance in Poland (1984)

Dov Levin, Fighting Back: Lithuanian Jewry's Armed Resistance
to the Nazis, 1941-1945 (1985)

Henri Michel, "Jewish Resistance and the European Resistance
Movement," Yad Vashem Studies, VII (1968), 7-16.

Yuri Suhl, ed., They Fought Back: The Story of Jewish Resistance
in Nazi Europe (1967)

Isaiah Trunk, "Note: Why Was There No Armed Resistance
Against the Nazis in the Lodz Ghetto?" Jewish Social
Studies, XLIII (Summer-Fall 1981), 329-34.
_____, Jewish Responses to Nazi Persecution (1982)

Nov. 23   DEATH CAMPS IN THE EAST (1): MACHINERY OF DESTRUCTION

*Raul Hilberg, Destruction of the European Jews, Ch. 6.
*Lucy Dawidowicz, Holocaust Reader, 104-20.

Yitzhak Arad, Belzec, Sobibor, Treblinka: The Operation
Reinhard Death Camps (1987)
Bruno Bettelheim, The Informed Heart (1960)
_____, Surviving and Other Essays(1980)
Tadeuz Borowski, This Way for the Gas, Ladies and Gentlemen
(1976)
Terrence Des Pres, The Survivor (1976)
Alexander Donat, ed., The Death Camp Treblinka (1979)
W. Glicksman, "Social Differentiation in the German
Concentration Camps," in Joshua A. Fishman, ed., Studies
in Modern Jewish History (1972)
Yisrael Gutman and Avital Saf, eds., The Nazi Concentration
Camps (1984)
Eugene Heimler, Concentration Camp (1979)
Eugen Kogon, The Theory and Practice of Hell (1980)
Miklos Nyiszli, Auschwitz: A Doctor's Eyewitness Account (1960)
Miriam Novitch, Sobibor: Martyrdom and Revolt (1980)
Anna Pawelzynska, Values and Violence in Auschwitz (1979)
Falk Pingel, "Resistance and Resignation in Nazi Concentration
Camps," in Gerhard Hirschfeld, ed., The Policies of
Genocide (1986).
Rudolf Vrba and Alan Bestic, I Cannot Forgive (1964)
Leon Weliczker-Wells, Janowska Road (1963)

Nov. 30   DEATH CAMPS IN THE EAST (2): THE SS EMPIRE

*Primo Levi, Survival in Auschwitz

Yitzhak Arad, Belzec, Sobibor, Treblinka: The Operation
    Reinhard Death Camps (1987)
Yisrael Gutman and Avital Saf, eds., The Nazi Concentration
    Camps (1984)
Rudolf Hoss, Commandant of Auschwitz (1959)
Robert Koehl, The Black Corps: The Structure and Power
    Struggles of the SS (1983)
Helmut Krausnick and Martin Broszat, Anatomy of the SS State
    (1968)
Gita Sereny, Into That Darkness (1977)
Albert Speer, Infiltration (1981)

Dec. 7   COUNTING THE VICTIMS: A BALANCE SHEET

*Primo Levi, Survival in Auschwitz

SECOND TERM: REACTIONS

Jan. 4   WHO KNEW WHAT? WHEN? WHERE? HOW?

*David Wyman, The Abandonment of the Jews, Parts 1 and 2.

Yehuda Bauer, "When Did They Know?" Midstream, April 1968,
    51-8.
Sarah Gordon, Hitler, Germans and the "Jewish Question" (1984)
Alex Grobman, "What Did They Know? The American Jewish
    Press and the Holocaust," American Jewish History,
    LXVIII 1979), 327-52.
Ian Kershaw, Popular Opinion and Political Dissent in the Third
    Reich (1983)
    _____, "The Persecution of the Jews and German Popular
    Opinion in the Third Reich," Leo Baeck Institute Year
    Book, XXVI (1981), 261-89.

Otto Dov Kulka, "'Public Opinion' in Nazi Germany and the
'Jewish Question'," Jerusalem Quarterly, 25 (1982), 121-44,
and 26 (1983), 34-45.
Walter Laqueur, "Hitler's Holocaust: Who Knew What, When,
Where?" Encounter, July 1980, 6-25.
_____, The Terrible Secret (1980)
_____, "Jewish Denial and the Holocaust,"
Commentary, December 1979, 44-55.
Deborah Lipstadt, Beyond Belief: The American Press and the
Coming of the Holocaust, 1933-1945 (1986)
Lawrence Stokes, "The German People and the Destruction of
the European Jews," Central European History, 6 (1973),
167-91.
Hans-Heinrich Wilhelm, "The Holocaust in National Socialist
Rhetoric and Writings -- Some Evidence against the
Thesis that before 1945 Nothing Was Known About the
'Final Solution'," Yad Vashem Studies, XVI (1984), 95-127.

Jan. 11   ALLIED REFUGEE POLICY, 1933-43

*David Wyman, The Abandonment of the Jews, Part 3.

Haim Avni, Spain, The Jews, and Franco (1982)
Irving Abella and Harold Troper, None is Too Many: Canada and
the Jews of Europe (1982)
Henry Feingold, The Politics of Rescue (1970)
Saul Friedman, No Haven for the Oppressed (1973)
Martin Gilbert, Auschwitz and the Allies (1981)
Michael Marrus, The Unwanted: European Refugees in the
Twentieth Century (1985)
Monty Penkower, The Jews Were Expendable: Free World
Diplomacy and the Holocaust (1983)
Bernard Wasserstein, Britain and the Jews of Europe, 1939-1945
(1979)

Jan. 18   OCCUPIED STATES IN THE WEST: HOLLAND AND DENMARK

Louis De Jong, "Jews and non-Jews in Occupied Holland," in Max
        Beloff, ed., On the Track of Tyranny (1960), 345-81.
Harold Flender, Rescue in Denmark (1963)
Michael Marrus and Robert Paxton, "The Nazis and the Jews in
        Occupied Western Europe," Journal of Modern History, 54
        (1982), 687-714.
Jacob Presser, The Destruction of the Dutch Jews (1969)
B.A. Sijes, "Several Observations Concerning the Postion of the
        Jews in Occupied Holland during World War II," in Yisrael
        Gutman and Efraim Zuroff, eds., Rescue Attempts during
        the Holocaust (1977)
Hugo Valentin, "Rescue and Relief Activities on Behalf of Jewish
        Victims of Nazism in Scandinavia," YIVO Annual of Jewish
        Social Science, VIII (1953), 224-51.
Leni Yahil, "Methods of Persecution: A Comparison of the 'Final
        Solution' in Holland and Denmark." Scripta Hierosolymita,
        23 (1972), 279-300.
_____, The Rescue of Danish Jewry (1969)

Jan. 25   SATELLITES OF THE REICH (1): VICHY FRANCE

Jacques Adler, The Jews of Paris and the Final Solution (1987)
Richard Cohen, The Burden of Conscience: French Jewry's
        Response to the Holocaust (1987)
_____, "The Jewish Community of France in the Face of
        Vichy-German Persecution, 1940-1944," in Frances Malino
        and Bernard Wasserstein, eds., The Jews in Modern
        France (1985)
_____, "A Jewish Leader in Vichy France, 1940-1943: The
        Diary of Raymond-Raoul Lambert." Jewish Social Studies,
        43 (1981), 291-310.
Michael Marrus and Robert Paxton, Vichy France and the Jews
        (1981)
Leni Yahil, "The Jewish Leadership of France," in Yisrael
        Gutman and Cynthia Haft, eds., Patterns of Jewish
        Leadership during the Holocaust (1979)

Feb. 1   HALF-HEARTED ALLIES: ITALY AND BULGARIA

Daniel Carpi. "The Catholic Church and Italian Jewry under the
    Fascists." Yad Vashem Studies, IV (1960), 43-54.
_____. "The Rescue of Jews in the Italian Zone of Occupied
    Croatia," in Yisrael Gutman and Cynthia Haft, eds.,
    Patterns of Jewish Leadership during the Holocaust (1979)
Frederick Chary, The Bulgarian Jews and the Final Solution,
    1940-1944 (1972)
Michael Marrus and Robert Paxton, Vichy France and the Jews
    (1981)
Meir Michaelis, Mussolini and the Jews (1978)
Nissan Oren, "The Bulgarian Exception: a Reassessment of the
    Salvation of the Jewish Community," Yad Vashem Studies,
    VII (1968), 83-106.
Vicki Tamir, Bulgaria and Her Jews (1979)
Susan Zuccotti, The Italians and the Holocaust: Persecution,
    Rescue, Survival (1987)

Feb. 8   SATELLITES (2): RUMANIA AND HUNGARY

Randolf Braham, The Politics of Genocide: the Holocaust in
    Hungary (2 vols., 1981)
_____. "The Jewish Question in German-Hungarian
    Relations during the Kallay Era," Jewish Social Studies,
    XXXIX (1977), 183-208.
Mario Fenyo, Hitler, Horthy, and Hungary: German-Hungarian
    Relations, 1941-44 (1972)
Andrew Handler, ed., The Holocaust in Hungary (1972)
Nicholas Nagy-Talavera, The Green Shirts and the Others (1970)

Feb. 15   READING WEEK

Feb. 22   THE CHURCHES AND THE HOLOCAUST

Owen Chadwick, "Weizsacker, the Vatican, and the Jews of
     Rome," Journal of Ecclesiastical History, 28 (1977), 179-99.
     _____, Britain and the Vatican during the Second
     World War (1987)
John Conway, "Records and Documents of the Holy See Relating
     to the Second World War," Yad Vashem Studies, XV
     (1983), 327-45.
Helen Fein, Accounting for Genocide (1979)
Saul Friedlander, Pius XII and the Third Reich (1966)
Judah Graubart," The Vatican and the Jews: Cynicism and
     Indifference," Judaism, 24 (Spring 1975), 168-80.
Leonidas Hill, "History and Rolf Hochhuth's The Deputy," in R.G.
     Collins, ed., From and Ancient to a Modern Theatre (1972),
     145-57.
John Morley, Vatican Diplomacy and the Jews during the
     Holocaust (1980)
Anthony Rhodes, The Vatican in the Age of the Dictators,
     1922-1945 (1973)

Feb. 29   THE POLITICS OF RESCUE (1): BARGAINING WITH THE NAZIS

*David Wyman, The Abandonment of the Jews, 209-87.

Yehuda Bauer, The Jewish Emergence from Powerlessness
     (1979)
     _____, The Holocaust in Historical Perspective (1978)
     _____, American Jewry and the Holocaust (1981)
     _____, "Jewish Foreign Policy during the Holocaust,"
     Midstream, December 11984, 22-5.
Randolf Braham, The Politics of Genocide: the Holocaust in
     Hungary (2 vols., 1981)
John Conway, "Between Apprehension and Indifference: Allied
     Attitudes to the Destruction of Hungarian Jewry," Weiner
     Library Bulletin, XXVII (1973/4), 37-48.
Amos Elon, Timetable (1980)

Yisrael Gutman and Efraim Zuroff, eds., Rescue Attempts during
the Holocaust (1977)
Alex Weissberg, Desperate Mission: Joel Brand's Story (1958)

Mar. 7   THE POLITICS OF RESCUE (2): MILITARY PROPOSALS

*Dino Brugioni and Robert Poirer, "The Holocaust Revisited,"
U.S. Central Intelligence Agency Report (1979) (on short
term loan)
*David Wyman, The Abandonment of the Jews, 288-307,
Conclusion.

Martin Gilbert, Auschwitz and the Allies (1981)
_____, "The Question of Bombing Auschwitz," in Yisrael
Gutman and Avital Saf, eds., The Nazi Concentration
Camps (1974)
Bernard Wasserstein, Britain and the Jews of Europe (1979)

Mar. 14   REACHING JUDGEMENT AT NUREMBERG

Tom Bauer, The Pledge Betrayed: America and Britain and the
Denazification of Postwar Germany (1982)
Joseph Borkin, The Crime and Punishment of I.G. Farben (1979)
Robert Conot, Justice at Nuremberg (1983)
Benjamin Ferencz, Less Than Slaves: Jewish Forced Labor and
the Quest for Compensation (1979)
Werner Maser, Nuremberg: A Nation on Trial (1979)
Bradley Smith, Reaching Judgement at Nuremberg (1981)

Mar. 21   SURVIVORS: THE END OF THE HOLOCAUST

Robert Abzug, Inside the Vicious Heart (1985)
Yehuda Bauer, "The Death Marches, Modern Judaism, 3 (1983), 1-
21.

_____, "Jewish Survivors in DP Camps and Sh'erith
   Hapletah." in Yisrael Gutman and Avital Saf. eds., The
   Nazi Concentration Camps (1984)
Leonard Dinnerstein, America and the Survivors of the
   Holocaust (1982)
Michael Marrus, The Unwanted: European Refugees in the
   Twentieth Century (1985)
Michael Selzer, Deliverance Day: The Last Hours at Dachau
   (1978)

Mar. 28 SUMMARY AND CONCLUSIONS

HISTORY 385:   HISTORY OF ZIONISM AND THE STATE OF ISRAEL

PROFESSOR ENDELMAN

WINTER 1987

Students should purchase the following books:

Walter Laqueur, A History of Zionism
Shlomo Avineri, The Making of Modern Zionism: The Intellectual
  Origins of the Jewish State
Stephen M. Poppel, Zionism in Germany, 1897-1933: The Shaping
  of a National Identity
Amos Elon, The Israelis: Founders and Sons

Lectures

Jan   7   Introduction

      9   Jewish Settlement in the Land of Israel before Zionism

     12   Zion in Pre-Modern Jewish Thought

     14   The Abandonment of Jewish Nationality in the West:
          Emancipation

             Reading: Laqueur, chap. 1; Avineri, intro.

     16   The Abandonment of Jewish Nationality in the West:
          Acculturation and Integration

     19   The Abandonment of Jewish Nationality in the West:
          Reform Judaism

     21   The Jewish Question in Western Europe

     23   The Jewish Question in Eastern Europe

     26   Jewish Responses to Antisemitism

     28   Precursors and Pioneers of the Nationalist Revival

             Reading: Avineri, chaps. 1-7

     30   Hebrew Renaissance

             Reading: Avineri, chap. 8

Feb   2   Hibbat Tziyyon

             Reading: Laqueur, chap. 2

4   The Strange Case of Theodor Herzl

    Reading: Laqueur, chap. 3; Avineri, chap. 9

6   Zionist Congresses and Diplomatic Activity

    Reading: Avineri, chap. 10

9   From the Death of Herzl to the First World War

    Reading: Laqueur, chap. 4

11 Midterm Examination

13 Ideological Currents and Parties within Zionism:
    Labor Zionism

    Reading: Avineri, chaps. 12-14, 17

16 Ideological Currents and Parties within Zionism:
    Cultural/Spiritual Zionism

    Reading: Avineri, chap. 11

18 Ideological Currents and Parties within Zionism:
    Religious Zionism

    Reading: Avineri, chap. 16

20 Competing Ideologies: Assimilationism

    Reading: Laqueur, chap. 8

Mar 2   Competing Ideologies: Socialism

4   Competing Ideologies: Diaspora Nationalism,
    Territorialism, Ultra-Orthodoxy

6   Zionism in the Diaspora: Germany

    Reading: Poppel

9   Zionism in the Diaspora: Poland

11 Zionism in the Diaspora: England

13 Zionism in the Diaspora: United States

    take-home midterm examinations to be distributed

16 The Growth of the New Yishuv

    take-home midterm examinations due at start of class

    Reading: Laqueur, chap. 6

18   Halutziyyut

       Reading: Elon, chaps. 1-7

20   The Seeds of Arab-Jewish Confrontation

       Reading: Laqueur, chap. 5

23   The Establishment of the British Mandate

25   Arab-Jewish Relations under the Mandate

27   The Weizmann Era

       Reading: Laqueur, chap. 9

30   Perfidious Albion

Apr 1   Jabotinsky and Revisionism

       Reading: Laqueur, chap. 7; Avineri, chap. 15

   3   The Impact of World War II and the Holocaust

       Reading: Laqueur, chap. 10

   6   Videotape: Pillar of Fire, episode 15,
                  "The Hundred Thousand"

   8   The Struggle for the State

       Reading: Laqueur, chap. 11 and conclusion

10   Ingathering and Absorption

13   Eastern and Western Jews

15   No Class (Passover)

17   Religious and Secular Jews

20   The Search for Peace and Security

       Reading: Elon, chaps. 8-12

22   Israel and Diaspora Jewry

       Reading: Avineri, epilogue

Final Examination: Monday, April 27, 1:30-3:30

```
Office Hours:        3625 Haven Hall

                     Mondays    1-2
                     Fridays    11-12

                     Phone 764-7308
```

The final grade for the course will be calculated as follows:

1st examination	25%
2nd examination (take-home)	30%
final examination	45%

PRINCETON UNIVERSITY

PROGRAM IN SCIENCE IN HUMAN AFFAIRS

SHA 294: Disease and Doctors in the Modern West

Professor Geison

Organization: Papers, Examinations, Grades

This course follows the standard format of two lectures and one precept each
week. There will be a final examination, but no midterm. In lieu of a midterm, each student will write an essay on a topic that falls within the pur-
view of the course. This essay, 15-25 double-spaced typed pages in length,
is due Friday, December 11th. Further instructions on the essay will be
distributed later. There will be no class meetings or additional assignments
during the reading period.

The final grade will be determined roughly as follows: final exam (40%),
essay (40%), precept (20%).

Readings

All readings below are required and, for the sake of precept discussion,
should be done in advance of the associated precept meetings. I will be
glad to suggest additional sources in connection with the required essay
and for those who may have special interest in particular topics.

The following works, which form part of the weekly reading assignments, are
required for purchase:

1.   Source Book of Medical History, compiled with notes by Logan Clendenning
        (Dover paperback, 1942).

2.   William H. McNeill, Plagues and Peoples (Doubleday paperback, 1976).

3.   Richard H. Shryock, The Development of Modern Medicine (Wisconsin
        paperback, 1979).

4.   Thomas McKeown, The Role of Medicine: Dream, Mirage, or Nemesis?
        (Princeton paperback, 1979).

LECTURE TOPICS AND READINGS BY WEEK

I.   Health, Doctors, and the History of Medicine

        Owsei Temkin, "The Meaning of Medicine in Historical Perspective,"
            in The Double Face of Janus and Other Essays in the History of
            Medicine (Baltimore, 1977), pp. 41-49.   R131.T4

        Owsei Temkin, "Health and Disease," in The Double Face of Janus,
            pp. 419-440. R131.T4

        McNeill, Plagues and Peoples, Chapters 1 and 2 (pp. 15-76).

II.   The Medical World of Antiquity and the Middle Ages

McNeill, Plagues and Peoples, Chapter 3 (pp. 77-148).

Henry Sigerist, The Great Doctors, Chapters 2, 8-9.   8954.857.4

Clendenning, Source Book of Medical History, pp. 1-94 (skim).

III.   The Renaissance Upheaval in Medical Thought and Practice

McNeill, Plagues and Peoples, Chapters 4 and 5 (pp. 149-234).

Sigerist, Great Doctors, Chapters 12-15.

Clendenning, Source Book of Medical History, pp. 95-141.

IV.   Medicine and the Scientific Revolution of the 17th Century

E.H. Ackerknecht, A Short History of Medicine, pp. 113-129. R131.A18.1968

Clendenning, Source Book of Medical History, pp. 142-169, 221-237.

Keith Thomas, Religion and the Decline of Magic (Charles Scribners' paperback, 1971), pp. 3-21, 177-211.   5511.902

Alfred White Franklin, "Clinical Medicine," in Medicine in Seventeenth Century England, ed. A.G. Debus (UCLA, 1974), pp. 113-145. R486.M43

V.   The Transition to Modernity: Health, Medicine, and Mortality in the 18th Century

Shryock, Development of Modern Medicine, pp. 57-108.

Clendenning, Source Book of Medical History, pp. 194-208, 204-253, 291-305, 441-468.

VI.   Life and Death in the 19th Century: Disease Patterns, Public Health, and Vital Statistics, 1800-1880

McNeill, Plagues and Peoples, Chapter 6 (pp. 235-291).

Shryock, Development of Modern Medicine, Chapter 12 (pp. 211-247).

Edwin Chadwick, Report on the Sanitary Condition of the Labouring Population of Great Britain (1842), ed. M.W. Flinn, pp. 18-26, 58-66, 75-79, 421-425.   89417.406.17.2

Robert Tomes, "Why We Get Sick (1856)," in Medical America in the Nineteenth Century: Readings from the Literature, ed. G.H. Brieger (Baltimore, 1972), pp. 256-262.   R151.B75

VII.   From Urine Flasks to Stethoscopes: Hospitals, Instruments, and the
       Social Role of Healers, 1800-1880

       Shryock, <u>Development of Modern Medicine</u>, Chapter 9 (pp. 151-169).

       Stanley Reiser, <u>Medicine and the Reign of Technology</u>, (London, 1978),
       pp. 23-44.   R145.R44

       Clendenning, <u>Source Book of Medical History</u>, pp. 306-330, 502-509,
       530-539, 572-587.

VIII. Quackery, Sects and Science, or Varieties of Response to Therapeutic
       Uncertainty: Medical Thought and Practice, 1800-1880

       Shryock, <u>Development of Modern Medicine</u>, Chapter 13 (pp. 248-272).

       Elisha Bartlett, "An Inquiry into the Degree of Certainty in Medicine;
       and into the Nature and Extent of Its Power Over Disease (1848),"
       in <u>Medical America in the Nineteenth Century</u>, ed. G.H. Brieger,
       pp. 98-106.   R151.B75

       Edwin L. Godkin, "Orthopathy and Heteropathy (1867)," in <u>ibid</u>., pp.
       75-83.   R151.B75

       Rudolf Virchow, "Scientific Medicine and Therapeutic Standpoints
       (1849)," in <u>Disease, Life and Man</u>, pp. 40-66.   8957.938

       Claude Bernard, <u>Introduction to the Study of Experimental Medicine</u>
       (1865), pp. 190-226.   8957.171

IX.   From Infectious to Chronic Diseases: Disease Patterns and Vital
       Statistics since 1880

       McKeown, <u>The Role of Medicine</u>, Chapters 3-6 (pp. 29-78) and 8 (pp.
       91-116).

       Judith W. Leavitt and Ronald L. Numbers, "Sickness and Health in
       America: An Overview," in <u>Sickness and Health in America: Readings
       in the History of Medicine and Public Health</u> (Wisconsin, 1978), pp.
       3-10.

       Shryock, <u>Development of Modern Medicine</u>, Chapter 15 (pp. 304-335).

X.   Specialization, Professionalization and Medical Education in the
       Brave New Medical World: The Organization and Social Role of
       Healers since 1880

       Shryock, <u>Development of Modern Medicine</u>, Chapters 16 (pp. 336-355)
       and 18-19 (pp. 381-430).

       Clendenning, <u>Source Book of Medical History</u>, pp. 634-675.

       Robert Hudson, "Abraham Flexner in Perspective: American Medical

Education, 1865-1910," Bulletin of the History of Medicine, 46 (1972), 545-561.

Abraham Flexner, Medical Education in the United States and Canada (1910), pp. 3-51, 156-166, 178-181.   8957.351.3

XI.   The Bacteriological Revolution and the Drama of Specific Cures:
       Medical Thought and Practice since 1880

Shryock, Development of Modern Medicine, pp. 273-303.

Clendenning, Source Book of Medical History, pp. 378-406, 603-621.

Hubert A. Lechevalier and Morris Solotorovsky, Three Centuries of Microbiology (Dover paperback, 1974), pp. 210-259, 437-492. 8954.998

Leo Zimmerman and Ilza Veith, Great Ideas in the History of Surgery (Dover paperback, 1967), pp. 461-518.   QR21. L4.1974

XII.   The Current Debate: Shifting Attitudes toward Health, Disease and
        Medicine

Shryock, The Development of Modern Medicine, pp. 432-457.

McKeown, The Role of Medicine, skim previously unassigned chapters.

Reiser, Medicine and the Reign of Technology, pp. 158-195. R145.R44

Walsh McDermott et al., "Health Care Experiment at Many Farms," Science 175 (1972), 23-31.   8001.863

Nick Eberstadt, "The Health Crisis in the USSR," New York Review of Books, February 19, 1981, pp. 23-31.

Highly recommended -- and not only because of its wonderfully apt title -- is Doing Better and Feeling Worse: Health in the United States, ed. John Knowles, Winter 1977 issue of Daedalus.

Also highly recommended is Susan Sontag, Illness as Metaphor.

SICKNESS AND HEALTH IN SOCIETY, 1492 TO THE PRESENT

Martin S. Pernick

Scope of the Course: Doctors, Disease, and Society

Medical history includes more than the history of doctors and their discoveries. It includes the history of sickness and health as well. From devastating epidemics of cholera and yellow fever, to the quiet suffering of malnutrition, diseases have deeply marked the evolution of society. In turn, social changes have dramatically altered the patterns of illness and health.

This course will study several different historical periods, exploring such issues as: the effect of personal habits, environmental conditions, and medical discoveries on human health; the changing health problems of specific social groups including Indians, women, blacks, children, immigrants, and the poor; the roles of ethics, economics, and politics in medical decisions; the spread and impact of medical discoveries; and the changing organization and power of the medical professions.

TOPIC OUTLINE

I.   1492-1790 The Old World and the New: Disease, Trade, and Conquest

"Childhood" Diseases and the Conquest of the Americas
New Diseases in Europe?: Plague, Syphilis
The Social Lessons of Medical History, and the Danger of Biodeterminism
Life and Death in Colonial America
Smallpox Inoculation: Medicine, Religion, and Responsibility
The Political Meaning of Health in the Age of Enlightenment

II.   1830-1880 Health, Society, and the Individual

Cholera: The Urban Revolution and the Environment of Disease
Health as an Individual Reform / Health as a Social Reform
Environmental Medicine: The Hospital and the Asylum
Changing Definitions of Disease
Women as Patients / Women as Doctors
Medicine and Slavery

III. 1880-1920 The Golden Age of Bacteria

From Big Truths to More Specific Truths: Germs, Genes, Hormones, Toxins,
      Vitamins and Drugs
Scientific Specificity and Medical Specialization
Health and the New Immigrant
Occupational Health in the New Factory
Science and Sex: VD, The Medicalization of Motherhood
Changing Health Behavior: Education, Persuasion, or Legislation
What Caused the Modern Rise in Life Expectancy
The Flu Epidemic of 1918

IV.   1930-1986 Decisions

Setting Priorities in Health Care: The March of Dimes and Polio
From Genetics to Genocide?: World Medicine and the Nazi Holocaust
Who Decides?: The Government Role in Medical Decisions
Who is Responsible for Health: Cancer, AIDS

TOPIC I: THE OLD WORLD AND THE NEW: DISEASE, TRADE AND CONQUEST 1492-1790

Read for 9/9 and 9/11

"Childhood" Diseases and the Conquest of the Americas
Part I: The Initial Epidemics

Alfred Crosby, The Columbian Exchange: Biological and Cultural Consequences
of 1492 (1972), pp. 35-62.

James P. Ronda, "'We Are Well as We Are': An Indian Critique of 17th Century
Christian Missions," William and Mary Quarterly (1977), pp. 66-82.

Part II: After 1492: The Long-Term Destruction

Virginia Allen, "The White Man's Road: Physical and Psychological Impact of
Relocation on the Southern Plains Indians," Journal of History of
Medicine and Allied Sciences (1975), pp. 148-63.

Sherburne Cook, "The Significance of Disease in the Extinction of the New
England Indians," Human Biology (1973), pp. 485-508.

Read for 9/16

Part I Syphilis: A Native American Disease in Europe?

Alfred Crosby, The Columbian Exchange, pp. 122-60.

Part II The Social Lessons of Medical History and the Danger of
Biodeterminism

P.M. Ashburn, The Ranks of Death (1937), epilogue pp. 210-12.

Read for 9/18

Death in the Colonies: "Our" View Versus "Their" View

Anne Bradstreet, Works, pp. 235-42.

Maris Vinovskis, "Angel's Heads and Weeping Willows: Death in Early
America," in The American Family in Social-Historical Perspective, ed. by
Michael Gordon (2nd ed 1978), pp. 546-63.

Read for 9/23

Part I Smallpox Inoculation: Medicine, Religion, and Responsibility

Increase Mather, William Douglass, Two documents on inoculation (1721, 1722).

John Blake, "The Inoculation Controversy in Boston," (1952), in Leavitt and
Numbers, Sickness and Health in America, pp. 347-55.

Part II The Political Meaning of Health in the Age of Enlightenment

George Rosen, "Political Order and Human Health in Jeffersonian Thought,"
Bulletin of the History of Medicine (1952), pp. 32-44.

TOPIC II: HEALTH, SOCIAL CHANGE, AND THE INDIVIDUAL, 1830-1880

Read for 9/25 and 9/30

Cholera, the Urban Revolution, and Social Medicine

Charles Rosenberg, The Cholera Years (1962), chaps. 1-6, 8-11.

Read for 9/30 (continued)

Personal vs. Public Responsibility?
Conflicting 19th Century Views on Who to Blame for Causing Sickness

"19th Century Statistics on Cholera and Immigration."

Lemuel Shattuck, Report of the Sanitary Commission of Massachusetts (1850), pp. 200-212, 266-272.

J.B.F. Walker, M.D., "Is It Wicked to be Sick?" The Water-Cure Journal (1861).

Read for 10/2

From Environmental Causes to Environmental Cures

Martin S. Pernick, A Calculus of Suffering (1985), pp. 9-22.

Charles Rosenberg, "Florence Nightingale on Contagion: The Hospital as Moral Universe," in Healing and History (1979), pp. 116-36.

Christopher Lasch, "The Origins of the Asylum," in The World of Nations (1974), pp. 3-17.

Read for 10/7

Part I: What is a Disease?

H. Tristram Engelhardt, "The Disease of Masturbation: Values and the Concept of Disease," in Leavitt and Numbers, Sickness and Health in America, pp. 13-21.

Martin S. Pernick, "Back from the Grave: Recurring Controversies Over Defining and Diagnosing Death in History," in When Are You Dead?: Whole Brain and Neocortical Definitions of Death, Philosophy and Medicine Series (Boston: D. Reidel, in press for 1987), edited by Richard Zaner and Charles E. Scott. Esp. pp. 16-22, 29-39.

Part II: Rival Medical Sects: Anti-monopoly or Anti-expertise?

Martin S. Pernick, A Calculus of Suffering, pp. 22-31.

Read for 10/9

Part I: Women as Patients

Charles Rosenberg and Carroll Smith-Rosenberg, "The Female Animal: Medical and Biological Views of Women," in No Other Gods (1973), pp. 54-70.

Part II: Women as Doctors

"Female Physicians," from <u>Philadelphia Bulletin</u> (1859).

Regina Markell Morantz, "The Connecting Link: The Case for the Woman Doctor
    in 19th Century America," in Leavitt and Numbers, <u>Sickness and Health in
    America</u>, pp. 161-172.

<u>Read for 10/14</u>

Medicine, Slavery, and Race

Todd L. Savitt, "Black Health on the Plantation: Masters, Slaves, and
    Physicians," in Leavitt and Numbers, <u>Sickness and Health in America</u>,
    pp. 313-30.

TOPIC III: HEALTH AND SOCIETY IN THE GOLDEN AGE OF SCIENTIFIC SPECIFICITY
1880-1930

Read for 10/21 and 10/23

From Big Truths to Little Truths: Germs and the Specific Cause of Infection

Paul De Kruif, <u>Microbe Hunters</u> (1926), chaps. 3-6.

Charles V. Chapin, "Dirt, Disease and the Health Officer," (1902).

James H. Cassedy, "The Flamboyant Colonel Waring: An Anticontagionist in the
Age of Pasteur and Koch," in Leavitt and Numbers, <u>Sickness and Health
in America</u>, pp. 451-58.

Charles Rosenberg, "Florence Nightingale on Contagion," review from Topic II

Read for 10/28 and 10/30

The Laboratory and the New Medical Profession

Abraham Flexner, <u>Report on Medical Education</u> (1910), pp. 43-59, 143-55, 178-
81.

Ronald Numbers, "The Fall and Rise of the Medical Profession," in Leavitt
and Numbers, <u>Sickness and Health</u>, pp. 185-196.

Virginia G. Drachman, "Female Solidarity and Professional Success: The
Dilemma of Women Doctors in Late 19th Century America," in Leavitt and
Numbers, <u>Sickness and Health</u>, pp. 173-182.

Susan Reverby, "The Search for the Hospital Yardstick: Nursing and the
Rationalization of Hospital Work," in Leavitt and Numbers, <u>Sickness and
Health</u>, pp. 206-216.

Read for 11/4

The "New Immigration" and the "New Public Health"

"Americanization by Bath," <u>The Literary Digest</u> (1913), pp. 280-81.

"The White Man's Burden" and "What Mississippi Has Done," <u>Journal of the
Outdoor Life</u> (1910), pp. 274-75, and (1914), p. 28.

"European Immigration by Country, Selected Years," from US Census.

Judith Leavitt, "Politics and Public Health: Smallpox in Milwaukee 1894-
1895," in Leavitt and Numbers, <u>Sickness and Health</u>, pp. 372-82.

Read for 11/6

Health in the Factory--Factory Methods in Public Health

David Rosner and Gerald Markowitz, "The Early Movement for Occupational
Safety and Health," in Leavitt and Numbers, <u>Sickness and Health</u>, pp. 507-
21.

Livingston Farrand, "Health and Productive Power," (1913), 6 pp.

"Consumptives Cost the Rest of Us $500,000,000 a Year," American City (1912), pp. 26-27.

"Standardization of Health Conservation," Journal of the Outdoor Life (1910), p. 119.

"Child Labor and the Laboratory," Charities (1903), p. 3.

John R. Shillady, "Cooperation of Tuberculosis Agencies with Labor Unions and Factories," Journal of the Outdoor Life (1913), pp. 228-31.

Read for 11/11

Part I: Science and Sex

John C. Burnham, "The Progressive Era Revolution in American Attitudes Towards Sex," Journal of American History (1973), pp. 885-908.

The End of the Road (1919). Film on videotape. Required viewing; schedule of showings at end of this handout.

Part II: Professionalism and Motherhood

Frances Kobrin, "The American Midwife Controversy," in Leavitt and Numbers, Sickness and Health, pp. 197-205.

Sarah Comstock, "Mothercraft: A New Profession for Women," Good Housekeeping (1914), selections.

Sheila Rothman, Woman's Proper Place (1978), pp. 97-106, 112-127, 135-153.

Judith Leavitt, "Science Enters the Birthing Room," in Leavitt and Numbers, Sickness and Health, pp. 81-97.

Read for 11/13

Changing Health Habits: Persuasion vs. Legislation

Part I: Persuasion

"The Awakening of Ivan Meyervitz," Fresh Air Magazine (1910), pp. 12-13.

William White, MD, "The Secret of Proper Tuberculosis Education," Journal of the Outdoor Life (1910), p. 41.

Martin S. Pernick, "The Ethics of Preventive Medicine--Thomas Edison's Tuberculosis Films: Mass Media and Health Propaganda," Hastings Center Report (June 1978), pp. 21-27.

Hope (1912) and The Temple of Moloch (1914). Films on videotape. Viewing required, showings listed at end of this handout.

Richard Shryock, "The Historical Significance of the Tuberculosis Movement," in Medicine in America (1966), pp. 13-48.

Part II: Legislation

Carl Scheffel, "Venereal Diseases--Educational vs. Sanitary and Legal Methods to Suppress," Modern Medicine (1921), pp. 248-49.

F. Cauthorn, "Some Thoughts Suggested by the Campaign Against Venereal Diseases," Medical Record of New York (1921), pp. 23-24.

Jacobson v. Massachusetts, 197 U.S. 11 (1905).

Read for 11/18

The Rise of Medical Science and the Rise of Life Expectancy:
What is the Connection?

Paul de Kruif, Microbe Hunters (1926), chap. 12.

Rene Dubos, Mirage of Health (1959), pp. 101-110, 151-165.

"Sickness and Health in America: An Overview," and Gretchen Condran et al., "The Decline in Mortality in Philadelphia from 1870 to 1930: The Role of Municipal Services," both in Leavitt and Numbers, Sickness and Health, pp. 3-10, 422-436.

Daphne Roe, "The Sharecropper's Plague," Natural History, pp. 52-54, 63.

Read for 11/20

1918: Flu, Fear and Force

Stuart Galishoff, "Newark and the Great Influenza Pandemic of 1918," Bulletin of the History of Medicine (1969), pp. 246-58.

The New York Times, selections from October 1918.

Alfred W. Crosby, Epidemic and Peace 1918 (1976), pp. 22-24, 203-207.

Read for 11/25

Health in Hard Times: Polio and Priorities

Part I: Setting Priorities Among Social Problems

Walter C. Clarke, MD, "Health Protection in Hard Times," script broadcast July 22, 1933, WEVD Radio New York.

Documents on Polio and Panic. A collection including the following:

    1920 Metropolitan Life Insurance, "Infantile Paralysis is Dangerous"
    1945 National Foundation-March of Dimes Fundraising Letter
    1946 "The Need is for More," New York World-Telegram
    1946 "Panic or Reason in Polio?" American Journal of Public Health
    1954 "Who Gets Your Charity Dollars?" Saturday Evening Post

Leonard Kriegel, The Long Walk Home, pp. 55-59. (Note-this is the first of two assigned selections from this book for today.)

Part II: Setting Priorities Among Individual Patients

John R. Paul, History of Poliomyelitis, pp. 324-34, 338-45, 308-312.

Leonard C. Hawkins, The Man in the Iron Lung (1956), pp. 13-15, 103-14.

Leonard Kriegel, The Long Walk Home, pp. 19-27. (Note-this is the second of two assigned selections from this book for today.)

Read for 12/2

From Genetics to Genocide?: The Medical Role in the Nazi Holocaust

Part I: Eugenics and Racism in World Medicine, 1880-1930

Mark Haller, Eugenics (1963), pp. 3-7.

Kenneth Ludmerer, Genetics and American Society (1971), chap. 5.

Part II: Medicine and Murder, 1933-45

Lucy Dawidowicz, The War Against the Jews (1975), chap. 7.

Part III: The Changing "Lessons" of History, 1946-1986

Leo Alexander, "Medical Science Under Dictatorship," New England Journal of Medicine 241 (July 14, 1949).

"Biomedical Ethics and the Shadow of Nazism: A Conference," Hastings Center Report (August 1976) supplement pp. 1-19.

"Health Professionals and Human Rights," Amnesty Action, Amnesty International, Fall 1985, p. 4.

<u>Read for 12/4</u>

Who Decides?: The Federal Government Role in Health Decisions

Stephen Strickland, <u>Politics, Science, and Dread Disease</u> (1972), pp. ix-xi, 233-59.

Ronald L. Numbers, "The Third Party: Health Insurance in America," in Leavitt and Numbers, <u>Sickness and Health</u>, pp. 233-45.

<u>Read for 12/9</u>

Who is Responsible for Health?: Cancer, AIDS, and the Continuing Debate

John Knowles, "The Responsibility of the Individual," in <u>Doing Better and Feeling Worse</u> (1977)

Samuel Epstein and Joel Swartz, "Fallacies of Lifestyle Cancer Theories," <u>Nature</u> (January 15, 1981), pp. 127-130.

Richard F. Spark, "Legislating Against Cancer," <u>The New Republic</u> (June 3, 1978), pp. 16-19.

Allan Brandt, <u>No Magic Bullet: A Social History of Venereal Disease in the United States Since 1880</u> (1985), pp. 179-185.

HEALTH AND DISEASE IN THE AGE OF VICTORIA, 1830-1900

Martin S. Pernick

The Victorian Era began with a devastating cholera epidemic, and ended with the revolutionary discoveries that shaped modern medicine. This course will examine the history of health and disease in Britain and the United States during this age of unprecedented medical and social change. Topics will include: the health effects of industrialization, immigration, urban growth, feminism, and colonialism; the influence of health and medicine on society, the arts, and politics; the growth of the organized healing professions; natural healing; hospitals and mental asylums; aging; sexuality; anesthesia; antisepsis; and evolution.

TOPIC OUTLINE

I   Victorian Health and Disease: An Overview

        Daily Life and Death
        Epidemics: Cholera
        Reformers: Public Health and Personal Hygiene

II   Treatments and Institutions

        The Role of Medication
        Environmental-Moral Medicine, Part I: Hospitals
        Environmental-Moral Medicine, Part II: Insane Asylums
        The Organization of a Profession

III   Patients and Diseases

        Definitions and Values: When Are You Sick, Old, Dead?
        Women's Diseases / Women Healers
        Disease, Race, Slavery, and Empire
        TB and Romanticism / TB and the Rise in Life Expectancy

IV   Innovations

        Anesthesia and Pain
        Evolution and Medicine
        Antisepsis, Germs, Specificity and Reductionism

TOPIC I: VICTORIAN HEALTH AND DISEASE: AN OVERVIEW

Read for January 20

DAILY LIFE AND DEATH

George Rosen, "Disease, Debility, and Death," in H.J. Dyos and Michael Wolff, eds., The Victorian City (1973) II, 625-667. (A1, UGLI)

F.B. Smith, The People's Health (1979), pp. 65-135, 195-223. (UGLI)
--OR--
Anthony Wohl, Endangered Lives (1983), pp. 10-79, 257-84. (UGLI)

Optional Background Reading

R.K. Webb, Modern England (UGLI)
Raymond Williams, Culture and Society 1780-1950 (UGLI)
Asa Briggs, The Age of Improvement

Read for 1/27

EPIDEMIC CHOLERA

R.J. Morris, Cholera 1832 (1976), esp. chaps. 1, 5-9; skim rest. (UGLI)

Individual Readings for 1/26

Charles Rosenberg, The Cholera Years: The United States in 1832, 1849, and 1866 (1962).
Michael Durey, The Return of the Plague (1979). Another view of Britain in 1832.
Margaret Pelling, Cholera, Fever, and English Medicine (1978). Physician's theories and treatments.
Geoffrey Bilson, A Darkened House: Cholera in 19th Century Canada (1980).

Read for 2/3

PUBLIC HEALTH AND PERSONAL HYGIENE REFORMERS
Part I: The Public Health Movement

Richard H. Shryock, "Medicine and the Public Health Movement," in The Development of Modern Medicine (1936), pp. 211-240. (A2, UGLI)

Edwin Chadwick, Report on the Sanitary Condition of the Labouring Population of Great Britain (1842), pp. 422-425. (A1, UGLI)

John M. Eyler, Victorian Social Medicine: The Ideas and Methods of William Farr (1979), pp. 1-36, 97-108, 123-149. (A2, UGLI)

Part II: The Personal Hygiene Movement

James C. Whorton, "Tempest in a Flesh-Pot: Formulation of a Physiological Rationale for Vegetarianism," reprinted from Journal of History of Medicine and Allied Sciences (1977) pp. 115-39. (A1)

J.B.F. Walker, "Is It Wicked to be Sick?" The Water-Cure Journal (1861).

Individual Readings for 2/2

1. The Politics of Public Health in Britain

Anthony Wohl, Endangered Lives (1983), pp. 142-204.   (UGLI)
Mark Brayshay and Vivien Pointon,   "Local Politics and Public Health in Mid-
19th Century Plymouth," Medical History 27 (1983), 162-78.

Steven J. Novak, "Professionalism and Bureaucracy: English Doctors and the
Victorian Public Health Administration," Journal of Social History
(Summer 1973).
Roy MacLeod,   "Law, Medicine, and Public Opinion: The Resistance to
Compulsory Health Legislation 1870-1907," Public Law (Summer, Autumn
1967), pp. 107-28, 189-211.

2. The Politics of Public Health in America

Barbara G. Rosenkrantz, Public Health and the State (1972), chaps. 1-3.   On
the first US state health board, in Massachusetts.
James Mohr, The Radical Republicans and Reform in New York During
Reconstruction (1973), pp. 1-115.   On the first US metropolitan health
board, in New York City.
Gert Brieger, "Sanitary Reform in New York City: Stephen Smith and the
Passage of the Metropolitan Health Bill," in Leavitt and Numbers,
Sickness and Health in America (1985), pp. 399-413.   (B, UGLI)

[Lemuel Shattuck], Report of the Sanitary Commission of Massachusetts (1850).
The "American Chadwick Report."

3. Politics and Responsibility for Occupational Disease

Friedrich Engels, The Condition of the Working Class in England (1842),
chap. 6. Karl Marx's collaborator.
Anthony Wohl, Endangered Lives (1983), pp. 257-84 (assigned for 1/20)
(UGLI)
George Rosen, "Medical Aspects of the Controversy Over Factory Conditions in
New England 1840-1850," Bulletin of the History of Medicine 15 (1944),
483-97.

4. British Public Health Leaders

R.A. Lewis, Edwin Chadwick and the Public Health Movement (1952).
Royston Lambert, Sir John Simon 1816-1904 (1963).

5. Personal Hygiene and Individual Responsibility

James C. Whorton, Crusaders for Fitness (1982), pp. 3-61, 92-131.   (UGLI)
Richard L. Schoenwald, "Training Urban Man," in Dyos and Wolff, The Victorian
City (1973), II, 669-92.   (UGLI). The psychohistory of plumbing.
Bruce Haley, The Healthy Body and Victorian Culture (1978).   Physical
fitness as a symbol in the writings of Victorian intellectuals.

Read for February 10

PART 1: MORAL-ENVIRONMENTAL THERAPY AND THE ROLE OF THE HOSPITAL

Martin S. Pernick, A Calculus of Suffering (1985), pp. 9-22.   (UGLI, B)

W. F. Bynum, "Hospital, Disease, and Community: The London Fever Hospital 1800-1850," in Charles Rosenberg, ed., Healing and History (1979), pp. 97-115.   (A2, UGLI)

Charles Rosenberg, "Florence Nightingale on Contagion: The Hospital as Moral Universe," in Healing and History (1979), pp. 116-36.   (A2, UGLI)

Morris Vogel, "Patrons, Practitioners, and Patients: The Voluntary Hospital in Mid-Victorian Boston," in Leavitt and Numbers, Sickness and Health in America (1985), pp. 287-97.   (UGLI, B)

PART 2: MEDICATIONS AND DRUGS

Charles Rosenberg, "The Therapeutic Revolution: Medicine, Meaning, and Social Change in 19th-Century America," in Leavitt and Numbers, Sickness and Health in America, pp. 39-52.   (UGLI, B)

Individual Readings for 2/9

John Woodward, To Do the Sick No Harm: A Study of the British Voluntary Hospital System to 1875 (1975).
Brian Abel-Smith, The Hospitals 1800-1948: A Study in Social Administration in England and Wales (1964).

F.B. Smith, Florence Nightingale: Reputation and Power (1982) revisionist attack.
John Eyler, "William Farr and Florence Nightingale," in Victorian Social Medicine (1979), pp. 159-89.   (UGLI)

*John Harley Warner, The Therapeutic Perspective: Medical Practice, Knowledge and Identity in America 1820-1885 (1986). Data on the actual drugs used, and on American ambivalence toward European medicine.

Read for February 17

MORAL-ENVIRONMENTAL THERAPY PART II: INSANITY AND THE ASYLUM

David Rothman, Discovery of the Asylum (1971), pp. 3-14, 109-54, 265-95. (UGLI, B)

Gerald Grob, "Rediscovering Asylums," in Morris Vogel and Charles Rosenberg, eds., The Therapeutic Revolution (1979).   (A2, UGLI)

Christopher Lasch, "Origins of the Asylum," in The World of Nations (1974), pp. 3-17.   (A2, UGLI)

Andrew Scull, ed., Madhouses, Mad-Doctors, and Madmen: Social History of Psychiatry in the Victorian Era (1981), chaps. 4-7, 13.   (UGLI, B)

Individual Readings for 2/16

W. Ll. Parry-Jones, <u>The Trade in Lunacy: A Study of Private Madhouses in England in the 18th and 19th Centuries</u> (1972).

*Andrew T. Scull, <u>Museums of Madness: Social Organization of Insanity in 19th Century England</u> (1979). Social construction of madness and asylums.

Mark Finnane, <u>Insanity and the Insane in Post-Famine Ireland</u> (1981).

S.E.D. Shortt, <u>Victorian Lunacy: Richard M. Bucke and the Practice of Late 19th Century Psychiatry</u> (1986). Psychiatry in Canada.

*Michel Foucault, <u>Madness and Civilization</u> (1965). Influential but difficult theoretical approach to Enlightenment roots of Victorian concepts.

*Andrew Scull, ed., <u>Madhouses, Mad-Doctors, Madmen</u>, chaps. 3, 10, 11. (UGLI, B). Scientific concepts, from phrenology to neurology.

Janet Oppenheim, <u>The Other World: Spiritualism and Psychical Research in England, 1850-1914</u> (1985).

Read for March 3

THE ORGANIZATION OF A PROFESSION

M. Jeanne Peterson, <u>The Medical Profession in Mid-Victorian London</u> (1978, chaps. 1, 4, 5.   (UGLI)

Martin S. Pernick, <u>A Calculus of Suffering</u> (1985), pp. 22-31, 241-48. (UGLI, B)

Individual Readings for 3/2

1. British and American Medical Professionalization Compared

*S.E.D. Shortt, "Physicians, Science, and Status: Issues in the Professionalization of Anglo-American Medicine in the 19th Century," <u>Medical History</u> 27 (January 1983), 51-68.

*Matthew Ramsey, "The Politics of Professional Monopoly in 19th-Century Medicine: The French Model and Its Rivals," in Gerald L. Geison, ed., <u>Professions and the French State</u> (1984), pp. 225-305. Despite the title, includes much on Britain and the USA.

Jeffrey L. Berlant, <u>Profession and Monopoly: A Study of Medicine in the United States and Great Britain</u> (1975). Tests sociological theories of Weber and Parsons against historical evidence.

2. Medicine Compared to Other Professions

W.J. Reader, <u>Professional Men: The Rise of the Professional Classes in 19th-Century England</u> (1966). Compares doctors, lawyers, clergy, military.

Margali Sarfatti Larson, <u>The Rise of Professionalism: A Sociological Analysis</u> (1977). More theoretical, historiographical, and critical.

William R. Johnson, "Education and Professional Life Styles: Law and Medicine in the 19th Century," <u>History of Education Quarterly</u> 14 (Summer 1974), 185-207. USA.

3. Medical Professionalization: Single Country Studies

Ivan Waddington, The Medical Profession in the Industrial Revolution (1985). British.

Ian Inkster, "Marginal Men: Aspects of the Social Role of the Medical Community in Sheffield, 1790-1850," in John Woodward and David Richards, eds., Health Care and Popular Medicine in 19th Century England (1977).

Joseph Kett, The Formation of the American Medical Profession: The Role of Institutions 1780-1860 (1968).

Ronald L. Numbers, "The Fall and Rise of the American Medical Profession," in Leavitt and Numbers, Sickness and Health (1985), pp. 185-196. (UGLI, B)

4. Medical Sects and Self-Cure

*W.F. Bynum and Roy Porter, eds., Medical Fringe and Medical Orthodoxy, 1750-1850 (1987). Compares US and Britain; may not yet be available.

Martin Kaufman, Homeopathy in America: The Rise and Fall of a Medical Heresy (1971).

Harris Coulter, Science and Ethics in American Medicine 1800-1914 (1973). A professional historian and practicing homeopath presents his side.

Robin Price, "Hydropathy in England, 1840-1870," Medical History (July 1981), 269-80.

Marshall Scott Legan, "Hydropathy in America," Bulletin of the History of Medicine 45 (1971), 267-80.

*Norman Gevitz, The D.O.s: Osteopathic Medicine in America (1982).

*Guenter Risse, et al., eds., Medicine Without Doctors: Home Health Care in American History (1977).

5. Medical Professionalism in Literature

*George Eliot, Middlemarch (1872). Major novel about a country doctor in early Victorian England.

Alvin Rodin and Jack Key, Medical Case-Book of Dr. Arthur Conan Doyle (1984). The medical career of the creator of Sherlock Holmes. How does the literary image of "professionalism" change from Middlemarch to Holmes?

TOPIC III: PATIENTS AND DISEASES

Read for March 10

DEFINITIONS AND VALUES: WHEN ARE YOU SICK, OLD, DEAD?

H. Tristram Engelhardt, "The Disease of Masturbation: Values and the Concept
   of Disease," in Leavitt and Numbers, Sickness and Health in America, pp.
   13-21.   (UGLI, B)

Carol Haber, Beyond Sixty-Five: The Dilemma of Old Age in America's Past
   (1983), pp. 1-7, 28-108.   (UGLI, B)

Martin S. Pernick, "Back from the Grave: Recurring Controversies Over
   Defining and Diagnosing Death in History," in When Are You Dead?: Whole
   Brain and Neocortical Definitions of Death, Philosophy and Medicine Series
   (Boston: D. Reidel, in press for 1987), edited by Richard Zaner and
   Charles E. Scott. Esp. pp. 16-22, 29-39. (typescript copies at UGLI)

Individual Readings for 3/9

1. Defining Disease

*Sander L. Gilman, Difference and Pathology (1985).
*H. Tristram Engelhardt, "The Concepts of Health and Disease," Evaluation
   and Explanation in the Biomedical Sciences (1984), 125-141.

Vern Bullough and Martha Voght, "Homosexuality and Its Confusion with the
   'Secret Sin' in Pre-Freudian America," Journal of the History of
   Medicine and Allied Sciences (1973), 143-55.
Leila J. Rupp, "'Imagine My Surprise': Women's Relationships in Historical
   Perspective," in Judith Leavitt, Women and Health, pp. 90-102.   (UGLI)

Karl Figlio, "Chlorosis and Chronic Disease in 19th Century Britain: The
   Social Construction of Somatic Illness in a Capitalist Society," Social
   History 3 (1978), 167-97.
Joan Jacobs Brumberg, "Chlorotic Girls 1870-1920: A Historical Perspective on
   Female Adolescence," in Judith Leavitt, Women and Health in America
   (1984), pp. 186-195.   (UGLI)   Two different views of a Victorian
   disease of young girls, with some epidemiological similarities to
   anorexia nervosa today.

Terry Parssinen and Karen Kerner, "Development of the Disease Model of Drug
   Addiction in Britain 1870-1920," Medical History 24 (July 1980), 275-96.

2. Concepts of Death and Practices of Mourning

J.J. Farrell, Inventing the American Way of Death 1830-1920 (1980).
D.E. Stannard, ed., Death in America (1975), chaps by Lewis Saum on
   cemeteries and Ann Douglas on consolation literature.

WOMEN AND VICTORIAN MEDICINE
Part I: Women's Diseases

Charles Rosenberg and Carroll Smith-Rosenberg, "The Female Animal: Medical
and Biological Views of Women," in No Other Gods, pp. 54-70 (1973), or in
Judith Leavitt, Women and Health (1984), pp. 12-26. (A2, UGLI)

Part II: Women Doctors

Regina Markell Morantz-Sanchez, Sympathy and Science (1985), pp. 184-231,
363-67. (A2, UGLI)

"Female Physicians," Philadelphia Bulletin (1859). (A1)

Individual Readings for 3/16

1. Medical Theory and Gender Roles in Society

Peter Gay, The Bourgeois Experience, Volume 1, Education of the Senses
(1984), pp. 71-168, 403-460. Europe and America.
*Charles Rosenberg, "Sexuality, Class and Role in 19th-Century America,"
(1973), in No Other Gods, chap 3. (UGLI)
Elaine Showalter, "Victorian Women and Insanity," in Scull, Madhouses, Mad-
Doctors, and Madmen (1981), chap. 12. (UGLI, B)

Peter Cominos, "Late Victorian Sexual Respectability and the Social System,"
International Review of Social History 8 (1963), 18-48, 216-50. Sex and
economics.
Barbara Ehrenreich and Deirdre English, Complaints and Disorders: The Sexual
Politics of Sickness (1973). Feminist and working-class critique.

2. Medical Theory and Female Sexuality

*Nancy F. Cott, "Passionlessness: An Interpretation of Victorian Sexual
Ideology, 1790-1850," and
Carl N. Degler, "What Ought to Be and What Was: Women's Sexuality in the
19th Century," all in Leavitt, Women and Health, pp. 40-69. (UGLI)

3. Gender Differences in Treatment of Patients

Ann Douglas Wood, "'The Fashionable Diseases': Women's Complaints and their
Treatment in 19th-Century America," and
Regina Markell Morantz, "The Perils of Feminist History," both in Leavitt,
Women and Health, pp. 222-245. (UGLI)
Martin S. Pernick, A Calculus of Suffering: Pain, Professionalism, and
Anesthesia in 19th-Century America (1985), pp. 174-76, 238-39
(UGLI, B)

4. Childbirth

Judith Walzer Leavitt, Brought to Bed: Childbearing in America 1750-1950
(1986), chaps. 1-6, 8.
Judith Schneid Lewis, In the Family Way: Childbearing in the British
Aristocracy 1760-1860 (1986)

Virginia Drachman, "The Loomis Trial: Social Mores and Obstetrics in the Mid-19th Century," in Leavitt, Women and Health, pp. 166-174. Male obstetrics vs. female modesty. (UGLI)

Jean Donnison, Midwives and Medical Men (1977), chaps. 4-9. English debate on licensing midwives.

Jane Donnegan, Women and Men Midwives: Medicine, Morality, and Misogyny (1978), chaps. 5-8. USA.

5. Contraception and Abortion

Angus McLaren, Birth Control in 19th Century England (1978).

Linda Gordon, "Voluntary Motherhood: The Beginnings of Feminist Birth Control Ideas in the United States," in Leavitt, Women and Health, pp. 104-116. (UGLI)

James Reed, From Private Vice to Public Virtue: The Birth Control Movement and American Society (1978), chaps 1-3.

Carl Degler, At Odds: Women and the Family in America (1980), chaps 7-10.

Peter Gay, The Bourgeois Experience Vol 1, Education of the Senses (1984), pp. 226-77. Includes Europe.

Norman E. Himes, Medical History of Contraception (1936). Technical development of early methods.

James Mohr, Abortion in America (1978), pp. 46-119, 147-70, 182-226.

George K. Behlmar, "Deadly Motherhood: Infanticide and Medical Opinion in Mid-Victorian England," Journal of the History of Medicine and Allied Sciences (1979), 403-27.

6. VD and Prostitution

*Judith Walkowitz, Prostitution and Victorian Society (1980). British policy.

Frances Finnegan, Poverty and Prostitution: A Study of Victorian Prostitutes in York (1979). Lives and backgrounds.

David Pivar, Purity Crusade (1973). USA.

7. Sex and Social Reform

Lewis Perry, "Progress Not Pleasure is Our Aim: The Sexual Advice of an Antebellum Radical," Journal of Social History 12 (1979), 354-67.

William Leach, True Love and Perfect Union: The Feminist Reform of Sex and Society (1981), chaps. 1-4, 9, 11, 12, epilogue.

8. Women and Health Reform

Martha Verbrugge, "The Social Meaning of Personal Health: The Ladies' Physiological Institute of Boston," in Susan Reverby and David Rosner, eds., Health Care in America (1979).

Regina Markell Morantz-Sanchez, Sympathy and Science (1985), chap. 2 on women and health reform.

Ronald L. Numbers and Rennie B. Schoepflin, "Ministries of Healing: Mary Baker Eddy, Ellen G. White, and the Religion of Health," and
John B. Blake, "Mary Gove Nichols, Prophetess of Health," both in Leavitt, Women and Health, pp. 359-90. (B, UGLI)

Helene E. Roberts, "The Exquisite Slave: Clothes and the Making of the Victorian Woman," and
David Kunzle, "Dress Reform as Anti-Feminism: A Response to Helene Roberts," both in Signs (1977), pp. 554-79.

9. Women Healers

William Barlow and David O. Powell, "Homeopathy and Sexual Equality: The Controversy Over Coeducation at Cincinnati's Pulte Medical College, 1873-1879," and
Kathryn Kish Sklar, "All Hail to Pure Cold Water!" and
Sarah Stage, "The Woman Behind the Trademark," all in Leavitt, Women and Health, pp. 246-69, 422-28. (UGLI)

Mary Walsh, Doctors Wanted: No Women Need Apply (1977), chaps 1-4. Boston case study with national background.
Virginia Drachman, Hospital With a Heart: Women Doctors and the Paradox of Separatism at the New England Hospital 1862-1969 (1985), chaps on 19th century.

*George Fredrickson, The Inner Civil War (1965), chaps 6-7. Contrasts male and female approach to wartime nursing.
*Martha Vicinus, Independent Women: Work and Community for Single Women 1850-1920 (1985), sections on British hospital nursing and Florence Nightingale.

Read for 3/24

RACE, DISEASE, SLAVERY AND EMPIRE

Dennis Carlson, African Fever (1984), pp. 1-32, 43-60, 85-92. (A2, UGLI)

Todd L. Savitt, "Black Health on the Plantation: Masters, Slaves, and Physicians," in Leavitt and Numbers, Sickness and Health in America, pp. 313-30. (B, UGLI)

Individual Readings for 3/23

Kenneth Kiple and Virginia King, Another Dimension to the Black Diaspora (1981). Modern view of health conditions of slaves.
Kenneth Kiple, The Caribbean Slave: A Biological History (1985). Ditto for West Indies, esp. British islands.
*Philip Curtin, "Epidemiology and the Slave Trade," Political Science Quarterly (1968), pp. 190-216.

John Harley Warner, "The Idea of Southern Medical Distinctiveness: Medical Knowledge and Practice in the Old South," in Leavitt and Numbers, Sickness and Health in America (1985), pp. 53-69.

Virginia Allen, "The White Man's Road: Physical and Psychological Impact of Relocation on the Southern Plains Indians," Journal of History of Medicine and Allied Sciences (1975), pp. 148-63.
Sherburne Cook, "The Significance of Disease in the Extinction of the New England Indians," Human Biology (1973), pp. 485-508.

Read for 3/31

PART 1: TUBERCULOSIS AND ROMANTICISM

Rene and Jean Dubos, The White Plague: Tuberculosis, Man and Society (1953),
    pp. 3-10, 44-66.   (A2, UGLI)

PART 2: THE DECLINE IN TB AND THE RISE IN LIFE EXPECTANCY

Leavitt and Numbers, Sickness and Health in America (1985), pp. 3-10.
    (B, UGLI).
Gillian Cronje,   "Tuberculosis and Mortality Decline in England and Wales,
    1851-1910, in Robert Woods and John Woodward, eds., Urban Disease and
    Mortality in 19th Century England (1984), chap. 4.   (UGLI, A2)

Individual Readings for 3/30

1. The Poetry of Health and Disease: Conflicting Views

Edgar Allen Poe, "Annabel Lee," (1850).   In any edition of collected works.
Walt Whitman, "Song of Myself," in Leaves of Grass. Any edition.

Susan Sontag, Illness as Metaphor (1978).

2. The Decline of Other Infections

*Erwin Ackerknecht, Malaria in the Upper Mississippi Valley 1760-1900 (1945).
    Classic study, which includes Michigan.

Anne Hardy, "Smallpox in London: Factors in the Decline of the Disease in the
    19th Century,"   Medical History 27 (1983), 111-38.
Gretchen Condran, et al., "The Decline in Mortality in Philadelphia from 1870
    to 1930:   The Role of Municipal Services," in Leavitt and Numbers,
    Sickness and Health (1985).   (B, UGLI)

*Thomas McKeown, The Modern Rise of Population (1976).

Read for 4/7

PAIN, MEDICINE, AND ANESTHESIA

Martin S. Pernick, A Calculus of Suffering: Pain, Professionalism, and
    Anesthesia in 19th-Century America (1985), chaps. 3, 5, 7, 8, 11, skim
    remainder.   (UGLI, B)

Individual Readings for 4/6

1. Anesthesia in Britain

A.J. Youngson, The Scientific Revolution in Victorian Medicine (1979), chaps.
    2-3.

2. Medicine and Suffering

George M. Fredrickson, The Inner Civil War (1965), chaps. 6-7. Nursing and
    the organization of relief for the wounded.

*James Turner, Reckoning with the Beast: Animals, Pain and Humanity in the
    Victorian Mind (1980), esp. chap. 5.
Richard D. French, Antivivisection and Medical Science in Victorian Society
    (1975).

3. Discrimination in Therapy

Ann Douglas Wood, "'The Fashionable Diseases': Women's Complaints and their
    Treatment in 19th-Century America," and
Regina Markell Morantz, "The Perils of Feminist History," both in Leavitt,
    Women and Health, pp. 222-245.   (UGLI)

John Harley Warner, "The Principle of Specificity," in The Therapeutic
    Perspective (1986).

Read for 4/14

MEDICINE AND EVOLUTION

John C. Greene, The Death of Adam: Evolution and Its Impact on Western
    Thought (1959), recommended chap. 9, required chap. 10.   (B, UGLI)

Anthony Wohl, Endangered Lives (1983), pp. 329-41. (A2, UGLI)

John Haller, American Medicine in Transition (1981), pp. 296-319. (A2, UGLI)

John Eyler, Victorian Social Medicine: The Ideas and Methods of William Farr
    (1979), pp. 154-58.   (A2, UGLI)

Individual Readings for 4/13

1. Social Darwinism

Richard Hofstadter, Social Darwinism in American Thought (1959).
Robert C. Bannister, Social Darwinism: Science and Myth in Anglo-American
    Social Thought (1979).
John C. Greene, Science, Ideology and World View (1981), chaps. 1, 3-6.
Gertrude Himmelfarb, Marriage and Morals Among the Victorians (1985), chs 3-4.
J.W. Burrow, Evolution and Society: A Study in Victorian Social Theory (1970).
P. Abrams, Origins of British Sociology 1834-1914 (1968).
Stephen Jay Gould, Ontogeny and Phylogeny (1977) or The Mismeasure of Man.

2. Eugenics

Mark Haller, Eugenics (1963), esp. chaps. 1-6, 10.
Kenneth Ludmerer, Genetics and American Society (1972), esp. chaps. 1-3.
Daniel Kevles, In the Name of Eugenics (1985), chaps. 1-5.
Pauline Mazumdar, "The Eugenicists and the Residuum: The Problem of the Urban
    Poor," Bulletin of the History of Medicine 54 (Summer 1980), 204-215.
    British.

3. Evolution and Race

John Haller, Outcasts from Evolution: Scientific Attitudes Toward Racial
    Inferiority.
*George M. Fredrickson, The Black Image in the White Mind (1971), chaps. 3, 8-
    10.

4. Evolutionary Biology

Dov Ospovat, The Development of Darwin's Theory (1980).
*Ernst Mayr, "The Nature of the Darwinian Revolution," Science 176 (1972), 981-
    89.

5. Evolution and Religion in Victorian Society

*Frank M. Turner, Between Science and Religion: The Reaction to Scientific
    Naturalism in Late Victorian England. (1979).
*David C. Lindberg and Ronald L. Numbers, eds., God and Nature: Historical
    Essays on the Encounter Between Christianity and Science (1986),
    Victorian chaps.
James R. Moore, The Post-Darwinian Controversies: A Study of the Protestant
    Struggle to Come to Terms with Darwin in Great Britain and America 1870-
    1900 (1979).
Neal C. Gillespie, Charles Darwin and the Problem of Creation. (1979).

ANTISEPTIC SURGERY, THE GERM THEORY, AND THE TRIUMPH OF SPECIFIC CAUSES

A.J. Youngson, <u>The Scientific Revolution in Victorian Medicine</u> (1979, chaps. 4-5.   (A2, UGLI)

Joseph Lister, "On a New Method of Treating Compound Fracture," (1867) and "On the Antiseptic Principle of the Practice of Surgery," (1867) in Clendening, ed., <u>Source Book of Medical History</u>, pp. 610-21.   (A1)

Jeanne L. Brand, <u>Doctors and the State: The British Medical Profession and Government Action in Public Health 1870-1912</u> (1965), pp. 37-64. (A2, UGLI)

Also, briefly review responses to the germ theory by William Farr, Florence Nightingale, Edwin Chadwick, Elizabeth Blackwell, and others we have studied, in readings for 2/3, 2/10, and 3/17.

Individual Readings for 4/20

1. Antisepsis and Germs

J.K. Crellin, "The Dawn of the Germ Theory," and F.F. Cartwright, "Antiseptic Surgery," both in F.N.L. Poynter, ed., <u>Medicine and Science in the 1860s</u> (1968), pp. 57-104.
Wangensteen and Wangensteen, <u>History of Surgery</u> (1979), "Antisepsis."

2. The Bacteriological Paradigm and Clinical Medicine

*Donald Fleming, <u>William Welch and the Rise of Modern Medicine</u> (1954). USA.
*Edmund Pellegrino, "The Sociocultural Impact of 20th Century Therapeutics," and Russell C. Maulitz, "Physician versus Bacteriologist: The Ideology of Science in Clinical Medicine," both in Vogel and Rosenberg, eds., <u>The Therapeutic Revolution</u> (1979), pp. 91-108, 245-268.   (UGLI)

3. The Health Effects of Antisepsis

David Hamilton, "The Nineteenth-Century Surgical Revolution: Antisepsis or Better Nutrition?" <u>Bulletin of the History of Medicine</u> (1982), 30-40.

History 123
Revised: 1986

M.A. Miller
207 E. Duke Bldg.
684-3575, 3626

Madness & Society in Historical Perspective

General Works:

Ackerknecht, E., A Short History of Psychiatry
Alexander, F., The History of Psychiatry
Altschule, M., Roots of Modern Psychiatry: Essays in the History
of Psychiatry
Chertok, L., The Therapeutic Revolution
Doerner, K., Madmen and The Bourgeoise: A Social History of Insanity
and Psychiatry
Ellenberger, H. The Discovery of the Unconscious
Fine, Reuben, A History of Psychoanalysis
Foucault, M., Madness and Civilization
Gilman, S., Seeing the Insane (uses works of art as source material)
Rosen, G., Madness in Society
Zilboorg, G., A History of Medical Psychology

Documentary Collections on Psychiatric History:

Bateson, G. (ed.) Perceval's Narrative
Burton, R. The Anatomy of Melancholy
Conolly, J. The Treatment of the Insane Without Mechanical Restraints
(1865)
Galt, J., The Treatment of Insanity (1946)
Coshen, C.E. (ed.), Documentary History of Psychiatry
Grob, G. (ed.) Origins of the State Mental Hospital in America
Hunter, R. and I. Macalpine (eds.), Three Hundred Years of Psychiatry
Jarvis, E., Insanity and Idiocy in Massachusetts (1855)
Peterson, D., A Mad People's History of Madness
Skultans, V. (ed.), Madness and Morals
Szasz, T. (ed.), The Age of Madness

SYLLABUS AND BIBLIOGRAPHY

1. Introduction: An Overview of the History of Mental Illness

Robert Baker, "Conceptions of Mental Illness," Encyclopedia of Bioethics
(ed. Warren T. Reich), III, 1090-1098
Peter Conrad and Joseph Schneider, Deviance and Medicalization, chapter
3, pp. 38-72: "The Emergence of Mental Illness" (Medical Model of
Madness)
R.E. Kendell, "The Concept of Disease and its Implications for Psychiatry,"
British Journal of Psychiatry (1975), 127, 30515.
H. Miller, "The Abuse of Psychiatry," Encounter, May 1970, pp. 24-31.
G. Mora, "Historical and Theoretical Trends in Psychiatry," Comprehensive
Textbook of Psychiatry, 2nd edition, II, volume 1, pp. 1-75.

Theodore Sarbin, "The Scientific Status of the Mental Illness Metaphor,"
  Stanley C. Plog & Robert B. Edgerton (eds.), Changing Perspectives
  in Mental Illness, pp. 9-31.

2. Madness Among the Ancients

  G. Zilboorg, History of Medical Psychology, pp. 36-58; Greece, from
      Hippocrates to Aristotle; pp. 58-92; Rome, through Galen,
  Bennett Simon, Mind and Madness in Ancient Greece
  E.R. Dodd, The Greeks and the Irrational
  George Rosen, Madness in Society, pp. 71-136 ("Greece and Rome")

3. Medieval and Renaissance Madness

  G. Zilboorg, pp. 93-143 (Dark Ages and Demonology); pp. 144-174
      (Witchcraft)
  G. Rosen, Madness in Society, 1-18 ("Psychopathology in the Social
      Process"), 139-150 ("Western & Central Europe during the Late
      Middle Ages and the Renaissance"), 195-225 ("Psychic Epidemics").
      _____, "Emotion and Sensibility in Ages of Anxiety," American Journal
      of Psychiatry, 124, 6 (Dec. 1967), pp. 771-784.
  William Bouwsma, "Anxiety & the Formation of Early Modern Culture," B.C.
      Malament (ed.), After the Reformation, 215-46.
  Guido Ruggiero, "Excusable Murder: Insanity and Reason in Early
      Renaissance Venice," Journal of Social History (Fall 1982): 109-
      119.
  Stanley W. Jackson, "Unusual Mental States in Medieval Europe: Medical
      Syndromes of Mental Disorder, 400-11000 A.D.," Journal of the
      History of Medicine 27 (1972): 262-97.
  Robert S. Kinsman, "Folly, Melancholy and Madness, 1450-1675," The Darker
      Vision of the Renaissance, 273-320.
  Jerome Kroll, "A Reappraisal of Psychiatry in the Middle Ages," Archives
      of General Psychiatry, 29 (Aug., 1973), 276-283.

4. Early Modern Europe: Spiritual and Secular Madness

  Zilboorg, pp. 175-244, "The First Psychiatric Revolution" (on Vives,
      Paracelsus, Agrippa and Weyer)
  Rosen, Madness in Society, pp. 151-94: "Irrationality and Madness in
      17th and 18th Century Europe"; "Some Origins of Social Psychiatry:
      Social Stress and Mental Disease from the 18th Century"
  R. Neugebauer, "Medieval and Early Modern Theories of Mental Illness,"
      Archives of General Psychiatry, 36 (April, 1979): 477-83.
  M. Foucault, Madness and Civilization, chapts. 1-5.
  D. Peterson, A Mad People's History of Madness, pp. 3-63
  Michael MacDonald, Mystical Bedlam: Madness, Anxiety and Healing in
      17th Century England
  D.P. Walker, Unclean Spirits: Possession and Exorcism in France and
      England in the Late 16th and Early 17th Centuries
  Max Byrd, Visits to Bedlam: Madness and Literature in the 15th Century
  Richard Hunter and Ida Macalpine (eds.) Three Hundred Years of Psychiatry
      (documents from the 16th through the 18th Centuries, pp. 1-564).

5. The Formation of Modern Psychiatry and Psychiatric Institutions

A. General

Zilboorg, pp. 311-341 ("Age of Reconstruction" on Pinel); pp. 342-378
    ("The Discovery of Neurosis," on Mesmer and Charcot); pp. 379-
    478 ("The Era of Systems," from Esquirol & Tuke to Kreapelin)
Peterson, pp. 64-135.
Szasz, Age of Madness, pp. 18-126
Robert M. Young, "The Functions of the Brain: Gall to Ferrier (1808-
    186)," Isis, 59, 1968: 251-268.

B. France

Henri Ellenberger, The Discovery of the Unconscious, chapters 1-6
Dora Weiner, "Health and Mental Health in the Thought of Philippe
    Pinel," Charles Rosenberg (ed.), Healing and History: Essays
    for George Rosen, pp. 59-85.
Jan Goldstein, "The Hysteria Diagnosis and the Politics of Anti-Cleri-
    calism in Late 19th Century France," Journal of Modern History,
    June 1982, pp. 209-39.
Theodore Zeldin, "Worry, Boredom and Hysteria," France, 1848-1945, II,
    823-75.

C. England

Vida Skultans, Madness and Morals, pp. 1-28.
Ida Macalpine and Richard Hunters, George III and the Mad-Business
    (espec. Part IV, "Georgian Psychiatry," pp. 267-363).
G. Bateson (ed.) Perceval's Narrative. A Patient's Account of his
    Psychosis, 1830-32
R. Hunter and I. Macalpine (eds.), Three Hundred Years of Psychiatry,
    (documents on the 19th Century), pp. 567-1084.

D. Germany

Gerlof Verway, Psychiatry in Anthropological and Biomedical Context:
    Philosophical Presuppositions and Implications of German Psychiatry,
    1820-1870
Geofrey Cocks, Psychotherapy in the Third Reich

E. United States

Ruth Caplan, Psychiatry & The Community in 19th Century America
Norman Dain, Concepts of Insanity in the U.S. 1789-1865
    _____, Disordered Minds. The First Century of Eastern State
    Hospital in Williamsburg, Virginia
Albert Deutsch, The Mentally Ill in America
Gerald Grob, The State of the Mentally Ill: A History of Worcester State
    Hospital, 1830-1920
    _____, Mental Institutions in America: Social Policy to 1875.
    _____, Edward Jarvis & the Medical World of 19th Century America
    _____, "Class Ethnicity and Race in American Mental Hospitals,
    1830-75." Journal of the History of Medicine 28 (July 1973), pp.
    207-29.

Todd Savitt, Medicine and Slavery, ch. 8, "Insanity," pp. 247-279.
S.P. Fullinwider, Techniques of the Finite: The Rise and Decline of
the Schizophrenic in American Thought, 1840-1960.

F. Russia and the Soviet Union

Joseph Wortis, Soviet Psychiatry
A. Galachyan, "Soviet Union," A. Kiev (ed.) Psychiatry in the Communist
World
Mark Field, "Soviet Psychiatry," American Journal of Psychotherapy, 21,
2 (April 1967): 230-43.
Nancy Rollins, Child Psychiatry in the Soviet Union, espec. pp. 1-45,
219-240.
Jimmie Holland, "A Comparative Look at Soviet Psychiatry," pp. 133-142,
and
Isidore Ziferstein, "Psychotherapy in the USSR," both in Samuel Corson
(ed.), Psychiatry and Psychology in the USSR.
Naomi Raskin, "Development in Russian Psychiatry before the First World
War," American Journal of Psychiatry, 120, 9 (1964): 851-5.
Gregory Zilboorg, "Russian Psychiatry: Its Historical and Ideological
Background," Bulletin of the N.Y. Academy of Medicine, 9 (1943):
713-28.
A. Kozulin, Psychology in Utopia
W. Lauterbach, Soviet Psychotherapy
Martin A. Miller, "The Theory and Practice of Soviet Psychiatry,"
Psychiatry, Feb., 1985, pp. 13-24.

6. "The Great Confinement": Revisionist Theory in Psychiatric Historiography

A. France

M. Foucault, Madness and Civilization, chapters 6-9
_____, Mental Illness and Psychology (espec. pp. 64-75: "The His-
torical Constitution of Mental Illness")
G. Bleandonu and G. de Gaufey, "The Creation of the Insame Asylums of
Auzerre and Paris," R. Forster ad O. Ranum (eds.) Deviants & The
Abandoned in French Society, 180-212.
H.C. Erick Midelfort, "Madness and Civilization in Early Modern Europe:
A Reappraisal of Michel Foucault," B.S. Malament (ed.), After the
Reformation, pp. 247-65.
P. Sedgwick, "Michel Foucault: The Anti-History of Psychiatry," Psycholo-
gical Medicine, 1981, 11: 235-48.

B. England

A. Scull, Decarceration
_____, Museums and Madness
_____, "Madness and Segregative Control: The Rise of the Asylum,"
Social Problems 24 (1977): 337-51
A. Scull (ed.), Madhouses, Mad-Doctors and Madmen: A Social History of
Psychiatry in the Victorian Era
William Parry-Jones, The Trade in Lunacy: A Study of Private Madhouses
in England in the 18th and 19th Centuries
Vieda Skultans, English Madness. Ideas on Insanity, 1580-1890

C. Ireland

Mark Finane, Insanity and the Insane in Post-Famine Ireland
Nancy Scheper-Hughes, Saints, Scholars and Schizophrenics.
   Mental Illness in Rural Ireland

D. United States

David Rothman, Discovery of the Asylum
_____, Conscience and Convenience
Richard Fox, So Far Disordered in Mind: Insanity in California, 1870-
   1930
Ervin Goffman, Asylums
Thomas Szasz, The Myth of Mental Illness
_____, The Manufacture of Madness
Gerald Grob, "Rediscovering Asylums," Morris Vogel and Charles Rosenberg
   (eds.), The Therapeutic Revolution, pp. 135-157.

7. Psychoanalysis

Hannah Decker, Freud in Germany
H. Ellenberger, chapters 7-11.
G. Zilboorg, pp. 479-525.
Reuben Fine, A History of Psychoanalysis
S. Freud, Introductory Lectures in Psychoanalysis
_____, On the History of the Psychoanalytic Movement
_____, and J. Breuer, Studies in Hysteria
Nathan Hale, Freud and the Americans, Vol. I: The Beginnings of Psycho-
   analysis in the U.S., 1876-1917
_____, James Jackson Putnam and Psychoanalysis (Correspondence
   with Freud)
"Historical Review of the Contribution of Psychoanalysis to Psychiatry,
   pp. 10-31 in Ida Macalpine and Richard Hunter, Schizophrenia 1677
   Published in 1956 in a limited edition of only 750 copies this book
   contains the translated diary of a 17th century painter, Christoph
   Haizmann, who recorded his psychotic experience of demonic possession.
   Nine of his paintings depicting his fantasies are also included.
   The book, in addition, contains Freud's analysis of the original
   diary and other related psychoanalytic material.)

Some recent studies on psychoanalysis of special historical interest
include:

Bruno Bettelheim, Freud and Man's Soul (a reinterpretation of psychoanalysis based on the argument that Freud has been inaccurately
   translated and thus misunderstood in English).
A. Carotenuto. A Secret Symmetry. Sabina Spielrein between Freud and
   Jung. (The story of a brilliant Russian student in analytic training with Jung whose affair with her mentor was brought to Freud's
   attention. Includes Speilren's recently discovered correspondence
   with Jung and Freud.)
Russell Jacoby. Social Amnesia. (A critical examination of post-Freudian
   psychoanalytic theory from Adler to Laing in whih Freud is praised
   for his revolutionary work.)
Russell Jacoby. The Repression of Psychoanalysis: Otto Fenichel and the
   Political Freudians

David Stannard. Shrinking History. On Freud and the Failure of Psychohistory. (A devastating critique of historians' efforts to apply psychoanalytic theory to historical study).

Shelly Turkle. Psychoanalytic Politics. Freud's French Revolution (An analysis of the conjecture between the 1968 upheaval in France and the popularity of Lacan's interpretation of Freud. Includes a discussion of the resistance to psychoanalysis in France prior to 1968.

Peter Gay, Freud for Historians (An argument in favor of the value of Freud's work for historical research.)

In addition, there are recent biographies of significant psychoanalytic theorists and practitioners, including the following:

Helen Swick Perry, Psychiatrist of America: The Life of Harry Stack Sullivan

Celia Bertin, Marie Bonaparte (a founder of psychoanalysis in France)

Myron Sharaf, Fury on Earth. A Biography of Wilhelm Reich

John Burnham, Jelliffe: American Psychoanalyst and Physician and his Correspondence with Freud and Jung (ed. William McGuire)

8. Twentieth Century Developments

A. The Critique from Within

Thomas Szasz, The Myth of Mental Illness
David Ingleby (ed.), Critical Psychiatry: The Politics of Mental Health
David Cooper, Psychiatry and Anti-Psychiatry
R.D. Laing, The Divided Self
Peterson, pp. 136-354
Szasz, Age of Madness, pp. 127-362

B. Psychiatric Epidemiology

G. Grob (ed.), Insanity and Idiocy in Massachusetts. Report of the Commission on Lunacy, 1855 by Edward Jarvis, 1-73
B. Malzberg and E.S. Lee, Migration and Mental Disease (Introduction by D.S. Thomas, 1-42)
H. Goldhamer and A. Marshall, Psychosis and Civilization
S.C. Plog, "Social Complexity," Plog and Edgerton, Changing Perspectives in Mental Illness, 285-312.
R.W. Fox, So Far Disordered in Mind: A History of Insanity in California, 104-134
D.P. Dohrenwend, "Social and Cultural Influences on Psychopathology," Annual Review of Psychology, 25 (1974): 417-452
_____, "Sociocultural and Social-Psychological Factors in the Genesis of Mental Disorders," Journal of Health and Social Behavior 16 (Dec. 1975): 365-392
_____, Mental Illness in America

9. Related Topics (with Selected Examples of the Literature)

A. The History of Mental Disorders

Ilse Veith, Hysteria. History of a Disease
Helmut Thomas, Anorexia Nervosa

236

A. Lewis, "Melancholia: A Historical Review," <u>The State of Psychiatry</u>,
pp. 71-110

O. Temkin, <u>The Falling Sickness: A History of Epilepsy from the Greeks
to the Beginnings of Modern Neurology</u>

B. **Psychiatric Biographies**

Jean Stouse, <u>Alice James</u>
Stephen Trombley, <u>All That Summer She Was Mad. Virginia Woolf, Female
Victim of Male medicine</u>
Bernard Straus, <u>The Maladies of Marcel Proust</u>

10. <u>Recent Evaluations of Psychiatric Treatment and Theory</u>

Walter Reich, "Psychiatry's Second Coming," <u>Psychiatry</u> 45 (Aug. 1982):
189-196
Richard Restak, "Psychiatry in America," <u>The Wilson Quarterly</u> 7, 4
(Autumn, 1983): 95-125

History 1261F

STUDIES ON THE EUROPEAN RIGHT

Thursday, 4-6   M.R. Marrus

Some works on fascism and the extreme right:

*Gilbert Allardyce, ed., The Place of Fascism in European History (1971)
_____, "What Fascism Is Not: Thoughts on the Definition of
        a Concept", American Historical Review, 48 (1979), 367-88, and
        comments by Stanley Payne., Ernst Nolte, and Allardyce, 389-98
 Hans Buchheim, Totalitarian Rule (1968)
*F.L. Carsten, The Rise of Fascism (1967)
*Alan Cassels, Fascism (1975)
*Renzo De Felice, Interpretations of Fascism (1977)
*_____, Fascism: An Informal Introduction to its Theory and
        Practice (1977)
*Charles Delzell, ed., Mediterranean Fascism (1970)
*Nathanael Greene, ed., Fascism: An Anthology (1978)
*A. James Gregor, Interpretations of Fascism (1974)
 Alastair Hamilton, The Appeal of Fascism (1971)
 H.R. Kedward, Fascism in Western Europe (1971)
*Martin Kitchen, Fascism (1976)
*Walter Laqueur, ed., Fascism: A Reader's Guide (1976)
*Walter Laqueur and George L. Mosse, eds., International Fascism (1966)
 Stein Ugelvik Larsen et al, eds., Who Were the Fascists? (1980)
*Arno Mayer, Dynamics of Counterrevolution in Europe (1971)
*George L. Mosse, ed., International Fascism (1979)
*Ernst Nolte, The Three Faces of Fascism (1966)
 Stanley Payne, Fascism: Comparison and Definition (1980)
 Amos Perlmutter, Modern Authoritarianism (1981)
*Nicos Poulantzas, Fascism and Dictatorship (1974)
*Hans Rogger and Eugen Weber, eds., The European Right (1965)
 W. Schieder, ed., Faschismus als soziale Bewegung (1976)
*Anthony D. Smith, Nationalism in the Twentieth Century (1979)
 H.-U. Thamer and Wolfgang Wipperman, Faschismus und neofaschistiche
        Bewegung (1977)
*Eugen Weber, Varieties of Fascism (1964)
*John Weiss, The Fascist Tradition (1967)
 Wolfgang Wippermann, Faschismustheorien (1975)
*S.J. Woolf, ed., European Fascism (1969)

*Denotes works available in paperback.

.....2

September 16   Introduction

September 23   The Nationalist Revival in France: Prefascism?

William C. Buthman, The Rise of Integral Nationalism
        in France
Michael Curtis, Three Against the Third Republic (1959)
Paul Mazgaj, The Action Française and Revolutionary
        Syndicalism (1979)
Rene Remond, The Right in France (1971)
David Shapiro, The Right In France (1890-1919)
Robert Soucy, Fascism in France: the Case of Maurice
        Barres (1972)
Zeev Sternhell, La droite révolutionnaire, 1885-1914
        (1978)
Eugen Weber, Action francaise (1962)
        _____, The Nationalist Revival in France (1959)

September 30   The Rise of Fascism in Italy

Tobias Abse, "Syndicalism and the Origins of Italian
        Fascism", Historical Journal, 25 (1982), 247-58
Paul Corner, Fascism in Ferrara (1975)
Renzo De Felice, Mussolini il rivoluzionario (1965)
        _____, Mussolini il fascista (1966)
A. James Gregor, Young Mussolini and the Intellectual
        Origins of Fascism (1979)
P. Milza and S. Bernstein, Le fascisme italien (1980)
*A. William Salomone, ed., Italy from the Risorgimento
        to Fascism (1970), chs. III, IV, V
Domenico Settembrini, "Mussolini and the Legacy of Revo-
        lutionary Socialism", Journal of Contemporary
        History, 11 (March 1976), 239-68
Frank M. Snowden, "From Sharecropper to Proletarian: the
        Background to Fascism in Rural Tuscany, 1880-1920",
        in John A. Davis, ed., Gramsci and Italy's Passive
        Revolution (1979)
Paolo Spriano, The Occupation of the Factories: Italy,
        1920 (1975)
Edward R. Tannenbaum, The Fascist Experience (1972),
        chs. 1, 2
Roberto Vivarelli, "Revolution and Reaction in Italy,
        1918-1922", Journal of Italian History, I
        (Autumn 1978), 235-63
S.J. Woolf, "Mussolini as Revolutionary", in Walter Laqueur
        and George L. Mosse, eds., Left-Wing Intellectuals
        Between the Wars (1966), 187-96

.....3

October   7   Mussolini's Fascist Regime, 1922-40

Alberto Aquarone, "Italy: the Crisis and Corporative
    Economy", Journal of Contemporary History,
    4 (1969), 37-58
Paul Corner, "Fascist Agrarian Policy and the Italian
    Economy in the Inter-War Years", in Davis, ed.,
    Gramsci and Italy's Passive Revolution
Renzo De Felice, Mussolini il fascista, Vol. II,
    L'organizzazione dello stato fascista (1968)
A. James Gregor, Italian Fascism and Developmental
    Dictatorship (1979)
Adrian Lyttelton, "Italian Fascism", in *Walter
    Laqueur, ed., Fascism: A Reader's Guide (1979)
    _____, "Fascism in Italy: the Second Wave",
    in *Walter Laqueur and George L. Mosse, eds.,
    International Fascism (1966), 75-100, and
    Roland Sarti, ed., The Ax Within (1974), 59-86,
    and George L. Mosse, ed., International Fascism
    (1979)
Piero Melograni, "The Cult of the Duce in Mussolini's
    Italy", Journal of Contemporary History, 11
    (March 1976), 221-37
P. Milza and S. Bernstein, Le fascisme italien (1980)
David Roberts, The Syndicalist Tradition and Italian
    Fascism (1979)
Giovanni Sabbatucci, "Fascist Institutions: Recent
    Problems and Interpretations", Journal of
    Italian History, 2 (Spring 1979), 75-92
Gaetano Salvemini, Under the Axe of Fascism (1971)
Roland Sarti, ed., The Ax Within (1974), passim.
    _____, "Fascist Modernization in Italy: Tradi-
    tional or Revolutionary?" American Historical
    Review, LXXV (April 1970), 1029-45
Denis Mack Smith, Mussolini (1982)
Edward R. Tannebaum, The Fascist Experience (1972),
    chs. 3, 4, 5, and passim.

October   14   The Origins of National Socialism in Germany

*William S. Allen, The Nazi Seizure of Power (1965)
Eberhard Jäckel, Hitler's Weltanschauung (1972)
Max H. Kele, Nazis and Workers: National Socialist
    Appeals to German Labor, 1919-1933 (1972)
Peter Loewenberg, "The Psychohistorical Origins of the
    Nazi Youth Cohort", American Historical Review,
    76 (1971), 1457-1502
Peter H. Merkl, Political Violence Under the Swastika
    (1975), esp. 668-716
*George L. Mosse, The Crisis of German Ideology (1964)

.....4

October 14

The Origins of National Socialism in Germany - cont'd

Detlef Mühlberger, "The Sociology of the NSDAP: the
     Question of Working-Class Membership", Journal
     of Contemporary History, 15 (July 1980), 493-511
Jeremy Noakes, The Nazi Party in Lower Saxony (1971)
Dietrich Orlow, The History of the Nazi Party, 1919-1933
     (1969)
*Geoffrey Pridham, Hitler's Rise to Power (1973)
Ronald Rogowski, "The Gauleiter and the Social Origins of
     Fascism", Comparative Studies in Society and
     History, 19 (1977), 399-430
*Peter Stachura, Nazi Youth in the Weimar Republic (1975)

October 21

The Hitlerian Revolution

Thomas Childers, "The Social Basis of the National Social-
     ist Vote," Journal of Contemporary History, 11
     (1976), 17-42
*Gordon Craig, Germany, 1866-1945 (1978), Chs. XV, XVI
*Theodor Eschenberg et alia, The Path to Dictatorship,
     1918-1933 (1966)
Peter Hayes, "A Question Mark with Epaulettes? Kurt von
     Schlieicher and Weimar Politics", Journal of
     Modern History, 52 (March 1980), 35-65
Detlef Mühlberger, "The Sociology of the NSDAP: the Ques-
     tion of Working-Class Membership, Journal of
     Contemporary History, 15 (July 1980), 493-511
*A.J. Nicholls, Weimar and the Rise of Hitler (1968)
Dietrich Orlow, The History of the Nazi Party (1969),
     esp. ch. 7
Nico Passchier, "The Electoral Geography of the Nazi Land-
     slide: the Need for Community Studies", in S.U.
     Larsen et alia, eds., Who Were the Fascists? (1980)
Peter D. Stachura, "'Der Fall Strasser': Gregor Strasser,
     Hitler, and National Socialism, 1930-1932," in Peter
     D. Stachura, ed., The Shaping of the Nazi State (1978)
Heinrich August Winkler, "German Society, Hitler, and the
     Illusion of Restoration, 1930-33," Journal of Contem-
     porary history, 11 (1976), 1-16; and also in *George
     L. Mosse, ed., International Fascism (1979), 143-60

October 28

Nazism as Regime, 1933-39

*Karl Dietrich Bracher, The German Dictatorship (1970), ch. V
Martin Broszat, The Hitler State (1981)
Gordon Craig, Germany, 1866-1945 (1978), ch. XVII
Sebastian Haffner, The Meaning of Hitler (1979)

.....5

October 28   Nazism as Regime, 1933-39 - cont'd

William Jannen, Jr., "National Socialists and Social Mobil-
        ity," Journal of Social History, 9 (1976), 339-66
Ian Kershaw, "The Führer Image and Political Integration:
        The Popular Conception of Hitler in Bavaria during
        the Third Reich", in Gerhard Hirschfeld and Lothar
        Kettenacker, eds., Der "Führerstaat": Mythos and
        Realität. Studien zur Struktur und Politik des
        Dritten Reiches (Stuttgart, 1981)
        _____, Der Hitler-Mythos, 1920-1945. Volksmeinung
        und Propaganda im Dritten Reich (Stuttgart, 1981)
Robert Koehl, "Feudal Aspects of National Socialism", in
        *Henry Ashby Turner, Ed., Nazism and the Third
        Reich (1972), 151-74
T.W. Mason, "The Primacy of Politics — Politics and Econo-
        mics in National Socialist Germany", in *Henry Ashby
        Turner, ed., Nazism and the Third Reich (1972),
        175-200
        _____, Sozialpolitik im Dritten Reich (1977)
*George L. Mosse, Nazism (1978)
Edward Peterson, The Limits of Hitler's Power (1969)
Wolfgang Sauer, "National Socialism: Totalitarianism or
        Fascism?" American Historical Review, LXXIII (1967),
        404-24, also in *Henry A. Turner, ed., Reappraisals
        of Fascism (1975), 93-116
*David Schoenbaum, Hitler's Social Revolution (1967)
Fred Weinstein, The Dynamics of Nazism (1980)

November 4   The Extreme Right in France in the 1930s

Gilbert Allardyce, "The Political Transition of Jacques
        Doriot", in *Walter Laqueur and George L. Mosse,
        eds., International Fascism (1966), 56-74
Serge Bernstein, Le 6 février 1934 (1975)
Henri Dubief, le decline de la IIIe Republique (1976), Part 3
William D. Irvine, French Conservatism in Crisis (1979)
        _____, "French Conservatives and the 'New Right'
        during the 1930s," French Historical Studies, VIII
        (Fall 1974), 534-62
Klaus-Jürgen Müller, "French Fascism and Modernization",
        Journal of Contemporary History, 11 (1976), 75-107
Antoine Prost, Les Anciens Combattants (1977)
René Rémond, The Right in France (1971)
Robert Soucy, "The Nature of Fascism in France", in *Walter
        Laqueur and George L. Mosse, eds., International
        Fascism (1966), 27-55, and in *Nathanael Greene, ed.,
        Faxcism: An Anthology (1968), 275-300

.....6

November 4   The Extreme Right in France in the 1930s - cont'd

Robert Soucy, "French Fascist Intellectuals in the 1930s:
    An Old New Left?" French Historical Studies, VIII
    (Spring 1974), 4454-58
Eugen Weber, "France", in Hans Rogger and Eugen Weber,
    eds., The European Right (1965), 71-127

November 11   The Authoritarian Right in Spain

Shlomo Ben Ami, "The Dictatorship of Primo de Rivera: A
    Political Assessment", Journal of Contemporary
    History, 12 (1977), 65-84
Raymond Carr, Spain, 18089-1939 (1966)
    _____, The Spanish Tragedy (1977)
*Gabriel Jackson, The Spanish Republic and Civil War (1965)
Stanley Payne, Falange: A History of Spanish Fascism (1966)
    _____, "Spanish Fascism in Comparative Perspec-
    tive," in *Henry A. Turner Jr., ed., Reappraisals
    of Fascism (1966), 174-69
Hugh Thomas, "The Hero in the Empty Room: Jose Antonio and
    Spanish Fascism" in *George L. Mosse, ed., Inter-
    national Fascism (1979), 345-54, and in *Walter
    Laqueur and George L. Mosse, eds., International
    Fascism (1966), 174-82
    _____, "Spain", in S.J. Woolf, ed., European Fascism
    (1969), 280-301

November 18   Vichy: The Authoritarian Right in France

Robert Aron, The Vichy Regime (1958)
Roger Bourderon, "Was Vichy Fascist? A Tentative Approach
    to the Question", in *John C. Cairns, ed., France:
    Illusion, Conflict, and Regeneration (1978),
    200-227
Stanley Hoffman, "Collaborationism in France during the
    Second World War", Journal of Modern History, 40
    (1968), 375-95
Fred Kupferman, Pierre Laval (1976)
Michael R. Marrus and Robert O. Paxton, Vichy France and
    the Jews (1981)
*Robert O. Paxton, Vichy France: Old Guard and New Order
    (1972)
Geoffrey Warner, Pierre Laval and the Eclipse of France
    (1969)

.....7

November 25   Hungary and Rumania: Fascism on the Periphery

George Barany, "The Dragon's Teeth: The Roots of
    Hungarian Fascism", in *Peter F. Sugar, ed.,
    Native Fascism in the Successor States (1971),
    73-81
Randolph Braham, The Politics of Genocide: The Holocaust
    in Hungary, 2 vols. (1981)
Istvan Deak, "Hungary", in Hans Rogger and Eugen Weber,
    eds., The European Right (1965), 364-407
Miklos Lacko, "Ostmitteleuropäischer Faschismus", Viertel-
    jahrshefte für Zeitgeschichte, 21 (1973) 39-51
    _____, Arrow-Cross Men, National Socialists (1969)
NicholA M. Nagy-Talavera, The Green Shirts and the Others:
    A History of Fascism in Hungary and Rumania (1970)
György Ranki, "The Problem of Fascism in Hungary", in *Sugar,
    ed., Native Fascism (1971), 65-72
    _____, "The Fascist Vote in Budapest in 1939", in
    S.U. Larsen et alia, Who Were the Fascists? (1980)
Henry L. Roberts, Rumania (1951)
*Joseph Rothschild, East Central Europe Between the Wars
    (1974)
*Peter F. Sugar, ed., Native Fascism in the Successor States
    (1971)
Eugen Weber, "Rumania", in Rogger and Weber, eds., The
    European Right, 501-76
    _____, "The Men of the Archangel", in *George L. Mosse,
    ed., International Fascism (1979) 317-44, and in
    *Walter Laqueur and George L. Mosse, eds., Interna-
    tional Fascism (1966), 101-26

December 2   Hungary and Rumania: Fascism on the Periphery - cont'd

R.O.Paxton
Fall 1986

Wednesdays 4:10 - 6
302 Fayerweather

SEMINAR: FASCISM

COURSE ASSIGNMENTS:
      (1) Reading (200-250 pages per week)
      (2) Participation in weekly classroom discussions
      (3) 3 essays (choice of 3 topics out of 4)
          About 8 - 10 pages. Topics to be distributed
          on first day of class.

All readings are available in the College Library (225 Butler)
under the CAPITALIZED name. Books marked with an asterisk (*)
are available in local bookstores.

I. HOW FASCISM CAME TO POWER
    Sept. 10: At the Grassroots: a German case
      *Wm. Sheridan ALLEN, The Nazi Seizure of Power, (1984 ed.),
        Part I, (pp. xii-147), and Chapts. 12 - 15 (pp. 184-237)

    Sept. 17: At the Grassroots: an Italian case
      Paul CORNER, Fascism in Ferrara, pp. ix-47, 76, 83, 86-97,
        100-03, 107-14, 121-23, 135-74, 181-82, 206-10, 215-20,
        233-34, 244-48, 250-52, 285-88.

    Sept. 24: At the Top: Germany and Italy
      Karl Dietrich BRACHER, The German Dictatorship, pp. 16-28,
        57-97. 152-202.
      *Alan BULLOCK, Hitler: A Study in Tyranny (2nd ed.),
        Chap. 4 (pp. 187-250.
      Adrian LYTTELTON, The Seizure of Power. pp. 1-93.
      *Eugen WEBER, The Varieties of Fascism, Readings 1A, 1C,
        2A, 5, 6, 7A, 8A.

    Oct. 1: "Second Revolutions;" Van der Lubbe and Matteotti
      *BULLOCK, Hitler (2nd ed.), Chapt. 5 (pp. 253-311).
      LYTTELTON, Seizure, Chapt. 10 (pp. 237-68).
      Jeremy NOAKES and G. Pridham, Documents on Nazism,
        Chapts. 5 - 7 (pp. 155-200).
      (as possible) Hans Mommsen, "The Reichstag Fire and its
        Political Consequences," in Hajo HOLBORN, ed., Republic
        to Reich, pp. 129-210, or in Henry A. TURNER, ed.,
        Nazism and the Third Reich, pp. 109-50.

      essay #1 due

II. THE NATURE OF FASCIST RULE
Oct. 8: The Police State
    INSTITUT FÜR ZEITGESCHICHTE, Anatomy of the SS-State ,
        pp. 127-40, 188-203, 305-96.
    LYTTELTON, Seizure, Chapt. 11, "Defeat of the Party,"
        (pp. 269-307).
    NOAKES, Documents. Chapt. 10 (pp. 265-95).

Oct. 15: Who Profited? Corporatism and Capitalism
    *Walter LAQUEUR, Fascism: A Reader's Guide, pp. 379-412
        (Alan Milward article, "Fascism and the Economy")
    LYTTELTON, Seizure, Chapts. 9, 12, 13 (pp. 202-36, 308-63).
    Stephen Salter, "Class Harmony or Class Conflict?" in Jeremy,
        Noakes, ed., GOVERNMENT, PARTY, AND PEOPLE IN NAZI GERMANY,
        pp. 76-97.
    NOAKES, Documents, Chapts. 13-14 (pp. 375-459).

Oct. 22: War
    *BULLOCK, Hitler, Chapts. 8 - 9 (pp. 490-559).
    Alan Bullock, "Hitler and the Origins of the Second World War,"
        in Henry A. TURNER, ed., Nazism and the Third Reich
    LYTTELTON, Seizure, pp. 421-34.
    John F. COVERDALE, Italian Intervention in the Spanish Civil
        War, pp. 6-18.

essay #2 due

III. IDEOLOGY, CONFORMITY AND PROTEST
    Oct. 29: The Ideology of the Volk
        Saul FRIEDLÄNDER, "From Anti-Semitism to Extermination"
            (xerox edition)
        Helmut Krausnick, "The Persecution of the Jews," in INSTITUT
            FÜR ZEITGESCHICHTE, Anatomy of the SS-State, pp. 1-124
        George MOSSE, The Crisis of German Ideology.
            (1981 ed.), pp. 1-50 (and browse as possible)
        (optional) Hannah ARENDT, Origins of Totalitarianism
        NOAKES, Documents, Chapt. 15 (pp. 460-93).

    Nov. 5: Leni Riefenstahl, The Triumph of the Will (film)

    Nov 12: Students
        Rudi KOSHAR, "Two Nazisms" (xerox edition)
        Geoffrey Giles, "The Rise of the National Socialist Students'
            Association," in Peter Stachura, SHAPING OF THE NAZI STATE,
            pp. 160-85.
        LYTTELTON, Seizure, chapt. 15, pp. 394-415.
        Edward R. TANNENBAUM, The Fascist Experience, Chapt. 5,
            "Socialization and Conformity," pp. 119-47.
        Melitta MASCHMANN, Account Rendered (as posssible)

Nov. 19: Fascism and the Arts
   Barbara Miller LANE, Architecture and Politics in Germany,
      pp. 1-12, 27, 41-56, 67, 147-67, 185-216.
   James JOLL, Three Intellectuals in Politics, "Marinetti"
   NOAKES, Documents. pp. 341-8

Nov. 26: Resistance
   Karl Dietrich BRACHER, The German Dictatorship. pp. 370-99,
      431-60.
   Ian Kershaw, "Popular Opinion in the Third Reich," in Jeremy
      Noakes, ed., GOVERNMENT, PARTY, AND PEOPLE IN NAZI GERMANY,
      pp. 57-75.
   Jeremy Noakes, "The Oldenburg Crucifix Struggle," in Peter
      Stachura, SHAPING THE NAZI STATE, pp. 210-33.
   *BULLOCK, Hitler. pp. 416-20, 448-52, 735-52
   TANNENBAUM, The Fascist Experience, Chapt. 11, pp. 305-25

essay #3 due

IV. SOME COMPARISONS
   Dec. 3: Fascist Movements Elsewhere in Europe
   *Eugen WEBER, Varieties of Fascism. Chapts. 8 - 13 (pp.
      88-139.
   Eugen Weber, "The Men of the Archangel," in Walter LAQUEUER,
      ed., International Fascism, pp. 101-26.
   Read further about fascism in one country, using:
   S.J.WOOLF, ed., Fascism in Europe
   Stein LARSEN et al., eds., Who Were the Fascists?

   Dec. 10: Where and When is Fascism Possible?
   Stanley G. PAYNE, Fascism: Comparison and Definition,
      Chapt. 7, "Fascism Outside Europe?" (pp. 161-76)
   Juan J. Linz, "Some Notes Toward a Comparative Study of
      Fascism," in *W. LAQUEUR, ed., Fascism: A Reader's
      Guide. pp. 3-121.
   B. Hagtvet and R. Kuhnl, "Contemporary Approaches to Fascism,"
      in LARSEN, ed., Who Were the Fascists? pp. 26-51.

essay #4 due

247

REVOLUTION AND FASCISM IN SPAIN, ITALY AND PORTUGAL

History 340   Mr. Payne

Description: This course examines the dramatic political and social conflict
of Spain, Italy and Portugal in modern times. No other countries present such
a broad and full gamut of radical ideologies, movements and institutional
changes since the nineteenth century. Main emphases will be on the breakthrough of modern liberalism, the rise of the revolutionary left, the onset of
fascism, the Spanish Civil War, the Portuguese revolution and the contemporary
challenge of terrorism. The course will conclude with a brief analysis of the
contemporary democratic systems in all three countries and the serious conflicts that face them. Study will be to some extent topical and comparative,
analyzing all three countries in terms of similar conflicts, movements and
phases of development.

Lectures: There will be three lectures each week, about 40-45 minutes in
length, punctuated and/or followed by questions or discussion. In addition,
there will be a fourth hour of discussion section.

Exams and Assignments: There will be six- and twelve-week exams (each one
hour) and a two-hour final exam. In addition, all students must submit a
three-page essay by December 2 analyzing a major aspect of their reading.

   Students registered for four credits must also prepare a brief research
paper or a longer essay on reading, defined by individual consultation with
the instructor no later than September 25. This will be due on December 2.

   Graduate students should consult with the instructor about their own
requirements.

Grading: For 3-credit students, each of the first two exams will make up 25%
of the final grade. The final will amount to 40 to 50%, and the 3-page essay
5 to 10%.

   For 4-credit students, the first two exams will each make up nearly 20%
of the grade, the paper 20 to 25%, and the final nearly 40%.

Required Reading (paperbacks):

S. G. Payne, A History of Spain and Portugal (UW) Vol. 2
Salvatore Saladino, Italy from Unification to 1919 (AHM)
A. J. Gregor, Italian Fascism & Developmental Dictatorship
Burnett Bolloten, The Spanish Revolution (North Carolina)
R. Carr & J. P. Fusi, Spain: Dictatorship to Democracy (Allen & Unwin).

Schedule of Topics:

August
31 Background   Readings
                                                          Payne, 351-414

September
2 The Liberal Revolution in Spain & Portugal   Payne, 415-52, 513-25
4 The Carlist Counterrevolution   ---
9 Democratic Revolution & Two-Pary
     Liberalism   Payne, 453-505, 525-47
11 The Risorgimento & Unification of Italy   Saladino, 1-23
14 Oligarchic Liberalism & Trasformismo   Saladino, 24-51
16 Stagnation of Liberalism & the Colonial
     Problem: 1) Spain & Portugal   Payne, 508-12, 547-50
18   2) Italy   Saladino, 52-93
21 Open
23 Origins of the Revolutionary Left in
     Spain and Italy   Payne, 601-03; Gregor, 3-31
25 Giolittismo & Liberal Democracy, 1902-
     1914   Saladino, 94-133
28 Maura's "Revolution from Above" and
     Liberal Reformism in Spain   Payne, 578-601
30 The Portuguese Republic, 1910-1918   Payne, 550-68

October
2 Open
5 Six-Weeks Exam
7 Italian Nationalism & the Great War   Saladino, 134-63; Gregor, 32-95
9 The Postwar Crises: 1) Socialist Maximalism
     & the Rise of Fascism in Italy   Gregor, 96-126
12 The Postwar Crises: 2) Spain, 1917-1923   Payne, 607-18
14 The Postwar Crises: 3) Portugal, 1918-1926   Payne, 568-77
16 Mussolini's Triumph   ----
19 Institutionalization of the Mussolini Regime   Gregor, 127-213
21 Democratic Breakthrough & Political Break-
     down: A Comparative Perspective   Payne, 618-29
23 Salazar's "New State"   Payne, 663-83
26 Fascist Italy at Mid-Passage   Gregor, 214-99
28 Open
30 The Second Spanish Republic: Opening to
     the Left, 1930-33   Payne, 630-36

November
2 The Regionalist Problem in Spain   Payne, 505-08, 605-07 .
4 The Effort to Stabilize the Republic,
     1933-36   Payne, 636-41
6 From Popular Front to Civil War   Payne, 614-46; Bolloten, 1-51
9 The Spanish Revolution   Payne, 646-57; Bolloten, 52-236
11 Franco's Victory   Payne, 657-62; Bolloten, 237-477
13 Open

November
16 TWELVE WEEKS EXAM
18 Mussolini and Hitler   Gregor, 300-34
20 Italy and Spain in World War II   Payne, 684-87
23 The Franco Regime   Payne, 687-97; Carr-Fusi, 1-48
25 The Real Spanish Revolution   Carr-Fusi, 49-167
30 Italian Democracy and Terrorism   ——

December
 2 The Portuguese Revolution, 1974-75   ——
 4 Portugal from Revolution to Democracy   ——
 7 The Democratization of Spain   Carr-Fusi, 168-258
 9 Current Problems   ——
11 Open

Reserve Reading:

SPAIN

Carr, Raymond	Spain, 1808-1939
——	The Spanish Tragedy
——	Modern Spain
—— & J. P. Fusi	Spain: Dictatorship to Democracy
Hennessy, C. A. M.	The Federal Republic in Spain
Ullman, Joan C.	The Tragic Week
Boyd, Carolyn	Pretorianism in Liberal Spain
Meaker, Gerald	The Revolutionary Left in Spain, 1914-1923
Malefakis, Edward	Agrarian Reform and Peasant Revolution in Spain
Jackson, Gabriel	The Republic and Civil War in Spain
Thomas, Hugh	The Spanish Civil War
Bolloten, Burnett	The Spanish Revolution
Robinson, R. A. H.	The Origins of Franco's Spain
Trythall, J. W. D.	El Caudillo
Coverdale, John F.	The Political Transformation of Spain after Franco
Payne, S. G.	Falange: A History of Spanish Fascism
——	Politics and the Military in Modern Spain
——	The Spanish Revolution
——	Franco's Spain
——	Basque Nationalism
Clark, Robert	The Basques: The Franco Years and Beyond
Harrison, Joseph	An Economic History of Modern Spain

ITALY

Hostetter, R.	The Italian Socialist Movement
Clough, S. B.	Economic History of Modern Italy
Neufeld, Maurice	Italy: School for Awakening Countries
Salomone, A. W.	Italian Democracy in the Making
Thayer, John	Italy and the Great War
Seton-Watson, C.	Italy from Liberalism to Fascism
Lyttleton, Adrian	The Seizure of Power

Roberts, David	The Syndicalist Tradition and Italian Fascism
Tannenbaum, Edward	The Fascist Experience
Gregor, A. J.	The Ideology of Fascism
————	Interpretations of Fascism
————	The Fascist Persuasion in Radical Politics
————	Italian Fascism and Developmental Dictatorship
Cassels, Alan	Fascism
Payne, S. G.	Fascism: Comparison and Definition
Allum, P. A.	Italy—Republic without Government?
Blackmer, Donald and Sidney Tarrow	Communism in Italy and France

PORTUGAL

Marques, A. H. de Oliveira	History of Portugal, v. II
Kay, Hugh	Salazar and Modern Portugal
Wiarda, H. J.	Corporatism and Development
Robinson, Richard	Contemporary Portugal
Wheeler, Douglas	Republican Portugal
L. Graham and H. Makler	Contemporary Portugal
Porch, Douglas	The Portuguese Armed Forces and the Revolution
Harvey, Robert	Portugal: Birth of a Democracy
Morrison, R. J.	Portugal: Revolutionary Change in an Open Economy

UNIVERSITY OF TORONTO
Department of History

History 345H
1987

FASCISM: A COMPARATIVE HISTORY

TR 9   M.R. Marrus
W 7-9

This course examines European fascism in such countries as Germany, Italy,
France, Rumania, Hungary and Spain, considering the interrelationship of
social forces, political movements and nationalist ideologies. Looking at each
national experience in turn, lectures will address specific problems of
historical interpretation, international comparisons, and the applicaability of
analyses of fascism in the literature of social science. There are two one-
hour lectures per week and no tutorial groups.

Recommended Preparation: HIS 242H/249Y

Term Work: There are no essays to be written in this course, but there is a
relatively heavy assignment of readings. Students should purchase copies of
the following books, which will be available in the Textbook Store:

    Alan Bullock, Hitler: A Study in Tyranny (Penguin pb)
    Alexander De Grand, Italian Fascism (Univ. of Nebraska pb)
    Walter Laqueur, ed., Fasicsm: A Reader's Guide (Univ. of California pb)

In addition to the above, students are to read Hans Rogger and Eugen Weber,
eds., The European Right, chapters on France, Spain, Hungary and Rumania.

There will be a term test, worth one-third of the final grade, in late October,
examining students on material covered to date, including Bullock, Hitler and
De Grand, Italian Fascism.

Final Examination: There will be a three-hour final examination, to be held
in the examination period, worth two-thirds of the final grade. For this
examination students are responsible for: material covered in lectures; the

works by Bullock, De Grand, the above-noted chapters in Rogger and Weber; plus the following chapters in Laqueur, Fascism: 1-5, 8-12.

Supplementary Reading: For those with the time, energy, and inclination, I append to the weekly topics, listed below, a short list of supplementary works in English. Please note that these are not alternatives to the regular course readings noted above.

WEEK OF	LECTURE TOPIC
September 14	ITALY (1): FASCISM AS MOVEMENT P. Corner, Fascism in Ferrara (1975) A. Kelikian, Town and Country Under Fascism (1986) A. Lyttleton, The Seizure of Power: Fascism in Italy (1973) E. Tannenbaum, The Fascist Experience (1972)
September 21	ITALY (2): FASCISM AS REGIME C. Delzell, ed., Mediterranean Fascism (1970) A. James Gregor, Italian Fascism and Developmental Dictatorship (1979) D. Mack Smith, Mussolini (1982) R. Sarti, ed., The Axe Within (1974)
September 28	GERMANY (1): THE KAMPFZEIT W. Allen, The Nazi Seizure of Power (1965) G. Craig, Germany, 1866-1945 (1978) P. Merkl, Political Violence Under the Swastika (1975) G. Mosse, The Crisis of German Ideology (1964) J. Noakes, The Nazi Party in Lower Saxony (1971) D. Orlow, The History of the Nazi Party (1969) G. Pridham, Hitler's Rise to Power (1973)

October 5   GERMANY (2): THE FUHRER AND SOCIETY
                     M. Broszat, Hitler and the Collapse of Weimar
                          Germany (1987)
                     T. Childers, The Nazi Voter (1983)
                     R. Hamilton, Who Voted for Hitler? (1982)
                     E. Jackel, Hitler's Weltanschauung (1972)
                     M. Kater, The Nazi Party (1983)

October 12   GERMANY (3): THE NAZI REGIME
                     K. Bracher, The Nazi Regime (1970)
                     M. Broszat, The Hitler State (1981)
                     K. Hildebrand, The Third Reich (1984)
                     I. Kershaw, The Nazi Dictatorship (1985)
                     E. Peterson, The Limits of Hitler's Power (1969)

October 19   TERM TEST;
                 IMAGERY OF FASCISM (1)

October 26   FRANCE (1): OBSTACLES AND CONDUCEMENTS
                     W. Irvine, French Conservatism in Crisis (1979)
                     R. Rémond, The Right in France (1971)
                     R. Soucy, French Fascism: The First Wave (1986)
                     Z. Sternhell, Neither Right Nor Left (1986)
                     G. Wright, France in Modern Times (1960)

November 2   IMAGERY OF FASCISM (2);
                 WAS VICHY FASCIST?
                     M. Marrus and R. Paxton, Vichy France and the
                          Jews (1981)
                     R. Paxton, Vichy France (1972)
                     J. Sweets, Choices in Vichy France (1986)
                     G. Warner, Pierre Laval and the Eclipse of France
                          (1969)

November 9   FRANCE (3): HIGH FASCISM
      Patrick McCarthy, Céline (1975)
      R. Soucy, Fascist Intellectual: Drieu La Rochelle
        (1979)
      R. Tucker, The Fascist Ego: A Political Biography of
        Robert Brasillach (1975)
      E. Weber, Action Francaise (1962)

November 16   SPAIN: A MARGINAL CASE?
      S. Ben Ami, Fascism from Above (1983)
      R. Carr, Spain, 1808-1939 (1982)
      S. Payne, Falange: A History of Spanish Fascism
        (1961)
      P. Preston, The Spanish Civil War (1986)

November 23   HUNGARY: FASCISM ON THE PERIPHERY
      R. Braham, The Politics of Genocide (1981)
      N. Nagy-Talavera, The Green Shirts and the Others
        (1970)
      A. Polonsky, The Little Dictators (1975)
      J. Rothschild, East Central Europe Between the Two
        World Wars (1974)
      P. Sugar, ed., Native Fascism in the Successor States
        (1971)

November 30   RUMANIA: RURAL FASCISM
      N. Nagy Talavera, The Green Shirts and the Others
        (1970)
      A. Polonsky, The Little Dictators (1975)
      J. Rothschild, East Central Europe Between the Two
        World Wars (1974)
      P. Sugar, ed., Native Fascism in the Successor States
        (1971)

December 7 TOWARD A THEORY OF FASCISM

    R. De Felice, _Interpretations of Fascism_ (1977)
    A. James Gregor, _Interpretations of Fascism_ (1974)
    M. Kitchen, _Fascism_ (1976)
    A. Mayer, _Dynamics of Counterrevolution in Europe_
     (1971)
    E. Nolte, _Three Faces of Fascism_ (1966)
    S. Payne, _Fascism: Comparison and Definition_
     (1980)

HISTORY W4157y

Spring 1985   R. O. Paxton

THE EUROPEAN LEFTS SINCE 1830

Course assignments: (1) keep up with reading for class
                     (2) mid-term – Wed. March 6
                     (3) choice of final or research paper (see instructor)
            GRADUATE STUDENTS: two review essays (see instructor)

Required reading:
   (1) texts: Albert H. Lindemann, A History of European Socialism
               Peter N. Stearns, European Society in Upheaval (2nd ed.)
        Available in bookstores. Read at your own pace.

   (2) readings for each class: as scheduled below.
        All available in reserve library, Butler 225, under CAPITALIZED name
        Those marked (#) also available in bookstores.

Class schedule

Mon. Jan. 21: Introduction to the course. What is the Left?

I. BEFORE THE FACTORY SYSTEM
   Wed. Jan. 23: Early Forms of Protest, I: crowd justice
        E.P.THOMPSON, "The Moral Economy of the English Crown in the
            18th Century
        Louise TILLY, "Food Riots as a Form of Collective Protest in
            France"
        John Merriman, "The Demoiselles of the Ariège," in EIGHTEEN-
            THIRTY IN FRANCE, ed. John M. Merriman.

   Mon. Jan. 28: Early Forms of Protest, II: Luddism
        Eric HOBSBAWM, "The Machine Breakers"   in
            HOBSBAWM, Labouring Men.
        #E.P.THOMPSON, The Making of the English Working Class, pp. 484-602,
            (part of Chapter 14, "An Army of Redressers")
        Frank MANUEL, "The Luddite Movement in France"
        Adrian J. RANDALL, "The Shearmen and the Wiltshire Outrages of
            1802"
        William J. REDDY, "Skeins, Scales, Discounts, Steam, and other
            Objects of Crowd Justice in early French Textile Mills"

II. FROM CORPORATION TOWARDS CLASS (1830s, 1840s)
   Wed. Jan. 30: Corporate Solidarities: Neighborhood, Craft
        Craig CALHOUN, "Transition in the Social Foundations of
            Collective Action"
        Peter N. STEARNS and Daniel J. Walkowitz, Workers in the
            Industrial Revolution, pp. 75-137 (William H. Sewell,
            Jr., "The Working Class of Marseille under the Second
            Republic," and Charles Tilly, "The Changing Place of
            Collective Violence")

        Robert J. Bezucha, "The Preindustrial Labor Movement: The
            Canuts of Lyon," in BEZUCHA, ed., Modern European Social
            History
        Cynthia TRUANT, "Solidarity and Symbolism among Journeyman
            Artisans"

Mon. Feb. 4: Conspiratorial Solidarity: "minorités agissantes"
Elizabeth Eisenstein, The First Professional Revolutionary:
Michele Buonarotti, pp. 1 - 7, 25-54
Alan B. Spitzer, The Revolutionary Theories of Louis-Auguste
Blanqui, pp. 3-27, 112-34, 157-84.

Wed. Feb. 6: Phalansteries and Utopian Communities
Mark POSTER, ed., Harmonian Man: Selected Writings of Charles
Fourier, pp. 1-29, 75-90, 115-44, 150-96, 202-14, 281-338.
Eileen Yeo, "Robert Owen and Radical Culture," in Sidney POLLARD
et al., eds., Robert Owen: Prophet of the Poor
J.F.C.HARRISON, "The Owenite Social Movement in Britain and in
the United States"
#Barbara TAYLOR, Eve and the New Jerusalem, pp. 83-117 (Chapter
IV: "The Men are as Bad as their Masters")
Christopher JOHNSON, Utopian Communism in France: Cabet and
the Icarians, pp. 158-206
Sidney Pollard, "Nineteenth Century Cooperation: From Community-
building to Shopkeeping," in Asa BRIGGS and John Saville,
Essays in Labour History

Mon. Feb. 11: From Tactics to Strategy: Karl Marx
#David McLELLAN, Karl Marx (Modern Masters Series)
#Robert C. Tucker, ed., The MARX-Engels Reader, 2nd edition,
pp. xix-xxxviii, 302-438 ("Capital," Vol. I)
Robert L. HEILBRONER, "Inescapable Marx"

III. STRATEGIES FOR A POTENTIAL MAJORITY (1860s-1914)
Wed. Feb. 13: The Strike. From Craft Unionism to Industrial Unionism
Clark Kerr and Abraham Siegel, "The Interindustry Propensity
to Strike," in A. KORNHAUSER, ed., Patterns of Industrial
Conflict
Henry PELLING, A History of British Trade Unionism, 3rd ed'n.,
pp. 89-148 (Chapters VI - VII)
David CREW, Town in the Ruhr, pp. 159-220 (Chapters 5-6)
Michael P. HANAGAN, The Logic of Solidarity, pp. 62-8, 165-208.
Margot B. STEIN, "The Meaning of Skill: The Case of the French
Engine Drivers, 1837-1917"
David Douglass, "The Durham Pitmen," in Raphael SAMUEL, ed.,
Miners, Quarrymen, and Saltworkers

Mon. Feb. 18: Anarchism
#George WOODCOCK, Anarchism, pp. 145-221, 275-355
Gerald BRENAN, The Spanish Labyrinth, pp. 131-169

Wed. Feb. 20: Syndicalism
Alan B. SPITZER, "Anarchy and Culture: Fernand Pelloutier
and the Dilemma of Revolutionary Syndicalism" (xerox ed)
Pierre J. PROUDHON, Selected Writings, ed. Stewart Edwards,
pp. 13-36, 56-79, 88-113, 147-83.
Gerald BRENAN, The Spanish Labyrinth, pp. 170-202
James D. YOUNG, "Daniel DeLeon and Anglo-American Socialism"

Mon. Feb. 25: Electoral Politics and Working-class Parties
   Harvey MITCHELL and Peter Stearns, The European Labor Movement:
      The Working Class and the Origins of Social Democracy,
      pp. 1-106, 192-218, 221-35.
   Theodore S. HAMEROW, The Social Foundations of German Unification,
      Vol. I: Ideas and Institutions, pp. 222-65 (Chapter 6)
   Peter NETTL, "The German Social Democratic Party as a Political
      Model"
   #Karl MARX, The Marx-Engels Reader, ed. Robert C. Tucker, 2nd ed'n.,
      pp. 382-98 (Marx, "Critique of the Gotha Program") and pp.
      556-73 (Engels, "Tactics of Social Democracy")

IV. PROBLEMS OF SOCIAL DEMOCRACY (1890s - 1914)
   Wed. Feb. 27: The Left and White-collar Workers
      Peter GAY, The Dilemma of Democratic Socialism, pp. 7-8. 19-21,
         110-40, 191-8, 204-19, 250-70.
      John H. LOCKWOOD and David Goldthorpe, The Black-coated Worker,
         pp. 13-37, 67-8, 125-55 (skim 155-94), 194-213.

   Mon. Mar. 4: The Left and Bureaucracy
      Robert MICHELS, Political Parties, study table of contents and read
         pp. 63-77, 129-48, 277-304, 333-56 (I-A2, II-2, IV-5,6, VI-1,2)
      Carl SCHORSKE, German Social Democracy, pp. 1-27, 88-145 (Chaps. 1,4,5)
      J.P.NETTL, Rosa Luxemburg (unabridged ed.), Vol. II, pp. 494-547
         (Chapter 12)

   Wed. Mar. 6: MID-TERM

   (spring vacation)

   Mon. Mar. 18: The Left and the Peasantry
      Oskar J. HAMMEN, "Marx and the Agrarian Question" (xerox edition)
      David MITRANY, Marx Against the Peasant, pp. 40-50, 66-104
         (Chapters 3,5,7)
      James SCOTT, "Hegemony and the Peasantry"

   Wed. Mar. 20: Women Workers and Women's Work
      #Louise TILLY and Joan Scott, Women, Work, and the Family, pp.
         104-213 (Chapters 6,7)

   Mon. Mar. 25: The Left and National Loyalty: Social Imperialism
      Karl MARX, Karl Marx on Colonialism and Modernization, ed.
         Schlomo Avineri, pp. 1-31, 83-9, 125-31, 320-7, 423-48.
      Carl SCHORSKE, German Social Democracy, pp. 59-87 (Chapter 3)
      J.P.NETTL, Rosa Luxemburg (unabridged edition), Vol. I, pp.
         1-40, 63-111, 133-40, 172-84, 269-83; Vol. II, appendix
         2, pp. 842-62.
      James JOLL, The Second International, pp. 106-25 (Chapter 5)

Wed. Mar. 27: Class Consciousness
> Gwyn A. WILLIAMS, "The Concept of 'Egemonia' in the Thought
> of Antonio Gramsci"
> Jerome KARABEL, "Revolutionary Contradictions: Antonio Gramsci
> and the Problem of Intellectuals"
> Eric Hobsbawm, "The Labour Aristocracy," in HOBSBAWM, Labouring
> Men, pp. 272-315; or in Peter STEARNS and Daniel Walkowitz,
> Workers in the Industrial Revolution, pp. 138-76; or in
> John SAVILLE, ed., Democracy and the Labour Movement, pp.
> 201-39.
> Eric Hobsbawm, "Class Consciousness in History," in ASPECTS OF
> HISTORY AND CLASS CONSCIOUSNESS, ed. Istvan Meszaros
> Gareth Stedman JONES,"Working Class Culture and Politics in
> London, 1870-1900"
> Bertell OLLMAN, "Toward Class Consciousness Next Time: Karl
> Marx and the Working Class"

V. THE GREAT DIVIDE, 1914-23: WAR AND REVOLUTION
> Mon. Apr. 1: The Left and the Call to Arms, August 1914
> James JOLL, The Second International, pp. 126-98

> Wed. Apr. 3: War Government, "Union Sacrée," and "Organized Capitalism"
> Gerald D. FELDMAN, Army, Industry, and Labor in Germany, 1914-18,
> pp. 3-38, 197-249, 333-73, 407-20,428-58, 467-77, 521-33.
> James HINTON, The First Shop Steward Movement, pp. 23-55
> Alan BULLOCK, The Life and Times of Ernest Bevin, Vol. I, pp.
> 44-88 (Chapters 3-4)
> Jonathan Schneer, "The War, the State, and the Workplace: Brit-
> ish Dockers during 1914-18," in James E. CRONIN and Jonathan
> Schneer, eds., Social Conflict and the Political Order in
> Modern Britain, pp. 96-112.

> Mon. Apr. 8: The Leninist Challenge
> #V.I.LENIN, The Lenin Anthology, pp. xi-lxiv, 12-33, 67-79, 107-14,
> 120-47, 183-95, 204, 295-304, 418-76, 492-5, 503-10, 675-6
> (and as possible)
> J.P.NETTL, Rosa Luxemburg (unabridged), Vol. I, pp. 285-94, 223-8,
> Vol. II, 679-705, 716-19.

> Wed. Apr. 10: Revolution and Stabilization in Western Europe (1917-23)
> James E. CRONIN, "Labor Insurgency and Class Formation: Compara-
> tive Perspectives on 1917-20 in Europe"
> Gwyn A. WILLIAMS, Proletarian Order, pp. 99-209, 220-76, 291-7.
> James E. Cronin, "Coping with Labour, 1918-26," in CRONIN and
> Schneer, eds., Social Conflict and the Political Order in
> Modern Britain, pp. 113-45.
> Charles S. MAIER, Recasting Bourgeois Europe, pp. 3-15, 136-94.

VI. POWER, RESPONSIBILITY AND ALIENATION IN INDUSTRIAL EUROPE
> Mon. Apr. 15: The "Exercise of Power": Ramsay MacDonald, Léon Blum
> Robert SKIDELSKY, Politicians and the Slump, pp. xi-79, 167-182,
> 270-308, 375-95.
> Joel COLTON, Léon Blum, pp. 104-17, 129-41, 147-205, 232-5, 261-85.

Wed. Apr. 17: Welfare States, Affluence, and the "End of Ideology" (1945-65)
Asa BRIGGS, "The Welfare State in Historical Perspective"
George KATONA et al., Aspirations and Affluence, Chapter 2, "The
    Economic Environment of the Western Consumer"
John SAVILLE, "The Welfare State: An Historical Approach"
Dorthy THOMPSON, "The Welfare State" (reply to above)

Mon. Apr. 22: Shop-floor Radicalism and the "Hot Years" (1968-69)
Harry BRAVERMAN, Labor and Monopoly Capital: The Degradation of
    Work in the Twentieth Century, pp. 3-39, 56-69,85-151, 236-47,
    293-358
René Dubois, "New Forms of Industrial Conflict," in RESURGENCE OF
    CLASS CONFLICT IN W. EUR., eds. Colin Crouch and Alessandro
    Pizzorno, Vol. II, pp. 1-34 (Chapter 1).
Peter LANGE et al., Unions, Change and Crisis, pp. 1-141.

Wed. Apr. 24: De-Stalinization and Eurocommunism (1970s)
Howard MACHIN, ed., National Communism in Western Europe (as poss.)

Mon. Apr. 29: Depression, Women, and Immigrants: The Dual Labor Force (1980s)
Thierry Baudouin, "Women and Immigrants: Marginal Workers?" in
    RESURGENCE OF CLASS CONFLICT IN W. EUR., eds. Colin Crouch
    and Alessandro Pizzorno, Vol. II, pp. 71-99 (Chap. 3)
Michael J. PIORE, "Economic Fluctuation, Job Security, and Labor
    Market Duality"

VII. COMPARING EUROPE AND THE UNITED STATES
Wed. May 1: American Exceptionalism
Daniel Bell, "The Background and Development of Marxian Socialism
    in the United States, in Donald D. EGBERT, Socialism in Amer-
    ican Life, Vol. I, pp. 215-405, and pp. 483-6 (Paul Sweezy).
David Montgomery, "The Suttle and the Cross," in Peter N. STEARNS
    and Daniel Walkowitz, Workers in the Industrial Revolution,
    pp. 44-74
Melvyn DUBOVSKY, "Origins of Western Working-Class Radicalism"
C. Vann WOODWARD, "Home-grown Radicals" (xerox edition)
James HOLT, "Trade Unions in the British and U.S.Steel Industries"

Jerome KARABEL, "The Reason Why"

PRINCETON UNIVERSITY
Department of Politics

Politics 335 - Radical Thought: Marxism

Spring 1979-80   Professor Cohen

This is a course about Marxism as radical thought and as the ideology of political movements. The course will examine the development of Marxist ideas and movements in various historical and social settings.

Note that the readings sometimes involve a choice on your part. The literature designated as "recommended" is in no way required; it is cited for students who wish to do some additional or secondary reading. (Titles marked with an asterisk are on reserve for this course in Firestone Library.) For students who would like a general, introductory book on the history of Marxism, I recommend George Lichtheim's Marxism: An Historical and Critical Study. Finally, the following required and alternative titles, as well as a few copies of some recommended titles, are available for purchase at the University Store:

*R. Tucker (ed.), Marx-Engels Reader
*R. Tucker (ed.), Lenin Anthology
*G. Sorel, Reflections on Violence
*L. Trotsky, The Revolution Betrayed
*G. Orwell, Homage to Catalona
*A. Koestler, Darkness at Noon
*R. Debray, Revolution in the Revolution?
*F. Fanon, Wretched of the Earth
*S. Stojanovic, Between Ideals and Reality
*L. Kolakowski, Toward a Marxist Humanism
*H. Marcuse, One-Dimensional Man
*E. Genovese, Political Economy of Slavery
*E. Thompson, Making of the English Working Class
*E. Hobsbawm, Age of Revolution
*G. Lichtheim, Marxism
*S. Avineri, Social and Political Thought of Karl Marx
*C. Sigal, Going Away
*M. Markovic, From Affluence to Praxis
*L. Trotsky, My Life
*S. Cohen, Bukharin and the Bolshevik Revolution
*P. Nettl, Rosa Luxemburg
*V. Gornick, Romance of American Communism
*E. Bernstein, Evolutionary Socialism
*R. Medvedev, On Socialist Democracy
*P. Miliband, The State in Capitalist Society
*N. Poulantzas, Political Power and Social Class

SCHEDULE OF TOPICS AND READINGS

Week I-III
Feb. 5-21

The Radicalism of Marx and Engels
Reading: *R. Tucker (ed.), The Marx-Engels Reader
(I recommend that students read the whole volume.
For those who cannot, the following minimum readings
are recommended: pp. 3-6, 12-15, 66-125, 143-200,
203-217, 294-438, 469-500, 525-548, 556-573, 577-652,
665-675, 681-717, 730-759.)

Other Recommended Writings by Marx and Engels:
The Poverty of Philosophy
The Holy Family
The Grundrisse (ed. by D. McLellan)
*Capital, Vol. I
The Class Struggles in France
Anti-Duhring
Origin of the Family, Private Property, and the State

Recommended Secondary Literature:
*R. Tucker, Philosophy and Myth in Karl Marx
*R. Tucker, The Marxian Revolutionary Idea
*S. Avineri, The Social and Political Thought of
Karl Marx
S. Hook, From Hegel to Marx
B. Ollman, Alienation: Marx's Conception of Man in
Capitalist Society
*D. McLellan, Karl Marx: His Life and Thought
Z. Jordan, The Evolution of Dialectical Materialism
*G. Lichtheim, Marxism
G. Lichtheim, Origins of Socialism
M. Buber, Paths in Utopia
H. Lefebvre, The Sociology of Marx
H. Marcuse, Reason and Revolution
G. Lukacs, History and Class Consciousness
P. Sweezy, The Theory of Capitalist Development
E. Mandel, Marxist Economic Theory
K. Korsch, Karl Marx

Week IV
Feb. 26-28

Social Democratic Marxism and the Rise of the Mass
Movement
Reading: *Eduard Bernstein, Evolutionary Socialism

Recommended Secondary and Related Literature:
*P. Gay, The Dilemma of Democratic Socialism
K. Kautsky, The Class Struggle
C. Gneuss, "Bernstein," in Revisionism (ed. L.Labedz
R. Michels, Political Parties

J. Joll, The Second International
*R. Tucker, Marxian Revolutionary Idea, chap. 6
R. Kindersley, The First Russian Revisionists
O. Bauer, The Austrian Revolution
C. Schorske, German Social Democracy, 1905-1917
*G. Lichtheim, Marxism, Part 5, chaps. 5-6
T. Bottomore & P. Goode (eds.), Austro-Marxism

Week V   Sorel's Reradicalization of Marxism
Mar. 4-6   Reading: *Georges Sorel, Reflections on Violence

           Recommended Secondary Literature:
           I. Horowitz, Radicalism and the Revolt Against Reason
           H. S. Hughes, Consciousness and Society, chaps. 4-5

Week VI   The Rise of Communism: Bolshevism and the Reradicali-
Mar. 11-13 zation of Marxism
           Reading: Lenin, "What Is To Be Done?"; "Imperialism";
           "State and Revolution"; "Two Resolutions on Party
           Unity"; "The Proletarian Revolution and the Renegade
           Kautsky"; "'Left-Wing' Communism--An Infantile Disor-
           der"; and last writings of 1922-23--all in Tucker
           (ed.), The Lenin Anthology, pp. 12-114, 204-274, 311-
           398, 461-476, 496-502, 550-618, 703-748.

           Recommended Secondary and Related Literature:

              N. Bukharin, Imperialism and World Economy
             *S. Cohen, Bukharin and the Bolshevik Revolution,
                chaps. 1-2
              R. Luxemburg, The Mass Strike and the Junius Pamphlet
              R. Luxemburg, The Accumulation of Capital
              P. Nettl, Rosa Luxemburg
              F. Venturi, Roots of Revolution
              R. Luxemburg, The Russian Revolution and Leninism or
                Marxism
              L. Haimson, Russian Marxists and the Origins of Bol-
                shevism
              I. Deutscher, Prophet Armed: Trotsky, 1879-1921
              A. Meyer, Leninism
              A. Ulam, The Unfinished Revolution
              B. Wolfe, Three Who Made a Revolution
             *R. Tucker, The Marxian Revolutionary Idea, chaps. 4-6
              S. Baron, Plakhanov: The Father of Russian Marxism
              L. Trotsky, Permanent Revolution
              L. Trotsky, "The Lessons of October," in The Essen-
                tial Trotsky

Week VII   Bolshevik Utopianism and the Golden Era of Soviet
Mar. 18-20   Marxism

No Required Reading

Optional Reading (any of the following):
  N. Bukharin and E. Preobrazhensky, The ABC of Com-
    munism
  N. Bukharin, Historical Materialism
  L. Trotsky, Terrorism and Communism
  L. Trotsky, Problems of Everyday Life and Other
    Writings
  L. Trotsky, Literature and Revolution
  N. Bukharin, Economics of the Transformation Period
  E. Preobrazhensky, The New Economics
  M. Pokrovsky, Russia in World History: Selected
    Essays
  R. Daniels (ed.), Documentary History of Communism,
    I, pp. 217-321

Recommended Secondary Literature:
  D. Joravsky, Soviet Marxism and Natural Science
  L. Graham, The Soviet Academy of Sciences and the CP
  R. Maguire, Red Virgin Soil: Soviet Literature in
    the 1920's
 *S. Cohen, Bukharin and the Bolshevik Revolution,
    chaps. 3-9
  I. Deutscher, Prophet Unarmed: Trotsky, 1921-1929
  A. Erlich, The Soviet Industrialization Debate
  B. Moore, Soviet Politics: The Dilemma of Power
  R. Daniels, Conscience of the Revolution
  M. Lewin, Lenin's Last Struggle
  S. Fitzpatrick, The Commissariat of Enlightenment
  G. Wetter, Dialectical Materialism
  R. Tucker, Stalin as Revolutionary
  F. Borkenau, World Communism

Week VIII	**Stalinism, Fascism, and the Crisis of Marxist Analysis**
April 1-3	Reading: *Leon Trotsky, The Revolution Betrayed

Recommended Secondary and Related Literature:
R. Tucker, Soviet Political Mind, chap. 2
I. Deutscher, Prophet Outcast: Trotsky, 1929-1940
*S. Cohen, Bukharin and the Bolshevik Revolution, chap. 10
M. Djilas, The New Class
J. Burnham, The Managerial Revolution
N. Krasso (ed.), Trotsky: The Great Debate Renewed
C. Rakovsky, "Bureaucracy and the Soviet State," in Essential Works of Socialism (ed. by I. Howe)
R. Hilferding, "State Capitalism or Totalitarian State Economy?" ibid.
M. Shachtman, The Bureaucratic Revolution
H. Arendt, The Origins of Totalitarianism
J. Steinberg (ed.), Verdict of Three Decades
V. Serge, Russia Twenty Years After
R. Dahrendorf, Class and Class Conflict in Industrial Society, Part I
J. Stalin, Mastering Bolshevism and Works, Vols.12-13
R. Daniels, Documentary History of Communism, Vol. 2
H. Marcuse, Soviet Marxism
R. Medvedev, Let History Judge: The Origins and Consequences of Stalinism
History of the Communist Party of the Soviet Union (Short Course)
C. Friedrich (ed.), Totalitarianism
F. Borkenau, World Communism

Week IX	The Literature of Disillusionment and Exodus
Apr. 8-10	Reading (one of the following):

*R. Crossman (ed.), The God That Failed (on reserve)
*G. Orwell, Homage to Catalona
*A. Koestler, Darkness at Noon
*C. Charney, A Long Journey (on reserve)
*W. Leonhard, Child of the Revolution (on reserve)
*C. Sigal, Going Away
*M. Kempton, Part of Our Time (on reserve)
*E. P. Thompson, "Open Letter to Leszek Kolakowski," and L. Kolakowski, "My Correct Views on Everything" --in The Socialist Register for 1973 (pp. 1-100) and 1974 (pp. 1-20) (on reserve)
*V. Gornick, The Romance of American Communism
*J. Mitford, A Fine Old Conflict

Recommended Related Literature:
I. Deutscher, "The Ex-Communist's Conscience," in Russia in Transition
M. Merleau-Ponty, Humanism and Terror
D. Cante, The Great Fear
J. Cogley, Report on Blacklisting
J. Steinberg (ed.), Verdict of Three Decades
A. Gide, Return From the USSR
A. Koestler, The Yogi and the Commissar
H. Fast, The Naked God
E. Bentley (ed.), Thirty Years of Treason: Hearings Before the House Committee on Un-American Activities, 1938-68
M. Djilas, The Imperfect Society
R. Garaudy, The Crisis in Communism
G. Hicks, Where We Came Out
J. Freeman, An American Testament
A. Solzhenitsyn, Letter to the Soviet Leaders

Week X   Marxism and Peasant War
Apr. 15-17   Reading:
              *Lin Piao, Long Live the Victory of the People's War! (on reserve);
              and
              *R. Debrary, Revolution in the Revolution?
                            (or)
              *F. Fanon, Wretched of the Earth

Recommended Secondary and Related Literature:
L. Bianco, Origins of the Chinese Revolution
E. Wolf, Peasant Wars of the Twentieth Century
C. Guevarra, Guerrilla Warfare
B. Schwartz, Chinese Communism and the Rise of Mao
C. Johnson, Peasant Nationalism and Communist Power
S. Schram (ed.), Political Thought of Mao
B. Moore, Social Origins of Dictatorship and Democracy
F. Engels, The Peasant Question in France and Germany
F. Engels, The Peasant War in Germany
Mao Tse Tung, Selected Works
S. Avineri (ed.), Karl Marx on Colonialism and Modernization
A. Ulam, The Unfinished Revolution

Week XI   The Revival of Critical Marxism
Apr. 22-24   Reading (one of the following):
              *S. Stojanovic, Between Ideals and Reality
              *L. Kolakowski, Toward a Marxist Humanism
              *E. Fromm (ed.), Socialist Humanism
              *H. Marcuse, One-Dimensional Man
              *M. Markovic, From Affluence to Praxis
              *Roy Medvedev, On Socialist Democracy

              Recommended Secondary and Related Literature:
              P. Baran and P. Sweezy, Monopoly Capitalism
              A. DeGeorge, The New Marxism
              Praxis (a Yugoslav journal also published in English)
              Marxism Today (January 1967 issue of Survey)
              L. Labedz (ed.), Revisionism, Part III
              H. Parson, Humanist Philosophy in Contemporary
                Poland and Yugoslavia
              A. Schaff, Marxism and the Human Individual
              H. Marcuse, Eros and Civilization
              S. Firestone, The Dialectic of Sex
              J. Mitchell, Woman's Estate
              A. MacIntyre, Herbert Marcuse
              G. Petrovic, Marx in the Mid-20th Century
              H. Marcuse, Negations
              H. Marcuse, An Essay on Liberation
              H. Magdoff, The Age of Imperialism
              W. Leonhard, Three Faces of Marxism
              G. Sher, Praxis

Week XII   Academic Marxism
Apr. 29-May 1 Reading (one of the following or any other serious
                work of Marxist scholarship):
              *E. Genovese, Political Economy of Slavery
              *E. Thompson, Making of the English Working Class
              *R. Miliband, The State in Capitalist Society
              *N. Poulantzas, Political Power and Social Class
              *E. Hobsbawm, Age of Revolution (or another of his
                works)
              *C. Hill, Century of Revolution (Or another of his
                works)

              Or one of these secondary and related works:
              *A. Gouldner, The Coming Crisis in Western Sociology
              L. Althusser, For Marx
              D. Howard and K. Klare (eds.), The Unknown Dimension:
                European Marxism Since Lenin
              *M. Jay, The Dialectical Imagination: A History of
                the Frankfurt School and the Institute of Social
                Research 1923-1950

L. Graham, <u>Science and Philosophy in the Soviet Union</u>

A. Mayer, <u>Politics and Diplomacy of Peacemaking: Containment and Counterrevolution at Versailles, 1918-1919</u>

*R. Blackburn (ed.), <u>Ideology in the Social Sciences</u>

D. Horowitz (ed.), <u>Marx and Modern Economics</u>

P. Berger (ed.), <u>Marxism and Sociology: Views from Eastern Europe</u>

<u>Marx and Contemporary Scientific Thought: Essays</u>

Reading Period Assignment: Read an account--biographical, auto-
May 5-18   biographical, or fictional--of the life of a Marxist
                  thinker. For example:

*D. McLellan, <u>Karl Marx: His Life and Thought</u>

*I. Deutscher, <u>Prophet Outcast: Trotsky, 1929-1940</u>

*L. Trotsky, <u>My Life</u>

*S. Cohen, <u>Bukharin and the Bolshevik Revolution</u>

*P. Nettl, <u>Rosa Luxemburg</u> (one-vol. ed.)

*L. Fischer, <u>Life of Lenin</u>

*P. Gay, <u>Dilemma of Democratic Socialism: Eduard Bernstein's Challenge to Marx</u>

I. Getzler, <u>Martov</u>

J. Cammet, <u>Gramsci</u>

S. Daron, <u>Plekhanov</u>

*I. Howe, <u>Trotsky</u>

G. Steenson, <u>Karl Kautsky</u>

M. Salvadori, <u>Kautsky and the Socialist Revolution</u>

Syllabus

History 29

European Communism in the Era of the Comintern, 1919-1943

I. Introductory Session

September 6:

Discussion of syllabus and course requirements.

II. Historical Background: European Socialism before the Communist International, 1780-1917.

September 13:

1. Lecture #1: The Industrial Revolution and the development of the Socialist vision: early critics of capitalism from Owen to Marx.

2. Readings: Carl Landauer, European Socialism: A History of Ideas and Movements from the Industrial Revolution to Hitler's Seizure of Power, pp. 3-71.

   Sidney Hook, Marx and the Marxists, pp. 11-48, 133-163.

September 20:

1. Lecture #2: The Second Phase: the spread of Socialist ideas after 1848 - Marx, Lassalle, Bakunin, and the First International, 1848-1876.

2. Readings: Edmund Wilson, To the Finland Station, pp. 178-346.

   Hook, pp. 49-64.

September 27: The Second International.

James Joll, The Second International, 1889-1914.

Hook, pp. 65-75, 177-182.

III. V.I. Lenin.

October 4: Life (to 1917)

Adam Ulam, The Bolsheviks: The Intellectual and Political History of the Triumph of Communism in Russia, pp. 1-313.

October 11: Life (1917-1924)

Ulam, pp. 313-579.

Hook, pp. 182-198.

October 18: Doctrine.

    (On Party Organization)

    V.I. Lenin, What is to be Done?, in Helmut Gruber (ed.),
        International Communism in the Era of
        Lenin, pp. 9-29.

    Rosa Luxemburg, The Russian Revolution and Marxism
        or Leninism?, pp. 1-24, 81-108.

    Bertram D. Wolfe, "A Party of a New Type: The
        Foundation Stone of the Communist
        International", in Milorad M. Drachko-
        vitch and Branco Lazitch (eds.), The
        Comintern: Historical Highlights, pp.
        20-44.

    (On War and Nationalism)

    V.I. Lenin, "The Tasks of Revolutionary Social
        Democracy in the European War", and
        "Draft Manifesto Introduced by the
        Left-Wing Delegates at the International
        Conference at Zimmerwald", in Gruber,
        pp. 44-60.

    (On the Thirs International)

    V.I. Lenin, The Third International and its Place
        in History, pp. 5-13.

    Stefan T. Possony, "The Comintern's Claim to Marxist
        Legitimacy", in Drachkovitch and Lazitch,
        pp. 3-19.

IV. The Founding of the Third International, 1919.

    October 25:

    James W. Hulse, The Founding of the Communist
        International.

    Gruber, International Communism in the Era of Lenin,
        pp. 73-123 ("The Creation of the Third
        International", "Spartacus in Berlin",
        "Bela Kun's 133 Days").

V. The Ebb of the Revolutionary Tide in Europe: The Long Period of
Communist Defeat, 1920-1927.

    November 1:

    Franz Borkenau, World Communism, pp. 161-295.

    Gruber, International Communism, pp. 231-46, 365-42
        ("The Twenty-One Conditions", "A Second
        Red October").

    Issac Deutscher, The Prophet Unarmed: Trotsky, 1921-
        1929, pp. 140-151.

    Fernando Claudin, The Communist Movement: From Comintern
        to Cominform, v. I, pp. 103-25.

VI. The Triumph of Stalin in the USSR.

November 8:Life

Issac Deutscher, *Stalin: A Political Biography*, chaps. 1-9.

November 15: Stalin and "Stalinism", an analysis.

Deutcher, *Stalin*, chaps. 10-11.

Leon Trotsky, "Why Stalin Triumphed", in *The Revolution Betrayed*, pp. 86-94.

- - - - - - , "Stalinism and Bolshevism", in Irving Howe (ed.), *The Basic Writings of Leon Trotsky*, pp. 356-70.

Stephen Cohen, "Bolshevism and Stalinism", in Robert C. Tucker (ed.), *Stalinism: Essays in Historical Interpretation*, pp. 3-30.

Robert H. McNeal, "Trotskyist Interpretations of Stalinism", in Tucker, pp. 30-52.

Leszek Kolakowski, "Marxist Roots of Stalinism", in Tucker, pp. 283-98.

Robert C. Tucker, "Stalinism as Revolution From Above", in Tucker, 77-108.

Mihailo Markovic, "Stalinism and Marxism", in Tucker, 299-319.

VII. The Sixth Comintern Congress and the Destruction of German Communist Party, 1928-1934.

November 29:

Borkenau, *World Communism*, pp. 332-385.

Claudin, *The Communist Movement*, I, 126-166.

Rosa Levine-Meyer, *Inside German Communism: Memoires of Party Life in the Weimar Republic*, pp. 125-188.

Issac Deutscher, *The Prophet Outcast: Trotsky, 1929-1940*, pp. 33-45, 128-144, 198-202.

VIII. The Popular Front, 1934-1939.

December 6: France.

Claudin, *The Communist Movement*, I, 210-242.

Daniel Brower, *The New Jacobins: The French Communist Party and the Popular Front*.

John Santore, "The Comintern's United Front Initiative of May 1934: French or Soviet Inspiration?", in *The Canadian Journal of History/ Annales Canadiennes d'Histoire*, XVI, 3, 405-21.

December 13:Spain.

> Claudin, The Communist Movement, I, 210-242.

> George Orwell, Homage to Catalonia.

> Branco Lazitch, "Stalin's Massacre of Foreign
> Communist Leaders", in Drachkovitch
> and Lazitch, pp. 138-175.

> Boris Souvarine, "Comments on the Massacre", in
> ibid., pp. 175-183.

IX. The Second World War and the Third International: the Comintern's
last four years, 1939-1943.

December 20:

> (The War and the act of dissolution)

> Hugh Seton-Watson, From Lenin to Khrushchev: The
> History of World Communism, pp. 200-228.

> Franz Borkenau, European Communism, pp. 296-336.

> Claudin, The Communist Movement, I, 294-304, 15-45.

> (The Comintern: summary and overall assessment, 1919-
> 1943)

> Milorad M. Drachkovitch and Branco Lazitch, "The
> Communist International", in Milorad M.
> Drachkovitch (ed.), The Revolutionary
> Internationals, 1864-1943, pp. 159-202.

> George Lichtheim, A Short History of Socialism,
> pp. 249-66.

> Adam Ulam, The Unfinished Revolution: As Essay on
> the Sources of Influence of Marxism and
> Communism, pp. 196-250.

> Geoffrey Barraclough, An Introduction to Contemporary
> History, pp. 199-232.

M. A. Miller
207 E. Duke
University

HISTORY OF RUSSIAN ANARCHISM

I. Anarchist Theory and Practice in Historical Perspective
   G. Woodcock, Anarchism
   J. Joll, The Anarchists

II. Pre-revolutionary Russian Anarchism
   A. Lehning (ed.), Michael Bakunin: Selected Writings
   M. Miller (ed.), Peter Kropotkin: Selected Writings on Anarchism and
      Revolution
   M. Miller, Kropotkin
   Marx-Engels-Lenin, Anarchism and Anarcho-Syndicalism

III. Anarchism and the Russian Revolution
   P. Avrich, The Russian Anarchists
   P. Avrich (ed.), Anarchists in the Russian Revolution
   P. Avrich, Kronstadt
   Voline (B. Eichenbaum), The Unknown Revolution
   D. Cohn-Bendit, Obsolete Communism
   L. van Rossum, "Proclamations of the Makhno Movement, 1920," International
      Review for Social History, XIII, 1968, 246-268
   P. Arshinov, History of the Makhnovist Movement
   E. Goldman, My Disillusionment in Russia
   V. Serge, Memoirs of a Revolutionary

IV. Soviet Research on Anarchism and the Revolution in Russia
   S. N. Kanev, "Krakh russkogo anarkhizma," Voprosy istorii, 1968, no. 9
   S. N. Kanev, Oktiabr'skaia revoliutsiia i krakh anarkhizma
   M. Khudiakulov, "Bor'ba kommunisticheskoi partii protiv anarkhizma v
      gody stanofleniia i uprocheniia Sovetskoi vlasti," A. V. Kachurina,
      Bolsheviki v bor'be protiv melkoburzhuaznykh partii v Rossii
   A. D. Kosichev, Bor'ba Marksizma-Leninzma s ideologiei anarkhizma
   N. S. Prozorova, Bor'ba K. Marksa i F. Engel'sa protiv anarkhizma
   I. B. Zil'berman, Politicheskaia teoriia anarkhizma M. A. Bakunina

Professor Donald H. Bell
Department of History

History 150
Spring 1987

Syllabus

Political Terrorism in Historical Perspective:

The Case of Western Europe

This course deals primarily with the relationship between contemporary European terrorist activities and their historical context. To what degree has recent political violence in Europe been informed by previous tradition? To what degree are such activities a response to the specific strains and issues of late-twentieth century life? Can terrorist movements and actions be compared cross-nationally? What are the main theories which social scientists employ to explain the phenomenon of terrorism? How valid and valuable are these theories and how might they be improved?

Books marked with an asterisk are for student purchase. Unless otherwise noted, all books and articles are on Reserve at the Library.

Course Requirements: an hour midterm examination (bluebook), and a final (take home) exam of 10-12 typewritten pages.

My office hours are Tuesday 2:00-4:00 in Miner 01; my office phone is extension 2426.

NOTE: Although we will not specifically discuss course readings in class, you are expected to keep up with such readings and to be accountable for them on course examinations.

I. The Phenomenon of Terrorism:

Reading:

1. Walter Laqueur, Terrorism*, Ch. 1,3 (Ch. 5 optional).
2. Walter Laqueur, The Terrorism Reader, pp. 251-285.
3. Michael Walzer, Just and Unjust Wars, pp. 44-47, 127-151, 197-206.
4. "It Must Be Simple and Reliable": Special Report on Weaponry: Discover Magazine, June, 1986, pp. 22-31.

Recommended Reading:

> 1. Franz Fanon, The Wretched of the Earth, Ch. 1
> 2. Jan Schreiber, The Ultimate Weapon: Terrorists and the
>   World Order
>
> 3. Franklin Ford, "Reflections on Political Murder" and
>   E.J. Hobsbawm, "Political Violence and Political Murder,"
>   in W.J. Mommsen and G. Hirschfeld, eds., Social Protest,
>   Violence and Terror in 19th and 20th Century Europe

II. Historical Case Studies :

(A) Nineteenth-Century Russia: The Historical Context

Reading:

1. Cyril Black, "The Nature of Imperial Russian Society, ", in Bruce
   Mazlish, et al, Revolution: A Reader.
2. Martin Malia, "What is the Intelligentsia?" in Mazlish, Revolution:
   A Reader.
3. Walter Laqueur, Terrorism, Ch. 2.
4. Isaiah Berlin "Russian Populism," in Isaiah Berlin, Russian Thinkers
   (Aileen Kelly, ed.), or "Introduction," to Franco Venturi, The Roots of
   Revolution.

Recommended:

1. Paul Avrich, The Russian Anarchists, Ch. 1-2.
2. Franco Venturi, The Roots of Revolution, Ch. 1, 2, 13-18.

(B) Nineteenth-Century Russia: The Intellectual Context

Reading:

1. Ivan Turgenev, Fathers and Sons, Ch. 10, 11.
2. Walter Laquer, The Terrorism Reader*, pp. 47-90, 198-223.
3. Sergei Nechaev, "Catechism of a Revolutionist"

4. V.I. Lenin, "What is to be Done?" in Mazlish, Revolution: A Reader.
5. Norman Naimark, "Terrorism and the Fall of Imperial Russia"

Recommended:

1. Isaiah Berlin, "Herzen and Bakunin on Individual Russian Liberty,"
   "Fathers and Children," in Isaiah Berlin, Russian Thinkers.
2. Wolfgang J. Mommsen and Gerhard Hirschfeld, eds., Social Protest, Violence
   and Terror in Nineteenth and Twentieth Century Europe,
   Chapters 5, 6, 7, (On Narodnaya Volya and the SRS).

(C). Pre-World I Western Europe:

Reading:

1. Barbara Tuchman, The Proud Tower; Chapter 2, "The Idea and the Deed."
2. James Joll, The Anarchists, Ch. V-VII.
3. Walter Laqueur, The Terrorism Reader, pp. 90-112, 193-198.
4. Alexander Berkman, "Propaganda by the Deed"
5. Prince Kropotkin, "The Conquest of Bread"

Recommended:

1. George Woodcock, Anarchism, Chapter 10.

(D) Spain:

Reading:

1. Richard Herr, An Historical Essay on Modern Spain Ch. 9-10.
2. Gerald Brenan, The Spanish Labyrinth, Ch. 7-8.
3. Murray Bookchin, The Spainish Anarchists, Introduction, Ch. 6-8.
4. Walther L. Bernecker, "The Strategies of 'Direct Action' and Violence in Spanish Anarchism"

III. Contemporary Western Europe: The 1960s-1980s

(A) The Background:

Reading:

1. Stanley Hoffman,"Fragments Floating in the Here and Now"
2. Suzanne Berger, "Politics and Antipolitics in Western Europe in the Seventies"
3. Walter Laqueur, Terrorism, Chapter 5.
4. Walter Laqueur, The Terrorism Reader, pp. 159-172.

(B) Case Studies:

1). Paul Furlong, "Political Terrorism in Italy: Responses, Reactions, and Immobilism," in Juliet Lodge, ed., Terrorism: A Challenge to the State

2). Richard Drake, "The Red Brigades and the Italian Political Tradition," in Yonah Alexander and K.A. Myers, Terrorism in Europe, Ch. 5.

3). "A Kind of Stability:Italy in the 1980s". The Economist, July 23,1983

4). Thomas Sheehan, "Italy: Behind the Ski Mask," <u>New York Review of Books</u>, 8/16/1979

5). Thomas Sheehan. Italy: Terror on the Right," in <u>Ibid</u>. 1/22/1981

6). C.B. Pepper, "The Possessed," <u>New York Times Magazine</u>

Recommended:

1. George Woodcock, <u>Anarchism</u>, Ch. 11.
2. Martin Clark, <u>Modern Italy</u>, 1871-1982
3. Gianfranco Pasquino, Donatella Della Porta, "Interpretations of Italian Left-Wing Terrorism."
4. E. Wiskemann, <u>Italy Since 1945</u>

GERMANY

1. Bommi Baumann, <u>How it All Began</u> (Terror or Love)*, entire.
2. Walter Laqueur, <u>The Terrorism Reader</u>, pp. 176-179, 246-251.
3. Jillian Becker, <u>Hitler's Children</u>. Ch. 1-5, 15-17.
4. Geoffrey Pridham, "Terrorism and the State in West Germany during the 1970s," in Lodge, <u>Terrorism</u>
5. Ovid Demaris, <u>Brothers in Blood</u>, pp. 215-265

Recommended:

1. Gordon Craig, <u>Germany, 1866-1945</u>.
2. Michael Balfour, <u>West Germany</u>.
3. Jan Schreiber, <u>The Ultimate Weapon</u>, Ch. 7.

NORTHERN IRELAND

1. J. Bowyer Bell, <u>A Time of Terror</u>, Ch. 10.
2. Walter Laqueur, <u>Terrorism Reader</u>, pp. 112-116, 130-137.
3. E. Moxon Browne, "Terrorism in Northern Ireland; The Case of the Provisional IRA" in Lodge, <u>Terrorism</u>, Ch. 6
4. John Conroy, "Ulster's Lost Generation," <u>N.Y. Times Magazine</u>, 8/2/1981.
5. Conor Cruise O'Brien, "The Mirage of Peace," <u>New York Review of Books</u>, 4/24/1986.

Recommended:

1. Ovid Demaris, <u>Brothers in Blood</u>, Book 4.

SPAIN

1. Gerhard Bruun, "Nationalist Violence and Terror in the
   Spanish Border Provinces: ETA," in Mommsen and Ritter,
   eds., Social Protest, Violence and Terror (xerox).
2. Raymond Carr and Juan Pablo Fusi, Spain: Dictatorship
   or Democracy, Ch. 7.
3. Gerald Brenan, "Out of the Labyrinth," N.Y. Review of Books,
   9/27/1979
4. Richard Herr, An Historical Essay on Modern Spain, Ch. 15

Recommended:

1. Raymond Carr, Modern Spain, 1875-1980.

IV. Terrorism and Literature

1. Walter Laqueur, Terrorism, Chapter
2. Joseph Conrad, The Secret Agent, selections
3. Oriana Falacci A Man, selections
4. John Le Carre, The Little Drummer Girl, selections
5. Henry James, The Princess Cassamassima, selections

V. A "Terrorist International"?: Conclusions:

Reading:
1. Walter Laqueur, Terrorism, Conclusion
2. Claire Sterling, "Terrorism: Tracing the International
   Network" ., and review of Sterling's work by
   Daniel Shorr
3. J. Bowyer Bell, A Time of Terror, Chapter 12
4. Conor Cruise O'Brien, "Thinking About Terrorism,"
   Atlantic Monthly, June, 1986, 62-66
5. Christopher Hitchens, "Wanton Acts of Usage" Harper's
   Magazine, September, 1986, 66-70.

Recommended:

1. Juliet Lodge, "The European Community and Terrorism," in
   Lodge, ed., Terrorism (, on reserve), Ch. 7.
2. David Freestone, "Legal Responses to Terrorism" in Ibid.,
   Ch. 8, (on reserve).

Introduction to Historical   Mr. Loewenberg
Practice (Honors) 101H   Spring 1987
                                                    Wednesday 7:30-10:30

"The function of the historian is akin
to that of the painter and not of the
photographic camera: to discover and
set forth, to single out and stress
that which is of the nature of the thing,
and not to reproduce indiscriminately all
that meets the eye."

                              - Sir Lewis Namier

Course Purpose:

    This course will examine historical research and practice by articulating
how theory (explicit or implicit) determines the method and assumptions of
research, which in turn leads to how history is written and interpreted.

Assignments:

    All students are responsible for reading all of the material. Readings
which are hard to get, out of print, or too costly, will be distributed to you
and will be in the College Reserve Service of the Powell Library.

    Each student will be responsible to serve as resource person to initially
present and lead the discussion for one of the topics.

    Paper: Seminar members will make an oral presentation and write a paper
on an historiographic problem of their choice. The historiographic work-up
should have at least three dimensions: 1.) Temporal: how the problem was
treated in various historical periods of time; 2.) Political-ideological: how
social, intellectual, class, cultural and philosophical orientation conditioned
the historian's work; 3.) Biographical: how the explicit life development
situation of historians shapes their product. There may of course be other
dimensions such as technological innovations, current political conflict, etc.
An outstanding model that integrates many of these dimensions is Pieter Geyl,
Napoleon: For and Against. The historical problem you choose to write on may
be a very small one. The process itself is important. If you know how various
historians treated one problem, you will know much about their general
approach, method, and work. You may also choose to write on the work and
development of one particular historian or historical school.

    Papers are due on Friday, June 5.

    Office Hours: Mr. Loewenberg's office hours are in Ralph Bunche Hall 8246
on Tuesday from 3:15 to 5:00 and Thursday from 3:15 to 4:15. Telephone:
825-3175.

Meetings: After the initial meeting in Bunche Hall 3143, I would like to invite the seminar to meet in my home, 449 Levering Avenue, Westwood; Telephone: 471-3039. There is a free bus service from 5:00 p.m. until midnight running every 20 minutes from the University Research Library and dormitories to the corner of Levering and Kelton Avenues.

April 1:   Introduction and Assignments

April 8:   Peter Loewenberg, Decoding the Past: The Psychohistorical Approach (Berkeley and Los Angeles: University of California Press, 1985).

"Emotional Problems of Graduate Education", pp. 48-58.

"The Graduate Years: What Kind of Passage?", pp. 59-66.

"Love and Hate in the Academy", pp. 67-80.

"The Langer Family and the Dynamics of Shame and Success", pp. 81-95.

April 15:   E.H. Carr, What is History? (1961).

Jacob Burckhardt, Reflections on History (Liberty Fund), also published as Force and Freedom (New York: Meridian, 1955). V. "The Great Men of History", pp. 269-306. VI. "On Fortune and Misfortune in History", pp. 309-327.

The Letters of Jacob Burckhardt (New York: Pantheon, 1955). Letters to Von Preen of 26 April 1872, 28 June 1872, and 3 October 1872, pp. 151-155 (Hand out).

April 22:   No seminar

April 29:   R.G. Collingwood, The Idea of History (Oxford GBI), Read "Epilegomena", pp. 205-334.

Collingwood, "The Purpose of the Roman Wall", The Vasculum, Vol 8 (October, 1921), 4-9 (Hand out).

Marc Bloch, The Historian's Craft (New York: Knopf, 1941, 1953).

Bloch, French Rural History (1931, 1966), "Introduction: Some Observations on Method", xxiii-xxx, and his use of aerial photographic plates as evidence, 142-143 (Hand out).

Bloch, Strange Defeat: A Statement of Evidence Written in 1940 (New York: Norton, 1968).

May 6:   Guest Presentation by Professor J.W. Smit, Queen Wilhelmina
           Professor of History, Columbia University, on "The Person and
           Work of Pieter Geyl." Professor Smit was Geyl's last graduate
           student.

           Read:

           Pieter Geyl, "Looking Back", (March 1958), Section 6 of
           Encounters in History (New York: Meridan M114, 1961), pp.
           355-372 (Hand out).

May 13   Crisis Decision Making: History from new kinds of sources: Oral
           and visual documentation. We will hear tapes of the original
           White House Executive Committee meetings during the October
           1962 Cuban missle crisis and discussion by participants being
           interviewed 21 years later.

May 20, 27, June 3:   Seminar reports.

June 5:   Seminar papers due.

Best wishes for recreation and renewal this summer.

P. Loewenberg

University of Chicago

Department of History

Quantitative Methods for Historians
History 436

Mr. John Coatsworth
Mr. Edward Cook

Introduction

The purpose of this graduate course is to introduce students to quantitative methods of historical research. Since the use of quantitative methods requires both statistical and conceptual skills, attention will be devoted both to the technical aspects of data processing and manipulation as well as problems of research design, modeling, hypothesis testing, and the like.

No prior training in statistics, data processing, mathematics or computer science is required. Arrangements have been made to offer students enrolled in the course an opportunity to take a three week course (six sessions) at the University Computation Center in the use of the Statistical Package for the Social Sciences, the computer program most widely used by historians. The SPSS course costs $25.00, and will meet Tuesday and Thursday at 4 p.m. from October 16 to November 1. Students interested in taking this optional course should register immediately at the Computation Center Business Office at 5737 South University Avenue.

Optional tours of the University Computation Center and the Social Sciences Division terminal facilities in Pick Hall have also been arranged.

A limited budget for computer time is available to all students in the course. Extra time is allocated for those who enroll in the SPSS course. In addition students are entitled to register with the Computation Center for a "get acquainted" account of $25 per quarter.

Requirements

Each student taking the seminar (including auditors) will be required to submit a two to five page essay on his/her current research interests and possibilities for use of quantitative methods by Thursday, October 11. The purpose of this essay is to assist the instructors in selecting relevant materials for lectures and additional readings.

All students (including auditors) will be required to complete the statistical exercises distributed in class during the quarter.

Quantitative Methods for Historians   History 436

        Students who wish to receive a letter grade in the course are
required to submit a paper, not less than ten pages in length, demonstrating
the application of quantitative methods in historical research. Students
should select a topic that corresponds to a current research project or
interest, and must consult one of the instructors in the course for approval
of the paper topic by the third week of the quarter.

Books for Purchase

        The following books have been ordered for purchase at the Seminary
Bookstore. All readings are available in Regenstein Reserve.

    1. Hubert Blalock, Social Statistics (McGraw-Hill).
    2. Charles Dollar and Richard Jensen, Historians Guide to Statistics:
            Quantitative Analysis and Historical Research (Holt, Rinehart
            and Winston).
    3. Primer, Statistical Package for the Social Sciences (McGraw-Hill).
    4. Edward Shorter, The Historian and the Computer: A Practical Guide
            (Prentice-Hall).
    5. Roderick Floud, An Introduction to Quantitative Methods for
            Historians.

Course Outline

Week I. Introduction to Computer Technology and Research Design

    1. Dollar and Jensen, pp. 139-72, 1-26.
    2. Floud
    3. Blalock, Chapters 1, 2.
    4. Robert A. Berkhofer, A Behavioral Approach to Historical
            Analysis, esp. ch. 1, 12, 13.
    5. David Potter, "Explicit Data and Implicit Assumptions in
            Historical Studies," in Louis Gottschalk, ed., Generaliza-
            tion in the Writing of History, pp. 178-94.
    6. Edward Shorter, The Historian and the Computer: A Practical
            Guide (entire)

Week II. Text Manipulation by Computer (Michael Dalby)

        No new readings.

Quantitative Methods for Historians   History 436

Week III.   Descriptive Statistics and Frequency Distributions

1. Blalock, Chapters 3-6
2. Dollar and Jensen, pp. 27-55
3. Floud, Chapters 1-5
4. Richard McCormick, "New Perspectives on Jacksonian Politics,"
   Rowney and Graham, pp. 372-84
5. Maris Vinovskis and Richard Bernard, "Women in Education in
   Ante-Bellum America," paper on reserve
6. Burton Singer, "Exploratory Strategies and Graphical Displays,"
   Journal of Interdisciplinary History, 7 (1976), pp. 57-70

Week IV.   Introduction to Times Series

1. Floud, pp. 85-124
2. D. T. Campbell and H. L. Ross, "The Connecticut Crackdown on
   Speeding: Time Series Analysis in Quasi-Experimental
   Analysis," in Edward Tufte, ed., The Quantitative Analysis
   of Social Problems, pp. 110-25.
3. Charles Tilly and Edward Shorter, "The Shape of Strikes in
   France, 1830-1900," Comparative Studies in Society and
   History, V. 13 (1971)
4. Dorothy S. Thomas, "The Impact of the Harvest On Population
   Change," in Paul F. Lazarsfeld and Morris Rosenberg, eds.,
   The Language of Social Research (Glencoe, 1962), pp. 206-13

Week V.   Probability and Sampling, and Cross Tabulation

1. Blalock, Chapters 7, 15, 21 (Chapters 8-13 recommended)
2. Floud, pp. 125-33, 155-83
3. Melvyn A. Hammarberg, "Designing a Sample from Incomplete
   Historical Lists," American Quarterly, 23 (1971), pp. 542-61
4. R. S. Shofield, "Sampling in Historical Research," in E. A.
   Wrigley, Nineteenth Century Society, pp. 146-90
5. Richard S. Alcorn & Peter R. Knight, "Most Uncommon Bostonians:
   A Critique of Stephan Thernstrom's The Other Bostonians,"
   Historical Methods Newsletter, 8 (June 1975), pp. 98-120
6. Patrick L. R. Higonnet & Trevor B. Higonnet, "Class, Corruption,
   and Politics in the French Chamber of Deputies, 1846-1848,"
   Rowney and Graham, pp. 129-47
7. Daniel Smith and Michael Hindus, "Premarital Pregnancy in
   America, 1640-1771: An Overview and Interpretation,"
   Journal of Interdisciplinary History V (1975), pp. 537-70

Week VI. Scalograms and Clusters

1. Dollar and Jensen, pp. 106-26
2. Barbara Sinclair, "From Party Voting to Regional Fragmentation: The House of Representatives, 1933-1956," _American Politics Quarterly_, v. 6 (1978), pp. 125-46
3. Allan G. Bogue, "Some Dimensions of Power in the Thirty-Seventh Senate," in William O. Aydelotte, Allan G. Bogue and Robert W. Fogel, eds., _The Dimensions of Quantitative Research in History_ (Princeton, 1972), pp. 285-318

Week VII. Nonparametric Measures of Association

1. Blalock, Chapters 14, 15
2. Dollar and Jensen, pp. 56-87, 106-26
3. Richard Jensen, "Quantitative Collective Biography: An Application to Metropolitan Elites," Swierenga, pp. 398-405
4. Allan Kulikoff, "The Progress of Inequality in Revolutionary Boston," _William and Mary Quarterly_, 3rd ser. 28 (July 1971), pp. 375-412
5. John Modell, Frank F. Furstenberg Jr., and Theodore Hershberg, "Social Change and Transitions to Adulthood in Historical Perspective," in Milton Gordon, ed., _The American Family in Social-Historical Perspective_ (2nd edition), pp. 192-219

Week VIII. Analysis of Variance

1. Blalock, Chapter 16
2. Edward M. Cook, Jr., "Local Leadership and the Typology of New England Towns, 1700-1785," _Political Science Quarterly_, v. 86 (1971), pp. 161-75

Week IX. Linear Regression and Correlation

1. Blalock, Chapters 17-20
2. Floud, pp. 133-51
3. Dollar and Jensen, pp. 56-87
4. John L. Shover, "Was 1928 a Critical Election in California?" in Rowney and Graham, pp. 385-98

Week X.   Introduction to Multivariate Analysis

    1. Blalock, Chapter 19

    2. Dollar and Jensen, pp. 87-104

    3. S. Hackney, "Southern Violence," in Swierenga, pp. 348-65

    4. Paul Burnstein and William Frendenberg, "Changing Public Policy: The Impact of Public Opinion, Antiwar Demonstrations, and War Costs on Senate Voting on Vietnam War Motions," <u>American Journal of Sociology</u>, v. 84 (1978), pp. 98-122

    5. Carl Stone, "Political Determinants of Social Policy Allocations in Latin America," <u>Comparative Studies in Society and History</u>, v. 17 (1975), pp. 286-308

    6. Maris A. Vinovskis, "A Multivariate Regression of Fertility: Differentials Among Massachusetts Towns in 1860," (unpublished paper, 1972)

University of California
History 136G   Los Angeles   Mr. Loewenberg
Tu-Th, 11:00-12:15   Fall 1983
Bunche 3170

Psychohistory

The goal of this course is to introduce you to some depth psychological concepts and their uses in historical research. The course structure is designed to present a three-phase approach: 1) a theoretical concept; 2) a clinical demonstration; 3) a historical application. Thus you will see the mental mechanism of projection demonstrated in the Schreber case and applied in pre 1914 European diplomacy; the anal sadistic character demonstrated in the Rat Man Case and applied to Himmler and Nazism; the syndrome "Wrecked by Success" demonstrated on Henrik Ibsen's Rebecca West and applied to John C. Fremont and to the Confederacy.

Class Discussion: Each member of the class will be asked to organize and lead one session's topic.

Paper: You may write an optional paper on "Psychodynamics and Historical Understanding: A Critique and Evaluation" to count for one half of the grade, due on December 1.

Examinations: There will be no midterm. The final examination will be from 11:30 a.m. to 2:30 p.m. on Monday, December 12 in Bunche Hall 3170.

Guest Presenters: We will have three guest presenters, each an accomplished historian, who will discuss their work in psychohistory:

Oct. 25: Professor Judith Hughes, Department of History, U.C. San Diego, on "Emotions and High Politics."

Nov. 10: Professor Mauricio Mazon, Chairman, Department of History, U.S.C., on "Psychohistory and Chicano-American Culture."

Dec. 1: Andrew Rolle, Clelland Professor of History, Occidental College, on "John C. Fremont: A Man Wrecked by Success."

Audio-Visual: We will view the following films to accompany course material:

Oct. 4: "Mother Love," Harlow's Monkey.

Oct. 11: "Sudden Departure," parental deprivation.

Oct. 13: "John," Regression of a boy cut off from his mother during hospitalization.

Oct. 27: "Shyness," Adult to Child Case Studies

Nov. 8: "Four Families," Comparative Child Rearing in India, France, Japan and Canada.

Nov. 15: "The Rat Man," Freud's classic case.

Nov. 22: "Feelings of Depression," Case History.

Office Hours: Mr. Loewenberg's office hours are Tuesday and Thursday just after this class, 12:30 to 1:45 in 8246 Ralph Bunche Hall, telephone: 825-3175.

Outline and Readings

Oct. 4: Introduction
film: "Mother Love" (26 min.)

Oct. 6: Loewenberg, "On Psychohistory: A Statement on Method" in
Decoding the Past: The Psychohistorical Approach (N.Y.: Knopf, 1983),
pp. 3-8.

Loewenberg, "Psychoanalysis and History: The Scope of the Problem,"
Ibid., pp. 11-41.

Oct. 11: Loewenberg, "The Education of a Psychohistorian," Ibid., pp. 45-80.

Martin Duberman, "On Becoming an Historian,"
Evergreen Review, 13:65 (1969) and in his The Uncompleted Past
(New York, 1969), pp. 335-356.
In College Library Reserve.

film: "Sudden Departure" (28 min.)

Oct. 13: Loewenberg, "The Psychobiographical Background to Psychohistory:
The Langer Family and the Dynamics of Shame and Success,"
Decoding the Past. pp. 81-95.

film: "John" (45 min.)

Oct. 18: Sigmund Freud, "The Case of Schreber" in Three Case Histories
(Collier/Macmillan 07665).

Judith M. Hughes, Emotion and High Politics: Personal Relations
at the Summit in Late Nineteenth Century Britain and Germany
(Berkeley and Los Angeles: University of California Press, 1983),
pp. 1-76.

Oct. 20: Jonathan Steinberg, "The Copenhagen Complex,"
Journal of Contemporary History; 1:3 (1966), 23-46.
In College Library Reserve.

J. Hughes, Emotion and High Politics. pp. 78-162.

Oct. 25: Guest Presentation by Professor Judith M. Hughes,
Department of History, U.C. San Diego.

Oct. 27: Erik H. Erikson, "Identity Crisis in Autobiographic Perspective," in Life History and the Historical Moment (New York: W. W. Norton, 1975), pp. 17-47.

film: "Shyness" (23 min.)

Nov. 1: Points of Technique:

a) Watch the apparently trivial details: S. Freud, "The Moses of Michelangelo" (1914) in Character and Culture (Collier-McMillan, 07620), pp. 80-106.

b) Ambivalence: "Reflections upon War and Death" (1915), Ibid., pp. 107-133.

c) Father Rivalry: "A Disturbance of Memory on the Acropolis" (1937), Ibid., pp. 311-320.

Nov. 3: S. Freud, "Character and Anal Erotism" (1908), Character and Culture, pp. 27-33.

S. Freud, "On the Transformation of Instincts with Special Reference to Anal Erotism" (1917), Ibid., pp. 202-209.

Wilhelm Reich, "The Compulsive Character" in Character Analysis (New York: Noonday, 1949), pp. 193-200. In College Library Reserve.

Nov. 8: film: "Four Families" by Margaret Mead (60 min.)

Nov. 10: Guest Presenter: Professor Mauricio Mazon, Chairman, Department of History, U.S.C. on "Psychohistory and Chicano American History."

Nov. 15: S. Freud, "The Rat Man Case" in Three Case Histories.

film: "Rat Man," (53 min.)

Nov. 17: Discussion of Freud's papers of Nov. 3, Wilhelm Reich, the Rat Man.

Loewenberg, "The Unsuccessful Adolescence of Heinrich Himmler," Decoding the Past, pp. 209-239.

Nov. 22: film: "Feelings of Depression" (30 min.)

Stanley M. Elkins, "Slavery and Personality," in Robert J. Brugger, ed., Ourselves/Our Past: Psychological Approaches to American History (Baltimore: Johns Hopkins University Press, 1981), pp. 141-164.

Nov. 29: Sigmund Freud, "Some Character Types Met With in Psychoanalytic Work" (1916), in Character and Culture, pp. 157-181, especially "Those Wrecked by Success," pp. 162-179.

Kenneth M. Stampp, "The Southern Road to Appomattox," in
The Imperiled Union: Essays on the Background of the Civil War
(New York: Oxford University Press, 1980), pp. 246-269.
In College Library Reserve.

Loewenberg, "Austro-Marxism and Revolution: Otto Bauer, Freud's
'Dora' Case, and the Crises of the First Austrian Republic," in
Decoding the Past, pp. 161-204.

Dec. 1: Guest Presenter: Andrew Rolle, Clelland Professor of History,
Occidental College, on "John C. Fremont: A Man Wrecked By Success."

Dec. 6: Generational Theory and Psychohistory:

Loewenberg, "The Psychohistorical Origins of the Nazi Youth Cohort,"
in Decoding the Past, pp. 240-283.

George Forgie, "Abraham Lincoln and the Melodrama of the House
Divided," in Our Selves, Our Past, pp. 179-204.

Dec. 8: Open for review.

Dec. 12: Final Examination, 11:30 a.m. - 2:30 p.m.

J.W. Smit
Columbia University

HISTORY 4521v Spring 1983
Historiography

Requirements: midterm and final exam (take-home); one of the
questions of the final exam may be developed into a short,
10 page paper and be substituted for the final exam. Graduate
students who take the course for E-credit write one more, short,
paper. In the reading list the readings marked G, are required
for graduate students on top of what has been designated as
required for the whole class.

Background reading, reference etc.: some of the obvious choices
for textbooks and background reading are out of print. For a
general introduction I shall regularly refer to H. Stuart Hughes,
History as an Art and as a Science (available in bookstore).
The following titles for Philosophy of History, W.H. Walsh, Philosophy
of History, R. Aron, Introduction to the Philosophy of History; for
Historiography: G.P. Gooch, History and Historians in the Nineteenth
Century, Tr.R. Tholfsen, Historical Thinking, G.G. Iggers, New
Direction in European Historiography

Readings:

1) Introduction
   a) Myth and History:

   Required: E. Cassirer, An Essay on Man, Ch. 5, 7, 10 or
              idem, The Myth of the State, Part I
              M.J. Finley, "Myth, Memory and History", in
              History and Theory, 1965
              M. Mandelbaum, The Anatomy of Historical Knowledge,
              Part I/II
              B. Halpern, "Myth and Ideology in Modern Usage",
              in History and Theory
   Recommended: S. Toulmin, The Discovery of Time; R. Berkhofer,
              A Behavioral Approach to Historical Analysis,
              Ch. 10, 11; G.S. Kirk, Myth, its Meaning and
              Functions in Ancient and other Cultures, p 261-
              285. (G)

   b) The Claims of Scientific History

              D.H. Fischer, Historian's Fallacies. (G)
              H. Meyerhof ed. The Philosophy of History in our Time.
              (art. by Hempel, White, Nagel)

2) The New History of the 18th Century; a Mythical Structure?

   Required: C. Becker, The Heavenly City of 18th Century Philosopher:
              F. Stern, ed., The Varieties of History, on Voltaire
              P. Gay, The Enlightenment, Book III, Ch. 7

3) <u>The Ambiguity of the 18th Century Legacy</u>

    Required: G.A. Wells, " Herder's two Philospphies of History"
              Journal History of Ideas, 1960.
          R. Nisbet, <u>Social Change and History</u>, Intro., Part I,
          II sect. 4.
          J.B. Bury, <u>The Idea of Progress</u>, Ch. 7 through 11.

  Recommended: I. Berlin, <u>Vico and Herder</u> (G)
             F. Meinecke, <u>Historism</u>,Ch. on Montesquieu, Voltaire,
             Burke, Herder (G).
             Voltaire, <u>Essay sur les Moeurs</u>, Ch. LXXIV, CXCVII
             Montesquieu, <u>Spirit of the Laws</u>, Book I, II, XVII-XIX
             Vico, <u>New Science</u>, Introduction;I, 4;II, Introd.;
             II sect. 4;III;IV sect 1-12;V; Conclusion.
             J.G. Herder, <u>Reflections on the Philosphy of the
             History of Mankind</u>, Ch. I, II, VII, VII

4) <u>New Theoretical Concepts in the Early 19th Century</u>
    a)Ranke and Possibilist Historicism

    Required: G.G. Iggers, ed., <u>The Theory and Practice of History</u>,
          Intro. and selections p. 51-101
          idem   <u>The German Conception of History</u>,
          Ch. II, III, UV,
          relevant readings in Stern, <u>op. cit.</u>

  Recommended: Meinecke, <u>op. cit.</u>, Ch. on Ranke

    b)Determinist Historicism: Comte and Hegel

    Required: Hegel, <u>Philosophy of Right</u>, Part III sect. iii
          (The State)
          idem, <u>Reason in History</u>

  Recommended: W.H. Walsh, <u>op. cit.</u> Ch. VII
             S. Hook, <u>From Hegel to Marx</u>
             J. S Mill, <u>August Comte and Positivism</u>
             A. Comte, <u>Positive Philosophy</u>, Book VI (Social Physics)
             Ch. 3-12
             H. Th. Buckle, <u>Civilization in England</u>, Introductory
             Chapter, (in Stern, <u>op. cit.</u>)
             I. Berlin, <u>Historical Inevitability</u> **(G)**

    c)Determinist Historicism ??? The case of Marx

    Required: K. Marx, <u>German Ideology</u>
          idem, <u>The Grundrisse</u>, ed., D. McClellan, 16-46
          William H. Shaw, <u>Marx's Theory of History</u>
  Recommended: S. Avineri, <u>The Social and Political Thought of
             Karl Marx</u>
             S. Hook, <u>op. cit.</u>(G)
             G. Lichtheim, <u>From Marx to Hegel</u>
             K. Marx, <u>Precapitalist Economic Formations</u>, introductio:
             by E.J. Hobsbawm.

5) Ideological (or Mythical ???) structures of 19th Century Historiography
   a)Nationalism

   Read sections in Stern of 19th century historians; also
   introductory chapters in J. Michelet's History of the French
   Revolution; also required: P. Geyl, Debates with Historians
   on Ranke, Michelet, Macaulay.

   b)Conservatism and Progressivism

   Required: Geyl, op. cit.
            Ranke,

   Recommended: R. Hoffstadter, The Progressive Historians

6) Some Positions against Historicism

   Required: F. Nietzsche, "Use and Abuse of History: in
            Thoughts out of Season.
            K. Popper, The Poverty of Historicism

   Recommended: Berlin, Inevitability

7) The Crisis of Historicism: Epistemology and the Problem of Objectivity

   Required: W. Dilthey, Pattern and Meaning in History
            C. Becker, "What are Historical Facts: and "Written
            History as an Act of Faith" in: H. Meyerhof
            The Philosophy of History in Our Time
            R.G. Collingwood, The Idea of History, Part IV,
            and Part V.
            M. Mandelbaum,The Anatomy of Historical Knowledge,
            Part III

   Recommended: W. Walsh, op. cit.
            K. Popper, The Logic of Scientific Discovery
            Meyerhof, ed. op. cit.: articles Hempel, White,
            Nagel, Aron.(G)

8) The Crisis of Historicism: the Solution of Max Weber

   Required: M. Weber, "Objectivity in Social Science and
            Social Policy" in Methodology of the Social
            Sciences
            idem, "Science as a Vocation:, in H.H. Gerth and
            C. Wright Mills, From Max Weber
            H. Stuart Hughes, Consciousness and Society,
            chapter on Weber

   Recommended: R. Bendix, Max Weber.

9) **The Loss of Unity and Efforts at New Integration**
a) The consequences of specialization

Required: W.O. Aydelotte, "Quantification in History", in
American Hist. Review, 1966
R.W. Fogel, "The New Economic History:, in Econ. Hist. Review,
1966
A. Lovejoy, Introduction to the first issue of
Journal of the History of Ideas
J. Huizinga, "The Task of Cultural History" in Men
and Ideas '.
Recommended: B. Mazlish, ed., Psycho-Analysis and History
T.W. Fogel, Time on the Cross

b) New integration

Required: F. Braudel, The Mediterranean etc., Introduction,
Conclusion and a close reading of the Table
of Contents
M. Bloch, The Historian's Craft
G.G. Iggers, New Directions, last 2 chapters

Recommended: R. Berkhofer, A Behavourial Approach to History
L. Febvre, Pour une Histoire à part entière
A. Danto, Analytical Philosophy of History
F. Braudel, Ecrits sur l'Histoire (English translation
available), 41-84;175-238.

10) **Once more: History , Myth or Science?**

Required: K. Popper, op. cit.
Meyerhoff, ed., op. cit. the essays by Croce, Hempel
White, Nagel
M. Foucault, The Order of Things, Chs. I,V,VI,VII,X.
Hayden White, Metahistory

Recommended: A. Danto, op. cit.
R. van Zandt, The Metaphysical Foundation of American
History

HISTCRICGRPHY

Part I: General Issues

Week I   Introduction to the course

Week II   Vocation, Values, and Constructive Imagination

Max Weber, "Politics as Vocation" and "Science as Vocation," in Hands Gerth and C. Wright Mills, eds. From Max Weber (1958) pp. 77-128, 129-56.

William H. Dray, "Some Causal Accounts of the American Civil War," Daedalus, 91 (1962), 578-92.

Thomas Kuhn, The Structure of Scientific Revolutions (1962 et. seq.)

Lawrence W. Levine, "The Historian and the Culture Gap," in L.P. Curtis, ed. The Historian's Workshop (1970), 307-326.

Week III   Classic Social Thinkers and Historical Analysis

Karl Marx, The German Ideology (1846, 1947), part I (pp. 3-78)

Max Weber, The Theory of Social and Economic Organizsation (1947ed.), pp. 88-104.

Emile Durkheim, The Rules of Sociological Method (1895, 1938), Chap. I, "What is a Social Fact"

Week IV   History as Structure/History as Event

James Henretta, "Social History as Lived and Written," AHR (December, 1979), 1293-1322.

Emmanuel LeRoy Ladurie, "The 'Event' and the 'Long Term' in Social History: The Case of the Chouan Uprising," in his The Territory of the Historian (1979), pp. 111-31.

Joan Kelley-Gadol, "The Social Relation of the Sexes: Methodological Implications of Women's History,"Signs, 1 (1976), 809-23.

Lawrence Stone, "The Revival of Narrative," Past and Present (198).

Fernand Braudel, "History and the Social Sciences: The Long Term," in Fritz Stern, ed. The Varieties of History (1972), 403-29.

Week V   The Quest for Meaning and the Problem of Causation

Clifford Geertz, The Interpretation of Cultures (1973), pp. 3-30, 412-53.

Carlo Ginzburg, The Cheese and Worms (1976/1980)

J.G.A. Pocock, "Languages and their Implications: The Transformation of the Study of Political Thought," in his Politics, Language and Time (1973), pp. 3-41.

Part II Case Studies: Witchcraft

Week VI   Witchcraft, Witchhunts, and Social Tension

Paul Boyer and Stephen Nissenbaum, Salem Possessed

Alan McFarlane, Witchcraft in Tudor and Stuart England, chaps. 11-12

H. Trevor-Roper, "The European Witch-craze of the Sixteenth and Seventheenth Centuries, " in his The Crisis of the Seventeenth Century, pp. 90-192.

Week VII   Witchcraft and World Views

Keith Thomas, Religion and the Decline of Magic, chaps. 14-18, 21-22.

Clark, "Inversion, Misrule and the Meaning of Witchcraft," Past and Present, 87 (1980), 98-127.

Carlo Ginzburg, The Night Battles, selections

Week VIII   Witchcraft Reassessed

John Demos, Entertaining Satan (1982)

Part III Case Studies: The Rise of Capitalism

Week IX   Transition from Feudalism to Capitalism

Karl Marx, Capital, part VIII, "The So-called Primitive Accumulation."

Henri Pirenne, "Stages in the Social History of Capitalism," AHR, (1914), pp494-515.

Robert DuPlessis, "The Transition Debate," Radical History Review (Winter, 1977), 3-38.

Hans Medick, "The Proto-industrial Family Economy," Social History, 3 (October, 1976), 291-315.

David Levine, "Production, Reproduction and the Proletarian Family in England," (unpub. manuscript, copyright, February, 1983), 28pp.

Week X   Ideas, Ideologies, and Fconomic Change

             Max Weber, The Protestant Ethic and the Spirit of
                Capitalism,(1905, 1958)

             Albert Hirschman, The Passions and the Interests, (1977)

Week XI   States, Politics, and Paths of Transition

             Barrington Moore, Social Origins of Dictatorship and
                Democracy, (1966)

Part IV   Case Studies: Society, Culture, Ideas in Renaissance
                         Florence

Week XII   Study in the City

             Jacob Burckhardt, The Civilization of the Renaissance in
                Italy, (1860), vol. I, pp. 21 - 150.

             Samuel Kline Cohn, Jr., The Laboring Classes in Renaissance
                Florence, (1980)

Week XIII Society and Culture: Painting and Architecture

            .Richard Coldthwaite, The Building of Renaissance Florence,
                (1980)

             Michael Baxandall, Painting and Experience in Fifteenth
                Century Italy, (1972), esp. pp. 1 - 118, 151 - 153.

Week XIV   Social Origin, Meaning, and Implication of Ideas

             Felix Gilbert, Machiavelli and Cuicciardini, (1965),
                pp. 1 - 200.

             Quentin Skinner, Machiavelli, (1981)

             J.G.A. Pocock, "Civic Humanism and Its Role in Anglo-
                American Thought," in his: Politics, Language, and
                Time, (1973), pp. 80 - 103.

             Isaiah Berlin, "The Originality of Machiavelli," in his:
                Against the Current, (1980), pp. 25 - 79.

ABOUT THE EDITOR

John Santore received his Ph.D. in modern European history from Columbia University in 1976 and has taught at Rutgers University (1976-1977), Barnard College (1977-1981), and New York University (1982-1983). In 1981, he served as the Associate Director of the Columbia University Center for Italian Studies and was a Faculty Fellow in the Cornell University Western Societies Program in 1987. A specialist in Twentieth-century Europe, his reviews and articles have appeared in the <u>Canadian Journal of History</u>, <u>The Germanic Review</u>, <u>History Teacher</u>, and <u>History: Review of New Books</u>. Currently, he is Associate Professor of History and Coordinator of the Cultural History Program at Pratt Institute in New York City.

September 1989

TABLE OF CONTENTS

Volume One:
Chronological and National Courses

Introduction 7

General Survey

1. ROBERT MOELLER, University of California Santa Cruz*
   "European History, 1789-1980" 11
2. MARY NOLAN, New York University
   "History of Western Civilization Since 1648".......................................16
3. JOHN BROOMFIELD, University of Michigan
   "Progress or Decay? Conflicting Ideas on the Development
   of the Modern World" 26
4. ROBERT MOELLER, Columbia University
   "Contemporary Civilization: From Ancient Times
   of the Present"..27
5. DARLENE LEVY, New York University
   "The French Revolution" 35
6. ROBERT DARNTON, Princeton University
   "Readings in the Old Regime and the Revolution in France" 42
7. ISTVAN DEAK, Columbia University
   "The Revolutions of 1848" 47
8. ROBERT MOELLER, Columbia University
   "European Politics and Society, 1870-1919".......................................50
9. MICHAEL R. MARRUS, University of Toronto
   "Modern Europe, 1890-1956" 65
10. CHARLES S. MAIER, Harvard University
    "Europe Since The Second World War" 86
11. JOHN GILLIS, Rutgers University
    "History of Modern Britain" 91
12. JOE THOMPSON, University of Kentucky
    "Modern Britain: The 19th and 20th Centuries" 96
13. SIDNEY ASTER, University of Toronto
    "Britain: From Empire to Welfare State, 1906-Present"....................106
14. THOMAS METCALF, University of California, Berkeley
    "The British Empire and Commonwealth"..122
15. HERRICK CHAPMAN, Carnegie-Mellon University
    "Modern France, 1815 to the Present"..124
16. JOHN MERRIMAN, Yale University
    "Peasants, Workers, and Revolution in
    Nineteenth-Century France" 139
17. STANLEY HOFFMANN, Harvard University
    "France's Decline and Renovation, 1934-1946".................................147
18. DAVID H. PINKNEY, University of Washington, Seattle
    "The Making of Contemporary France"..146
19. HERRICK CHAPMAN, Carnegie-Mellon University
    "Problems in French History: A Graduate Colloquium"......................151
20. STANLEY HOFFMANN, Harvard University
    "French Thought About Politics and Society" 158

21. THEODORE HAMEROW, University of Wisconsin
    "History of Central Europe, 1648 to the Present" 164
22. MARION KAPLAN, Queens College, CUNY
    "Germany From 1870 to the Present" 169
23. MARY JO MAYNES, University of Minnesota
    "Society and Politics in Imperial Germany, 1871-1918" 172
24. MARY JO MAYNES, University of Minnesota
    "Topics in Modern German History: Society,
    Economy, and Politics in the 20th Century" 179
25. ISTVAN DEAK, Columbia University
    "Colloquium on Germany and East Central Europe
    in the 19th and 20th Centuries" 185
26. ROBERT F. BYRNES, Indiana University
    "Russia in the Nineteenth Century" 187
27. CYRIL E. BLACK and
    RICHARD S. WORTMAN, Princeton University
    "Modern and Contemporary Russia" 192
28. MARTIN MILLER, Duke University
    "The Russian Intelligentsia" 208
29. STEPHEN F. COHEN, Princeton University
    "Soviet Politics" 215
30. STEPHEN F. COHEN, Princeton University
    "Soviet Foreign Policy" 221
31. ROBERT F. BYRNES, Indiana University
    "Soviet-American Relations Since 1945" 229
32. ROLAND SARTI, University of Massachusetts
    "Modern Italy" 235
33. RICHARD HERR, University of California, Berkeley
    "Spain and Portugal Since 1715" 245
34. ISTVAN DEAK, Columbia University
    "History of the Hapsburg Monarchy, 1815-1918" 252
35. PETER J. LOEWENBERG, University of California, Los Angeles
    "Twentieth-Century Austria" 255
36. ISTVAN DEAK, Columbia University
    "History of Hungary, 1848-1956" 264
37. GABOR VERMES, Rutgers University
    "History of Poland" 267
38. JAN DE VRIES, University of California, Berkeley
    "History of the Netherlands" 272
39. PETER J. LOEWENBERG, University of California, Los Angeles
    "Switzerland in the Twentieth Century" 274

For the table of contents of Volume II, please refer to the end of the book.

*Institutional designations refer to the university or college at which the course was taught, and not necessarily to the school at which the author now teaches. In all but a few instances, the syllabi have been reproduced exactly as submitted, with little modification or change. All college courses, of course, are subject to annual revision and updating, and the reader is advised to check the syllabus for format and date. [Ed.]